RAFFI

(Hakob Melik-Hagobian, c. 1835-1888)

THE FOOL

Events from the Last
Russo-Turkish War
(1877–78)

translated by

Donald Abcarian

Gomidas Institute
London

GOMIDAS INSTITUTE - ARMENIAN LITERATURE IN TRANSLATION

ABOUT THE TRANSLATOR
Donald Abcarian was born and raised in Fresno, California, where his family was part of the extensive Armenian-American community that has settled there since the turn of the last century. His earliest influences, including the Armenian language, derived from that milieu. He graduated from the University of California at Berkeley with a degree in philosophy and has pursued a lifelong interest in languages and world literature. His translations also include Raffi's *Jalaleddin* and *The Golden Rooster*.

Published by Gomidas Institute, 2021.

ISBN 978-1-909382-56-5

For further comments and inquiries please contact:

Gomidas Institute
42 Blythe Rd.
London W14 0HA
Email: *info@gomidas.org*
Web: *www.gomidas.org*

INTRODUCTION

This third edition of *The Fool*, just like the earlier editions, is presented in loving memory of my father, Manoog Abcarian, born in the ancient town of Arghani near the upper reaches of the Tigris and raised in the city of Dikranagerd [Diarbekir]. The year of his birth, 1894, saw the first in a series of massacres of Armenians across Ottoman Turkey which were unprecedented in scale and consumed scores of thousands of innocent lives. At the age of seventeen, he left home in search of a more secure life and some means of contributing to the welfare of his family.

All that remains of the home he left behind is a large photo of his family with eleven individuals (sent to him in the United States) and a letter from his father dated March 1914 from Dikranagerd, carefully preserved by my mother for many years. In this letter, addressed "My Dear child, Manoog," my grandfather expresses his gratitude on receiving my father's last and long-awaited letter, reports on the state of his own health and business, conveys the best wishes and state of being of close family friends, and goes on both to congratulate and caution his son on his new-found trade as a barber in California. In 1915, my father received word that his entire family had been massacred by Ottoman troops.

Years later my father learned that one of his younger sisters, Serpoohy, had survived the massacre, being left for dead beneath her mother's body. She was subsequently taken in by Muslim neighbors, and after years of painstaking effort on the part of my father and of friends who were still in the Near East, she was able to overcome her eye disease enough to immigrate to the United States and be reunited with him. She would eventually marry and raise a family as Serpoohy Zooloomian in Providence, Rhode Island, haunted by her searing past until the end of her life several years ago.

My mother, Annie Hallaian Abcarian, was born in Kharpert in 1904 and came to the United States as a toddler in 1906. She therefore spoke English as a native language and was thoroughly steeped in American culture. Though she spoke Armenian fluently, she didn't read it and never had the chance to read an Armenian book. That is why I was struck several years after my father's death in 1952 that, in a conversation that touched on my university studies, my mother turned to me and in a particularly meaningful tone stated that Raffi had been my father's favorite author. That simple statement gave expression to something that had always been in the air during my upbringing, for it would be difficult to exaggerate the importance Raffi had to Armenians of my father's generation. Behind Raffi's brooding social darwinism and thundering rage over the cruelties inflicted on his people there lay a profound conscience, uncompromising and exacting, always ready to confront evil and recognize good wherever they were found. With a heart keenly attuned to the suffering of those whose finer human qualities had been shorn from them by the ravages of cultural, political and economic oppression, he was a fierce advocate for the dignity of women and a voice for the voiceless.

Though I am older now than my father was at his untimely death, I realize after all these years how deeply he communicated to me – and in the most wordless of ways – his love for Armenian national life and his profound concern for its destiny. This translation is offered in homage to him and his entire tortured generation, those who narrowly escaped the worst but were condemned to look on helplessly as their homeland, their loved ones, and the leading lights of their nation were destroyed in the final and most brutal chapter of Ottoman history.

The Fool had its origins in 1877 when Raffi undertook an assignment from a publisher to investigate the condition of the Armenian refugees from Alashgert who had ended up in the area of Yerevan as a result of the Russo-Turkish War. In 1878 in Vagharshapat, he met and interviewed Samson Der Boghosian, a veteran of the war and the individual on whom he would base the character of Vartan. Of his encounter with Raffi, Der Boghosian had the following to say: "He led me to a monk's cell and began interrogating me about my experiences the previous year in Bayazid... I tried to keep it short, but he wouldn't let me go." The impassioned story that grew out of this interview would become a novel of unprecedented importance in modern Armenian literature, a stunning wake-up call to a people slated for annihilation.

In connection with the opening scene of the novel, it should be borne in mind that it is set in a war between two great empires, not simply a war between two nations or ethnic groups. Therefore, deals were made and a mixture of ethnic and confessional groups could be found fighting on either side of the battle lines, depending on their perceived interests. It is undeniable, however, that the overall sympathies of the 'Russian Armenians' were with the Russian side, consistent with Russia's assertion that it had declared war on the Ottoman Empire on behalf of its long oppressed Christian minorities.

One other point should be clarified on the relationship between Echmiadzin and Vagharshapat. Echmiadzin is where the supreme cathedral of the Armenian Church and associated sites are located. It is part of the ancient town of Vagharshapat. Therefore, the two names are practically synonymous.

This translation is based primarily on the edition of the novel published by Hairenik Press, Boston, 1937. Very special acknowledgment is due to Khachik Samvelyan for the highly detailed notes he provided about Raffi and *The Fool* in the 1984 *Sovedagan Krogh* [Soviet Writer] edition of Raffi's collected works published in Yerevan.

My first thanks for the completion of this project go to my wife Marcia, my son Ravi, and my daughter Jacinda, who have lived it and breathed it with me from the start. Their understanding, support and counsel have been essential. I also wish to give special thanks to Eddie Arnavoudian, Ara Melkonian and Artsvi Bakhchinyan for the help and moral support they have offered me over the years in my work on Raffi. My final and heartfelt thanks go to Ara Sarafian. Without his forthright, unhesitating recognition that it was time for a new English translation of this work and his tenacity in making it a reality, Raffi and his masterpiece might, as far as the rest of the world was concerned, lie forever buried in the dust of Armenian libraries.

Donald Abcarian
Berkeley, California
November 2020

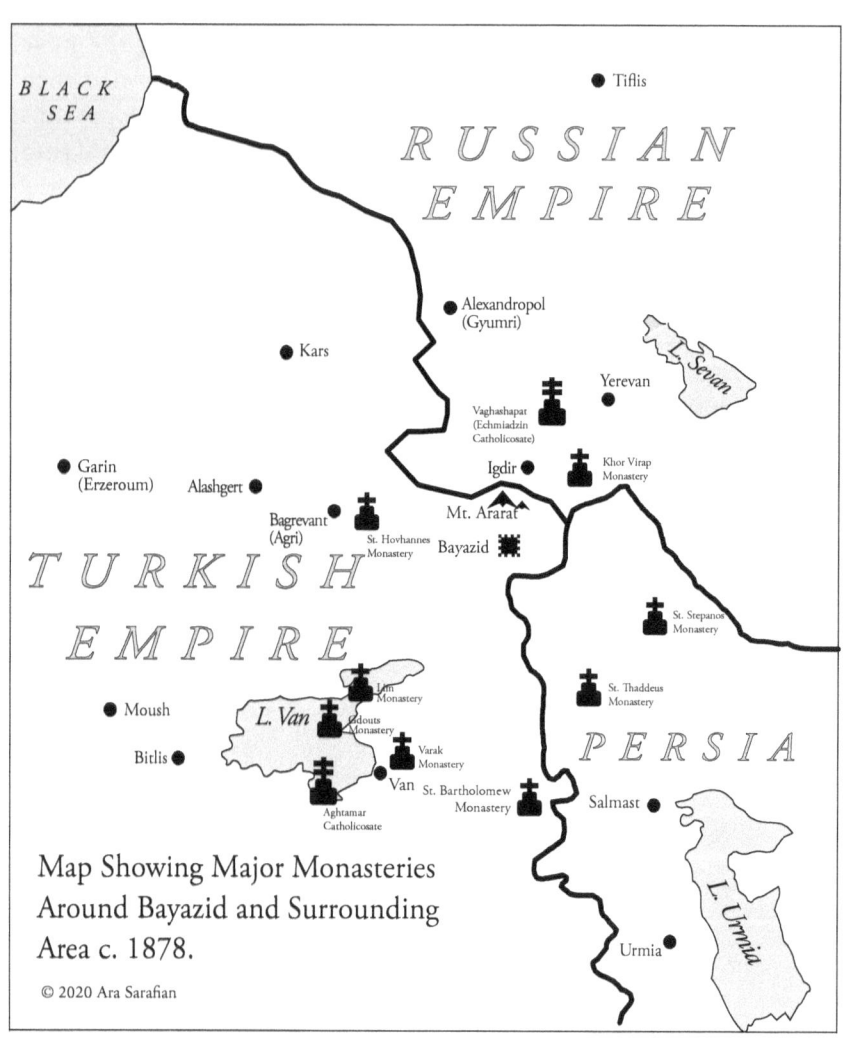

BLACK
SEA

RUSSIAN

EMPIRE

● Tiflis

● Alexandropol
(Gyumri)

● Kars

Vaghashapar
(Echmiadzin
Catholicosate)

Yerevan
●

● Garin
(Erzeroum)

Alashgert ●

Igdir ●

Khor Virap
Monastery

L. Sevan

Bagrevant
(Agri) ●

St. Hovhannes
Monastery

Mt. Ararat

Bayazid

TURKISH

EMPIRE

St. Stepanos
Monastery

● Moush

L. Van

Lim
Monastery

Ktouts
Monastery

St. Thaddeus
Monastery

Bitlis ●

Varak
Monastery

Van

St. Bartholomew
Monastery

Salmast ●

PERSIA

Aghtamar
Catholicosate

Urmia ●

L. Urmia

Map Showing Major Monasteries
Around Bayazid and Surrounding
Area c. 1878.

© 2020 Ara Sarafian

THE FOOL

Events from the Last
Russo-Turkish War
(1877–78)

*"A fool rolled a rock into a ditch
that a hundred wise men gathering around could not remove."*

*"While the prudent stand and ponder,
the fool has already crossed the river."*

"From the fool—a direct answer."

CHAPTER 1

Bayazid was under siege.

Turks, Kurds, Gypsies, Julos[1] and a rabble of more than twenty thousand *bashibozouks* had joined with Turkish regular troops to surround the half-destroyed town; it lay burning like one vast bonfire. The homes of the Christian Armenians were empty, annihilated by the sword and slavery of the barbarians. A small number of Armenians, getting early word of what was about to happen, had managed to save themselves by timely escape to the border town of Maku on Persian soil.

The citadel of Bayazid had remained impregnable. Inside, a small force of Russian soldiers together with Armenian and Turkish volunteer militiamen had fortified themselves and, with utmost dread, awaited the final, horrific outcome. The fortress was besieged on all four sides, as if caught in a ring of iron which grew ever tighter around it, inexorably closing in to choke off and destroy the hopeless defenders. All contact with the outside world was cut off.

This siege began on June 6th, 1877 and lasted for all of 23 days, taking place at a time when Russia's military fortunes in Armenia were suddenly reversed. The Mohammedans of the area, who at first had gone along with Russian rule, now rebelled and went over to Ismail Pasha's side. During this time, General Der-Ghugasov,[2] Commander of the Yerevan Division, was located in the area of Zetekan and Tali-Papa, his small regiment courageously battling the forces of Mukhtar Pasha which outnumbered his army five-to-one. The general seemed to have no news of what was happening in ill-fated Bayazid, a town whose defense he had left in the hands of commander Shedogvitch.

It was night.

The horns of the crescent moon had just disappeared from the horizon, casting everything into utter darkness—a darkness welcome to the besieged men; for the moon, beloved of the universe, had seemed to betray them with her glimmering beams. Yet the darkness did nothing to slow the fierce attack of the barbarians. The citadel of Bayazid was an obscure point, hardly discernible among the hills. The fire drew closer on every side; and from all sides cannon and rifles sent a hail of shells down upon it. The fortress murmured like some gigantic beast, assailed on all sides; confronting its last moments, it struggled on stubbornly; faced with death, it resolved to die with honor. About a thousand Russian troops and the same number of Armenian and Turkish volunteers faced Ismail Pasha's force of twenty thousand. Responses from the fortress were rare, since ammunition was almost exhausted. Cannons were used only as enemy positions were revealed by their fire. In the citadel was a damaged building that had served as barracks for the Ottomans at one time, but was left in ruins by them on being forced out by the attacking Russians. Here, on this night, a multitude of people who had come face to face with every horror was sprawled out on the floor.

"A drop of water… I'm fainting from thirst…" many of them could be heard sighing in distress. "A piece of bread… I'm starving to death," they clamored in their feeble voices.

This pitiful multitude had been without food or drink for an entire week. The siege had come so quickly, there had been no time to stock up on provisions. Now they had to battle three enemies: starvation and thirst on the inside, and the fire of the enemy on the outside. They had gone without a hot meal since the eighth of the month.

The commander's horse and all the artillery horses had already been slaughtered and eaten, their remaining feed portioned out among the soldiers. Finally, so little food was left that each man was given one eighth pound of biscuit and a spoon of water. The June heat was unbearable, and the condition of the healthy could hardly be distinguished from that of the sick in the infirmary.

There was no source of water inside the citadel. At a distance of three hundred paces outside the walls was a spring which had been closed off by the Turks. Every night, an attempt was made to descend from the citadel for water, but out of twenty or thirty who tried, few had ever returned.

"Bread… water," the cries of the afflicted could be heard once more; and then, again and again, the cannon roared and swallowed up their voices.

This was one of those moments in life when people lose compassion for their fellows, there being nothing they can do to help. No one paid attention to the starving or cared for the thirsty. Each man, in his own distress, awaited the decisive moment when the enemy would pour in like a flood, sword in hand, and finish them off.

Deployed around the ramparts, soldiers stood near gun slots watching the movements of the enemy, not daring to raise their heads. Fire came in from all over. The repugnant hot air from exploding shells blasted them in the face.

The town could be seen from here and presented a frightful spectacle, lit up as if for a great holiday, its light even reaching the nearby heights. But this was a holiday celebrating inhuman cruelty, a monstrous holiday created by the Muslims. Only hell—hell itself—with its scorching flames and evil spirits, with all its horrors, could rival the cruelty that was practiced here. The houses of the Armenians were burning. Rivers of fire seemed to flow from every door and window, mixing with the heavy smoke, then rising up into the sky and spewing torrents of sparks in every direction. As the fire intensified, it engulfed the entire Armenian quarter. Tongues of flame burst through roofs; burning rafters gave way and covered the people with an inescapable blanket of fire, their cries lost in the roar of the inferno. In the air, enormous flames turned this way and that like gigantic dragons, casting their terrible light in every direction. In that vast panorama, one horrendous sight after another came into view. The Muslims were exterminating the Armenians, killing those who tried to escape without regard to age or gender, dragging young girls from their homes by the hair. Cries of pain came from everywhere, yet the crying and the tears of the victims had no impact at all on the hearts of the attacking monsters... And the Kurdish men were not alone in these barbarities. Turkish regular troops joined in, as well; even more appalling than this, however, was the role played by the Kurdish women. Having completely forgotten feminine tenderness and care, they tore children from their mothers' arms and threw them into the flames. The slightest resistance to these barbarities brought swift punishment by the sword.

In the citadel, several Armenian volunteers were weeping as they looked down on this hellish sight. The massacre had gone on without stop for all of three days and three nights.

"Oh, what slaughter..." they were sighing.

But one young Armenian, who had like them witnessed all these barbarities, stood nearby without a tear in his eyes. There was no trace of sadness in the intensity of his expression; it was rather hatred that filled his heart—hatred not for the monsters who were burning and killing, but for the Armenians who allowed themselves to be slaughtered like so many sheep.

"Look... Just take a look," he said. "Out of all those people, there's not one who will lift a finger against the murderers. What more would it take to provoke vengeance? They burn our houses in front of us... They drag our women and girls from their homes.... and a young man just watches, then offers his neck to the sword... Oh, damn you! Aren't you a man, too? You too should kill and then be killed..."

"Vartan, you're always so heartless," commented one of his comrades.

Vartan said nothing, but walked away. The shameful spectacle of his people seemed to weigh very heavily upon him, and, as he walked away, he thought to himself, "These people don't know what it is to die with honor."

Not far away, in a remote corner of the citadel, the following conversation was taking place among a group of Armenian volunteers:

"If Bedros doesn't come back, that will make five people we've lost tonight..."

"The poor fellow is really late."

"But listen. That's his signal. Don't you hear the crow-call?"

"That's him. Let's put down the rope-ladder."

Within moments after the ladder was let down, a young man appeared at the rampart carrying an enormous water-skin over his shoulder. His comrades pulled him in and hugged him, covering his face with kisses. But one of them drew back with shock.

"Why is your face wounded, Bedros?" he asked

Just at that moment, the flames rose up and illumined Bedros's face.

"There's blood!" they all cried.

"It's nothing," Bedros said with a smile. "It's been a long time since I washed my face, but tonight it got a good cleaning!"

He recounted that on getting near the spring, he found a few Kurds guarding it, and that he had sustained the wound in the course of "shutting them up."

"But what happened to Haness, Atam, and Nerso?" they all asked.

"Oh, devil take them!" Bedros answered with his characteristic sarcasm. "They were talking some nonsense about going to join their dearly departed ancestors. One of them was hit by a bullet just at the moment he touched down, and the other one lost his grip and fell before he reached the bottom. He never had a chance. Another fellow was lying near the spring as still as a log. Not far away, Tomas was lying on the ground gripping a wound in his side and cursing the Kurds. It was from him that I took the water-skin."

(These four young Armenians had followed each other in successive attempts to get water, and not one of them had returned.)

This report had little effect on the young soldiers, since by now they had become so familiar with death and killing. They didn't promptly dress Bedros's wounded face, though it was still bleeding, and Bedros himself paid it no further attention.

"May those Kurds go to hell!" said Bedros. "Those bastards can see in the dark like wolves, and they fire a bullet at every little sound, no matter where it comes from."

Finally, only after this conversation in the darkness had ended did they remember to dress Bedros's wound; then they picked up the water-skin for which so many lives had been given and proceeded to the central square of the citadel.

"Fellows, we can't give one drop of this water to the Turks," said one of the young men in the group. "This is no joke. None of them was willing to leave the fortress for water, and we lost four people tonight."

"No, that's not right. We have to share it with them, too," said Bedros.

"But why should we? The other day they got some water and hid it away just for themselves."

"That was wrong, but we have to set an example of solidarity as soldiers."

"Here they come."

"Water! Water!" came the sound of happy voices approaching from all directions, and a crowd soon gathered around the young men.

It is impossible to describe the delight and mad joy with which that thirsty multitude approached the water-skin, jostling each other to get in front for the first drink.

"Strike up a torch and calm down. You'll all get some water," said the young water-bearer, and set the bag down on the ground.

A torch was lit and cast its weak, bluish light over the crowd of excited men, beside themselves with happiness.

A young Armenian took a tiny brandy glass and started distributing the water among them. The water had a repulsive smell and tasted bad. A few drank without comment, but one in the group finally exclaimed, "What is this color in the water?"

"Drink, the Kurds put that color in the water for us," said Bedros.

"What do you mean?" several men in the crowd asked.

"It's tinted with our blood. If you could only see how may bodies have fallen into that spring."

The men were shocked, but within a short time went back to drinking this water in which so much human blood had been spilled and so many corpses had decomposed. One in the crowd even had the audacity to say, "So much the better. It will have more nourishment for us."

The facetiousness of the light-hearted soldier was soon interrupted by the roar of guns in the distance. Shells began whistling overhead, and one of them landed near some of the soldiers, sending its deadly fragments in every direction.

At the same time, in one of the rooms of the fortress that once was the headquarters for the Ottoman command, the Russian garrison commander Shedogvitch had called together an officers meeting which included the leaders of the Armenian and Turkish volunteer militia. The dim light of a lamp set on the table illuminated their grim and anxious faces.

Over the past few days they had received repeated letters from the enemy advising them to surrender. The author of the letters was Lieutenant-General Shamil, the son of Shamil,[3] that great enemy of the Russians. He was now present in the enemy camp, serving as *aide-de-camp* for His Elevated Majesty the Sultan.

The subject of the meeting was what response should be given to the last such letter, which consisted of various threats and promises.

"We won't give up as long as we live," the commander said.

"But if this siege goes on much longer, it will be impossible to hold out," said another officer.

"Our situation is untenable right now," said another officer. "We're out of food and ammunition. Why don't the stupid Kurds just get it over with? How can we defend ourselves?" he said, his voice full of anxiety.

"Yes, we should have been more careful," said another.

"Nothing can be done about what's happened. We have to deal with the situation as it is," observed the commander who, according to military law, had enormous powers during times of siege and as presiding officer of the meeting. "We can't surrender as long as we live," he said, repeating himself.

"But if we don't get help from the outside, we're finished," said a khan, the commander of the Turkish volunteers.

"We're in no condition to wait for help," said a Kurdish *bek*. "As I see it, we should throw the gates open and battle our way through the encirclement. We'll either succeed and save ourselves or fall to the enemy."

"The latter seems more likely, and the consequences would be terrible," responded the leader of the Armenian volunteers. "This fortress is at least a bulwark against the further advance of the Ottoman army. If we give it up, we'll leave the way open for Ismail Pasha's *bashibozouks* to push on unopposed to Yerevan, Nakhichevan, and possibly even further. It's obvious to me that these self-invited guests will then be welcomed with open arms by the local Mohammedans, while the Christian Armenians of the area are entirely without arms. There are hardly any weapons left to defend our territory; all of our forces are concentrated to defend Kars and its region. By the time the Ottomans get there, they will have destroyed everything in their path."

The young Armenian leader's words provoked the Turkish khan, and he responded angrily:

"So you don't trust the Mohammedans!"

"My doubts aren't unfounded. I know of many cases that support what I'm saying. Right now among the Kurds besieging us, there are many from Zila who were Russian subjects before the war; and every night in Nakhichevan some crazy mullah has a dream of that area passing into Muslim control."

"We have to hold on and resist to our last breath," said the commander, putting an end to the dispute. "I'm confident that help will soon reach us. General Der-Ghugasov isn't far off. As soon as he finds out what our situation is, he'll move immediately to save Bayazid. It's just a matter of getting word to him as soon as possible."

"But how can that be done?" someone asked.

"With a letter," he answered.

"Who will carry it?"

"I would think that out of so many young men here, one has to be brave enough to do it."

"What if someone did step forward to carry the letter, how could he possibly get through? The enemy is everywhere."

"We have to try," the commander replied.

The decision to send a letter to General Der-Ghugasov was approved. Within fifteen minutes, the commander emerged from the meeting with the letter in hand and walked to the assembly grounds of the fortress.

A light tapping of the drum summoned all the troops to the square, and the commander addressed them in a loud voice:

"Fellows, our situation is clear to all of you and discussing it is useless. Our fate now rests in the hands of God and His power to send us help from the outside. If help is delayed, we perish. We have to do everything possible to get word out about our situation. This letter in my hand has to be carried to General Der-Ghugasov; he isn't far from here. As soon as he receives it, he'll send help. Which one of you has the courage to take on this grave responsibility? Step forward and take this letter from my hand. I pledge that you will receive an award befitting such a selfless act in saving the lives of everyone here. Speak up! Who will take it?"

There was utter silence. Not a sound was heard.

"I repeat," the general went on, this time in a more forceful voice, "Who will accept the honor of being the man who saves all our lives?"

Again, not a sound was heard.

"Am I to believe that not one of you has the courage to do this!" he shouted, his voice trembling now.

"I ," came a voice from the ranks, and a young Armenian stepped forward and took the letter from his hand. His name was Vartan.[4]

CHAPTER 2

The next morning, as the first rays of the sun spread over the landscape, a shocking spectacle was revealed in Bayazid. The aftermath of three days and three nights of barbarous destruction could now be seen. A funereal silence hung over the town, broken only by the occasional cawing of crows arriving to feed on the dead. The streets presented a tragic and heart-rending sight: houses reduced to smoking rubble, here and there small fires smoldering in materials not yet wholly consumed. The bodies of old people, women, and children lay near almost every house. Starving dogs dragged them off ravenously, growling and snapping to ward off flocks of descending crows. The stifling stench of decaying corpses flowed from every house, every shop, every yard.

Looking down on this dying town, the citadel of Bayazid stood awaiting its final hours.

The siege intensified. Hill and plain were filled with every sort of *bashibozouks* and marauding rabble. They broke up into separate groups, each rushing about on its own, murmuring and shouting. The brutality of war having been joined with the fanaticism of religion, barbarity had been pushed to its very limits. Men, transformed into monsters, extorted and killed their fellow beings.

Having satisfied themselves with bloodletting, they now began to indulge their greed. Any Armenians that seemed wealthy were laid out on the ground and subjected to every sort of torture to reveal where their money was hidden. When they wept and cried that they had given all they had, and had no more, they weren't believed. Children were killed in front of their parents to force divulgence of where their money was hidden. Elsewhere, the Kurds were dividing up the booty, and their women happily carried it off on horseback.

In another spot, Armenian slaves were being selected. Men with swords were disputing over attractive women or girls. Nearby, wolves and wild cats gathered together for breakfast around unburied bodies. Somewhere else, Mohammedan fighters in the grip of intense devotion performed their age-old prayers, raising their bloody hands to heaven in praise of the Allah of Islam.[5]

All of these things transpired inside the heavy pall of smoke produced by the spent gunpowder and flames, a dense cloud extending to the horizon and blocking out the sunlight. Cannons roared and pounded the gigantic fortress, but it remained unshaken on its heights, withstanding the fearsome assault of the enemy.

Yet, somewhere in the enemy camp, everyone's attention was turned to one man who was walking through the middle of the army, whistling, clapping his hands, and singing a childish Kurdish song:

"An old grandad turned into a frog,
Turned into a frog and jumped in the sea,
Then out of the sea, he fetched up some sand,
The sand turned into gold,
In exchange for the gold, he bought a goat,
A hobbling, itchy goat,
Little goat, little goat, dear little goat,
Offerings for you, my little goat,
Tell me how it was you got so itchy and lame."

"That crazy fellow!" said the soldiers to one another and encouraged him to sing on.

And, indeed, this man seemed a fool. He was dressed in the same manner as the clowns in our circuses who assist acrobats and amuse the audience with their antics below the ropes. He was tall, with a wild look on his face. On his head he wore a strange square cap made of felt, with little bells hanging from each corner, ringing with the slightest motion. His face was smeared with shoe polish accented by red, yellow and blue lines drawn over it. Aside from the cap, his only clothing was a tattered military overcoat covering his otherwise naked body. It was bound at the waist, not by a belt, but by a length of rope. His feet were bare.

"What a jack-ass that fellow is," the soldiers said.

The fool stuck his fingers in his ears; he opened his mouth wide and brayed as loud as he could like a donkey. Everyone laughed and dropped pennies near him. He picked up the coins, gave them a crazy look, then threw them aside and asked for bread. On being offered some, he took it, stuffed it into his mouth, and swallowed without chewing.

"I'll bet you can dance like a bear, too. Let's see what you can do," the soldiers said.

The fool began executing various eccentric movements—crawling on all fours, kicking up his heels, doing hand-stands—and uttering various curses in Kurdish. He cursed the Russians; he roared that all infidels should be killed; his voice rang throughout the camp until midnight. But the next morning, the fool was gone.

CHAPTER 3

The scorching midday sun was beating down, stifling and unbearable. This was the time of day when travelers are forced off the road to seek shelter in the shade. On the road that leads from Bayazid to Alashgert, there was only one person at this hour. The road led by twists and turns into the mountains and, with its constant rise and fall, was a severe challenge to the young traveler. Yet, though barefoot and without a horse, he didn't seem to tire. He continued at a brisk pace without stopping once to look around, as if impelled by some urgent mission which didn't allow for one wasted minute.

He was a young man with much the same look as the fool of the previous day, the same ragged military overcoat over his naked body, the same rope around his waist. But now he wore no eccentric garb nor had a painted face; on his head, fashioned from rushes with fresh leaves still attached, he wore the kind of hat that peasants weave for themselves at harvest time; it cast its protective shadow over his virile, though anxious, face. In contrast with the foolishness of the previous day, the severity of his expression betrayed some profound inner disturbance.

He came to a sudden stop at what sounded like the whinnying of a horse. He looked around; the sound repeated itself. It came from the direction of a little vale. At first, all he could see was a saddled horse grazing in a grassy spot near some bushes. On closer inspection, he noticed a long spear stuck in the ground near the bushes; its tip was gleaming in the sun. There must be a man nearby, he thought, and he must be alone, because there is only one horse. The man must be a Kurd, because the horse's saddle and stirrups are Kurdish. And, he thought, he must be sleeping, because his horse's legs are fettered to keep him from wandering off. Suddenly, the young traveler had an idea.

The little brook running through the vale was lined with a thick stand of rushes. He hid himself in them and crept toward the spot where the spear was stuck in the ground. A snake itself couldn't have surpassed the suppleness of this daring young man as he made his way through reeds. A light wind, setting up a rustle in the tips of the rushes, provided cover for whatever unavoidable sounds he might make. All the conditions were right.

Within a few moments he approached the bushes near which the spear was stuck in the ground. Still hidden, he parted the rushes and looked out. Indeed, a man was lying on the ground, half-visible in the shade of the bushes, driven to take shelter there by the midday heat. His clothing confirmed that he was a Kurd. He was facing in the opposite direction, making it hard to tell if he was asleep or not, and he lay on a thick patch of grass which was pressed into a comfortable bed beneath the weight of his body.

The young man surveyed the scene from his hiding place, still trying to determine if the man was awake or not. If only his face were visible, he would know. Suddenly some inner disturbance overtook him, and his eyes took on a look of madness. Beside himself with inner turmoil, he didn't know what to do. Unarmed and without real clothing, he would be at a great disadvantage in trying to deal with a monster who was armed from head to foot. Time was flying, and he had to do something. But what?

As he stood turning these thoughts over in his mind, he saw the Kurd raise his head to check on his horse. Seeing that all was well, he put his head back down on the saddle pack which served as his pillow.

So now the Kurd was definitely awake. The young man's face once again registered profound distress. His eyes dilated, and his cheeks trembled. But then he caught sight of the spear and saw it firmly planted in the ground not far away. With that discovery, his face relaxed, and there was the glimmer of something like happiness in his eyes. To get a weapon—that was his only thought. Suddenly, like a stalking tiger, he flew out of his cover, grabbed the spear out of the ground, and ran toward the Kurd.

"Give me your weapons!" he shouted, running toward the Kurd.

The Kurd, seeing this outrageous figure before him in a tattered military overcoat and ridiculous hat, gave him a contemptuous look and reached for his pistol.

"Sure, take it," he said, pointing the pistol directly at the young man.

With that, the gun roared and the bullet came close to hitting the fool.

"You bastard! You dare resist!" he shouted and drove the tip of the spear into the Kurd's neck. The Kurd's warm blood rushed out. His head quivered and fell to the ground.

He roused himself one more time and tried to draw his sword, but managed to get it only half-way out when his grip loosened.

"You dog! Why are you killing me?" he murmured in his death throes.

"You have killed so many of my people! You have plundered so many! It is from you that I learned to kill! I have a long way to go. You can see for yourself—I have no clothes, no weapons, no horse. I need your clothes, your weapons, that beautiful horse grazing there in the grass. I knew that as long as you drew breath, I'd get nothing from you, so I laid you to rest. Maybe you didn't participate in the massacre at Bayazid; but that doesn't matter, because your brethren were there, zealously doing their work."

The Kurd heard none of what he was saying. His eyes were already shut, and his lifeless body lay on the ground.

All of this had transpired in just a few moments. The young traveler stripped the victim's clothes off, then dragged his body into the reeds. He covered it with his tattered military overcoat. Then, putting on the Kurd's clothing and picking up his weapons, the young traveler sped off on his fine steed to continue his journey.

CHAPTER 4

The day after these events, a horseman clad in Kurdish dress flew into General Der-Ghugasov's camp at full gallop. He stated that he had a letter of utmost importance to deliver to the general. He was led to the general's tent, and an officer took the letter inside. The young man stayed outside to care for his horse, which was completely covered with sweat. Within a few minutes he was called inside.

Inside the tent was seated a middle-aged military man, thickset, and with the haughty look of a lion. This was Der Ghugasov himself. His white head was bent over a pile of freshly opened letters on his desk. He picked up the latest letter and read it over again, drawing heavily on his pipe. The uneasiness of his expression reflected profound distress.

"You are Armenian?" he asked, turning to the messenger.

"Not only Armenian, but the son of a priest," the young man answered.

The general gave the bold young man a sharp look, then continued with his interrogation.

"Was there any food left in the fortress?"

"They may be feeding on each other within a few days to avoid starvation."

"And what about water?" asked the general, sitting back in his chair to listen.

"There isn't any inside the fortress. It has to be brought in from outside, but it's impossible to get out during the day. At night ten or twenty men make the attempt to descend on a rope-ladder and come back with water. The Kurds know full well what's going on and they pick them off one after the other. Seldom does anyone make it back."

"What about the supply of ammunition? Do they have gun-powder and shells?"

"It was all used up, but then some Armenians—and may all Armenians be proud of them henceforth—found a sizable cache of weapons, gun-powder, and shells the Turks had hidden away. But that's being used up right now."

"How did you manage to leave the fortress?"

"At dawn, before the sun came up, I descended the wall of the fortress and went straight into the midst of the Kurdish army. For a whole day, I made them laugh; I entertained them; I sang them songs; I danced for them; I did a thousand different things to distract them, and, doing so, I was able to move at will through the entire army. When I had learned all that I could, I bid them good-bye and left."

Looking at the young man with astonishment, the general asked, "What kind of nonsense is this you're talking? You must be crazy!"

"Yes, sir," said the young man calmly, "My whole life, it's been my lot to play the fool. It hasn't been all bad, though, and sometimes it's actually saved me a lot of trouble; and so, accepting the role of a fool, I was able to mingle freely with the Kurdish army."

A slight smile transformed the general's stern countenance. "Where did you find those clothes?" he asked.

"They were provided by God. On the way here, I encountered a Kurd. It was from him I got the clothing, the weapons, and that fine horse standing outside," answered the young man; and then, continuing in a normal tone, he went on to recount how he had managed to kill the Kurd.

"You must be a very brave young man," the general said, and, returning to his previous pensive manner, continued the interrogation.

"Are there many Kurds?"

"I've heard about twenty thousand. But they aren't only Kurds; every sort of Mohammedan tribe is mixed in with them, anyone with a gun or a horse. They all hit the road for Bayazid, and they turned out to be an awesome number by the time they got there. As I made my way here, I could see ever new groups taking to the road for Bayazid."

"Do they have artillery?"

"Yes."

"What is their goal?"

"They're in a big hurry to take the citadel of Bayazid. After that they'll go on to Yerevan, and a week later they'll be in Tiflis because of their strong interest in Georgian and Armenian girls."

Again, a slight smile transformed the general's face, and he asked with contempt in his voice, "Do they think they can do all that with twenty-thousand? That's impossible!"

"If there aren't a hundred troops to slow their advance, twenty-thousand is no small number, general. Besides that, soon all of Ismail Pasha's troops will join up with them, while in our territory the Mohammedans can't wait to give a big welcome to their fellow believers."

Once again, a worried look came over the general's face, like a dark cloud. Though never a man to be greatly upset by reversals in fortune, he was now deeply troubled. He put his hand to his forehead and started to rub it unconsciously, as if trying thereby to rid himself of this great dilemma. After some moments of reflection, he lifted his white head and asked, "Did you get into the town of Bayazid itself?"

"Yes. There isn't a bit of life left among the Christian Armenians there. Young and old were massacred. Desirable girls and boys were taken into slavery. The houses were burned, and everything was stolen. Only about a hundred families managed to escape. They fled toward Maku in

Persia after learning what was going to happen. But they just barely escaped with their lives and left all their possessions to the enemy. Oh, how cruel the Mohammedans were to the Armenians!"

"What do you mean?"

"At the beginning of the war, while the Russians were moving toward Bayazid, the Mohammedans of the area were struck with fear that the Russians, like the Turks before them, would rob and plunder them. So they went to their Armenian neighbors and said, 'You are Christians; the Russians won't bother you, and our possessions will be safe in your homes,' and they handed their possessions over to their Armenian neighbors to keep for them. Then the Russians came, and, of course, took nothing away from anyone; they made no distinction between Mohammedans and Christians. Seeing this was so, the Mohammedans felt at ease and took their possessions back from their Armenian neighbors. Just then, however, word arrived that the Kurds were on their way. The Turks went to their Armenian neighbors and said, 'You did a good turn for us, and now it's time for us to repay you. The Kurds are coming, and they will rob you. Give us your possessions, and we will safeguard them for you.' Taking them at their word, the Armenians handed over their possessions, and, in some cases, hid their wives and daughters in their homes, too. But when the Kurds got there, the Turks said to the Armenians hiding in their homes, 'You'd better get out of here. If the Kurds find out we're hiding you, they'll make trouble for us, too.' They turned the Armenians out, but kept all their possessions. When the massacre began, it was these same Turks who were the first to set fire to the houses of their Armenian neighbors, the very same Turks who a month and a half before swore to you that they accepted Russian rule. Gunfire came from everywhere, even from the Turkish women."

The general listened silently as the young man continued.

"Oh, sir, if you only knew how many fine young men met their end in that battle before the Kurds even reached Bayazid! As you know, only a tiny force was left to defend the citadel, including the Armenian and Turkish volunteers. Shedogvitch, that hero of Bayazid, manned the fortress; it was up to the volunteers to protect the town itself. We soon got word that an enormous force of Kurds was on its way under the command of Sheikh Jalaleddin[6] and Sheikh Ibadullah.[7] We got this news from the Armenians of Van. We quickly advised those inside the fortress to strengthen their defenses and be ready to face the enemy. But certain individuals inside discounted this news; they tried to convince everyone that nothing special needed to be done. I don't know what these treacherous people had in mind in trying to keep us unprepared for the arrival of the enemy. You may very well find out some day, General. I can only say this. The Armenians were always loyal, and will always remain so."

It would seem there were certain points in the young man's story he had difficulty making clear.

"Tell me what you did once the Kurds got there."

"When they arrived, Shedogvitch tried several times to engage them in battle, but with little success. He quickly withdrew to the citadel to fortify it and defend it. Part of the militia stayed outside, because there wasn't enough space or provisions inside. Some of our Turkish comrades fled to Persia and others to Iktir. As for us Armenians, we made up our minds either to be killed or to keep the town from passing into the hands of the enemy. Though there were only a few of us, many of the Armenian inhabitants were ready to join us. Those poor people knew very well what would be in store for them if the Turks took over the town again. And you know, general, how enthusiastically the Armenians had welcomed the victorious Russian army when it entered the town the first time. The Ottomans couldn't forget this, and they were waiting to take full revenge on these people who preferred being subjects of the Russian eagle rather than the Ottoman crescent moon."

"You're straying from the subject again," said the general interrupting the young man's story. "I want to know what finally happened."

The young man continued after putting a check on this loquacity that sprang from a heart filled with so many tragic experiences.

"We might have succeeded by joining with the Armenians of the town, but they had no weapons. Despite that, many of them still joined us. And, I must say, the battle went very well at first; a tiny force fighting a much greater number. But suddenly our Mohammedan comrades began fleeing the field of battle. They seemed uneasy about firing on their fellow believers. But we Armenians remained alone, fighting stubbornly. Then hand-to-hand fighting began. Many fell, and many were taken prisoner. Those who remained, seeing that nothing more could be done, gave up and fled. That is when the enemy took over the town."

"That is understandable," said the general to himself as he stood up. Drawing a small chest toward him, he took a cross out of it and hung it around the young man's neck.

"You have earned this," the general said. "In addition, I'm going to recommend you to my superiors for promotion and honors. From now on, you'll stay with me, because I need brave men like you beside me."

The young man bowed his head in acknowledgement. "This cross is enough for me, general. You will do me a great favor by letting me go on my way now," he said.

Amazed by the young man's indifference to promotion and honor, the general asked, "Where do you have to go?"

"To save the life of someone who is more precious to me than anything in this world."

"It seems you have a secret, comrade," the general said with sympathy

"Yes, the secret of my heart..."

"Well then, accept this small gift. It may be useful to you," said the general, handing him a packet of gold coins wrapped in paper.

"I'd be obliged if I could go now," the young man said, declining the gift.

"Then go, and may the Lord be with you," the general said, giving him a handshake.

The young man bowed his head and left.

CHAPTER 5

Now let us go back a few years before the war.

In the province of Bagrevant, not far from the monastery of St. Hovhaness (Uch-Kilisah), was situated the Armenian village of O... on the banks of one of the upper tributaries of the Euphrates. This village was located in a great valley, richly endowed by nature with every sort of beauty. It lay between two chains of mountains which, encircling it with their snowy heights, gave it an oval shape.

Through this valley, wending its way this way and that, flowed the tributary river that, on account of its purity, was known by the locals as Eyin Agh Sou, or "White Water." The surrounding mountains contained countless pastures with excellent nourishment for the many herds of livestock there. The lowlands were planted in wheat, barley, flax, and several kinds of legumes. No piece of land had been left untouched by the tiller's hand. Several Armenian villages, spaced out from each other in the valley, were tucked away in the midst of their farms and orchards and, when seen from afar, stood out from the treeless valley, as beautiful green dots of forest.

The village of O— was nestled in a dale at the far end of the valley, and there the most imposing house, distinguished from all the others by its size and wealth, belonged to Danouder Khacho, his true name being Khachadour. Every morning, hundreds of animals were driven forth to pasture from this house. His cows, bulls, oxen and horses were the finest in the village. Nearly a thousand sheep were driven out each day to graze in mountain pastures under the watchful care of his shepherds. His household also owned the enormous olive press in the middle of the village as well as the beautiful watermill on the outskirts of the village which turned unceasingly through all the seasons. But of all Khacho's possessions, his seven sons were the most precious, each successively reaching maturity to become the pillars of his household. All his grown sons were married, and the home was full of children of every age. Some of his grandchildren were married as well and had their own children. And so, before him, Khacho saw several generations living together, making up a little world unto itself. There was a saying in this village, in the style of a proverb, that Khacho's children were as numerous as his animals.

Of all Khacho's sons, only one remained unmarried, and this was the youth Stepanig who had just turned sixteen. One did not see the kind of maturity in his face that is usually found in boys of his age, especially in this hot climate where boys reach manhood quickly. A charming, youthful freshness still lingered in his face. Khacho's other sons all had tasks of their own away from the house—tilling the fields or working with the livestock—and were rarely found at home. But Stepanig hardly ever took part in such tasks. He was Khacho's "Joseph the Fair," and the old father never let him far out of his sight. Stepanig and Joseph the Fair were similar not only in beauty, gentleness, intelligence, and a sympathetic nature, but also in the utmost attention reflected in their clothing and appearance. He could often be seen in robes made from the most florid and colorful textiles of Aleppo beneath a purple frock coat bound by a sash with gold needle-work. His full trousers were made of the most delicate cloth from Van, and on his feet were red shoes from Erzeroum. His head bore a red fez with a black silk tassel, wrapped with a colorful turban also of the finest silk. His auburn hair fell from the fez and rested on his shoulders. Just one thing distinguished Stepanig from Joseph the Fair: whereas Joseph's brothers were jealous of him, Stepanig was loved by all his brothers.

As seen from afar old Khacho's house resembled some ancient fortress. It stood on elevated ground, and both by its construction and its position provided its occupants with ample security from external foes. Its massive foursquare walls enclosed an extensive tract of land, and nothing could be seen from the outside but the four high towers at each corner. Inside those walls were all the living quarters and shelters necessary to support a well regulated domestic economy. There was an underground sheepfold; a barn divided into separate enclosures for the horses, cows, and oxen; a shed for farm equipment; lofts in which hay, fodder, and medicinal herbs for the animals were stored, as well many storehouses and cellars to receive the harvest. Here also were the cottages for the shepherds, the male servants and the female servants, all of whom were Kurdish youth. In one word, this fortress enclosed what amounted to a small village, with Danouder Khacho as its sole lord and master.

This home was plain in design, unlike the elaborate houses of our modern towns. With its stone composition, it still retained the simplicity of a family tent. There were no separate quarters for his sons, each of whom had sizable families of their own, and everyone lived within the same four walls, with the same massive beams overhead. It was here they made their fires and baked. It was here they made their meals and ate. And it was here they all slept. Here could be seen newborn calves together with toddlers, all mixed together, scampering about, and filling the house with a lively clamor. Sometimes the chickens came in and pecked around the floor for the crumbs dropped by the careless children. In short, this was Noah's ark where every sort of living thing could be found. Next to this dwelling place was another. This was different in only one respect; its front was entirely open and faced the courtyard. This was used as a parlor during summertime. There was a door between this room and the main quarters, and thus it served as an ante-room to the main dwelling. Next to this room was also a small guest room, used as an inn only when guests were on hand in the village, and always kept in a clean and attractive state.

CHAPTER 6

Despite its simplicity, life in this traditional home went on with joy and prosperity. Work proceeded at a steady pace, and God's blessings flowed down upon it. The store-rooms were kept full of wheat, oil, olives, and wine, supplying their needs through all the seasons. Whether it was hot or cold, all their needs were satisfied, and there was always work to do.

The mountain snows were melting, and the fields were already touched with a lovely green. It was Spring. The fragrant air spread its life-giving warmth everywhere. In the dales, a thousand noisy brooks twisted and turned their way through the valley. The newly returned swallows were inviting the farmers to work, and Khacho's sons were already prepared to plough the fields.

The sun was just beginning to rise, illuminating the snow-laden heights with its rose-colored rays. Old Khacho was just beginning his day, saying "God bless" to everyone he met. This was the day that, for the first time, his sons had the task of bringing the bulls and oxen out from their winter shelter where they had spent the whole time eating, putting on weight, and resting without seeing the light of day. This event was a great attraction to all the village folk, and they crowded around Khacho's house to see for themselves how well the animals had been cared for through the winter.

"Congratulations!" said one of the villagers to Khacho, "It looks like your sons are ready to bring the oxen out."

"Yes. It's time. There's no use keeping them inside any longer. I asked the priest's advice, and he said, 'This is the right day.' So I decided to bring them out," he said, giving special importance to the priest's advice.

From inside came the sound of bells, and the crowd drew back to make way.

"That's Zorah!", came shouts from the crowd.

Zorah was one of Khacho's lead oxen. On his forehead was a white moon-shaped spot, and he was reputed both for his size and strength. The enormous beast came bursting forth from the door, huffing and snorting. The earth trembled beneath his hoofs. Then, coming to a sudden halt outside, he lifted his head and looked around. Suddenly, old Khacho cracked a raw egg on him to protect him from the evil eye, and its yellow color spread over his forehead. Being startled by this, Zorah lowered his horns and, breaking away with an astounding move, charged at the gathered crowd. Within a moment, Khacho's sons caught up with him and tried to control the spirited animal with large sticks—human strength pitted against that of untamed nature. Having just emerged from the darkness of his winter quarters into the light of day, everything looked dim and indistinct to him. He didn't even recognize his own masters from whose hands he had meekly licked his food through the period of winter inactivity. Raving mad, he charged this way and that, and there was no controlling him. Six of Khacho's sons set upon him from all sides, but he took the blows of their great sticks as if they were so many flying chips of wood.

The old man stood at a distance, looking with delight on this scene that was worthy of a Roman circus. Before him, he saw two tremendous forces: on one side, the strength of his brave sons, and on the other, the power of this gigantic animal, both of whom were of equal importance. On these two forces depended the work of his entire household. And now the struggle intensified as the heavy chain around Zorah's neck broke, releasing him from the large wooden beam that had hung from it to constrain his bold movement. The villagers rushed at him with ropes to try to restrain him, but he snapped the ropes with ease and charged in every direction. The crowd fled before him like flies. In the midst of this frightful tumult, Khacho's son, Abo, made a bold move, running up with the speed of a lion and grabbing Zorah's tail. The provoked animal, seeing itself so daringly assaulted, quickly turned his head around to deal a blow against his opponent, but Abo just held on, following behind him. They made several fearsome turns together, and the bout continued for several minutes, filling the air with dreadful sounds. The distressed animal bellowed and left deep furrows in the earth from the movement of his hoofs. Both opponents were enveloped in the thick cloud of dust they threw up in their struggle. Finally, Abo's brothers arrived on the scene with chains and succeeded in hobbling Zorah. There were cheers everywhere from the villagers.

The old father went up to Abo, and, planting a kiss on his forehead, said, "May God favor you, my son, for you have honored me." In saying this, it was his intention to acknowledge that Abo had not allowed his father to be shamed in the eyes of the people, and then, going up to Zorah, he petted his head and said, "Naughty fellow! Why did you put up such a ruckus?"

But by now, Zorah had calmed down. The cloudiness in his vision had been dispelled, and having vented his distress, he now recognized his masters. A heavy chain with a beam attached was once again placed around his neck, and the beam hung between his front legs. Then he was led to the river to be washed and refreshed in the ice-cold water.

The crowd of villagers still remained, because the other oxen, even less tame, were still to be brought out. This time his sons were more careful in maintaining control of the situation, and no untoward incidents occurred. They brought the beautiful animals out in groups, each one healthy and plump and worthy of first place in any country fair. Khacho stepped forward and crushed a magical egg on each of their foreheads to ward off the evil eye, looking on them with admiration. In addition, he hung from each of their necks a green leather talisman with a prayer inscribed on it, made especially for the occasion by the priest. Seeing all of this, the gathered villagers voiced their praise for Khacho's sons who had taken such good care of the animals. Following this, it would be necessary to bring the animals out each day in just the same manner until they became gradually adjusted to the open air and sunlight and were ready to pull the plough.

CHAPTER 7

With April came warmer and brighter days. Red, gold, and white lilies had already bloomed in the mountains. Kurdish girls gathered them into bouquets and brought them to the Armenian villages to trade for bread. Mushrooms, asparagus, snake-weed, blue salsify, and other mountain vegetables were so plentiful this year that one donkey load could be traded by the Kurdish women for several pounds of flour.

Khacho's sons had set out to work in the fields. There was a bustle of activity everywhere as all carried out their respective tasks.

It was morning. The tonirs were lit. On one was placed a great copper kettle and earthenware crock to cook the meal, and in the other bread was placed to bake. Khacho's daughters-in-law were at work around the ovens with their helpers. The whole house, filled with the delicious smell of food, gave the impression of a huge kitchen busy at work to feed an army. In addition to Khacho's family, there were numerous shepherds and plough-men together with their entire families who would sit down to eat together. This was, indeed, an entire legion. Everyday the ovens were lit to prepare the same amount of food. Khacho's daughters-in-law were always busy; close attention was required in every detail.

There were, in addition, many other household chores that had to be done. One of the daughters-in-law was engaged in milking the cows and sheep and heating milk for madzoon on a small stove; another was making cheese; another churning butter. Meanwhile, the children were running to and fro, playing with the new-born lambs and calves—a picture of rural plenty sweet, indeed, to behold! Children and lambs growing up together—for the peasant, the two treasures that bring the greatest joy and pride.

Along a wall on the sunny side of the yard, hundreds of beehives were stacked on top of each other. The April sun cast its warm beams here, and while his daughters-in-law were occupied with their tasks, Khacho was opening up the hives. Thousands of bees promptly and gaily flew forth from them, and, swarming around the old man's white head, filled the air with their reverberation. Some of the more aggressive bees left stinging little kisses on the old man's wrinkled brow, but he wasn't overly troubled by them; he just waved them away with his hand, saying, "Oh, you little devils, what harm did Khacho ever do to you?"

At a distance, Stepanig stood watching his father with interest.

"You'd better leave before the bees sting you," his father warned.

"But why aren't they stinging you?" his son asked.

"They do, but it doesn't bother me much."

"Why not?"

"Because my body is used to it."

"May I get used to it, as well!" said his son with a laugh.

The old man laughed and gave his son a kiss.

Just at this moment, the kizir of the village came up and announced that the Kurdish Chieftain Fattah-Bek had sent a message that he was on his way to visit Khacho's house as a guest. The kizir noted that his guest could arrive at any moment, since he and his party had been hunting in the nearby mountains.

It seemed that some dark shadow passed over the old man's brow, and his clear face became clouded with sadness. But, maintaining his composure, he told the kizir to call his sons in from the fields so that they could help with preparations, and himself to make sure that all the horses were refreshed and fed when the party arrived.

Visits by Fattah-Bek were so familiar that everyone knew what had to be done. Therefore, as soon as the daughters-in-law found out about the impending visit, they had several sheep slaughtered and set to work making pilaf in large kettles, knowing the *bek* would be bringing twenty or thirty men with him.

Fattah-Bek was the leader of a Kurdish tribe whose sheep were grazing in the nearby mountains. On several occasions, conflicts had occurred between Armenian and Kurdish shepherds after Kurds had stolen sheep or encroached on pastures belonging to the Armenians. But these clashes were usually resolved before they got out of hand, since not only was Fattah-Bek a good friend of Khacho's but, as well, godfather to some of his grandchildren when they were baptized. Khacho, in turn, had been godfather to some of the *bek*'s sons at the time of their circumcision rites. Thus, between the Armenian elder and the Kurdish chieftain, friendly relations had been established.

But what made Khacho so unhappy on getting the news of the visit?

He wasn't the sort of person who, out of stinginess, would avoid entertaining the *bek* and all of his men. Like the patriarch Abraham himself, his table was open to everyone. Everyday many travelers and foreigners ate at his table. All through his life Khacho had stated many times that no table was to be set without guests present. "Food," he would say, "is given by God and belongs to God. God's poor must have their share in it." But what was it that troubled him so much on hearing of the *bek*'s imminent visit?

Engrossed in thought, he came out of the house and stood near the door waiting for his guest to arrive. A few of the villagers noticed him there and approached.

"They say the *bek* is coming. Who knows what kind of belly-ache he's going to have this time!" one of them said.

"Yes, when a Kurd comes calling at an Armenian's home, he'll always have some belly-ache," responded the old man in a troubled tone.

There was a glint of spear tips emerging from the nearby hills; within moments a group of horsemen could be discerned.

"There they come!" said one of the villagers.

The old man looked but, because of his declining vision, saw nothing.

"That's them!" cried another villager.

"Fellows," said Khacho to the villagers around him, "stay here and take their horses when they arrive. Offer them hay and barley. My sons are on their way in from the fields."

The *bek* drew near, accompanied by various kinds of hounds and more than twenty mounted men. These were his close and distant kin, and, like body-guards, were always at his side. Today he was mounted on a fine blue-hued Arabian horse with trappings decorated entirely in silver and gleaming precious stones. The *bek*, slightly over forty years of age, could easily have been taken for thirty—a large, well-built man with a virile face and clothed entirely in fine muslin and silk, sewn with gold thread.

On seeing him, Khacho went forward to the culvert, which was spanned by a bridge and had been dug to drain off water during storms. But instead of using the bridge, the *bek* spurred his horse to leap over the culvert. The horse flew over the culvert like a sparrow, and, landing on the other side, stopped with a flourish near Khacho after executing several impressive turns.

"What do you think of him, godfather Khacho? Do you approve of him?" asked the *bek* as he stroked the horse's beautiful mane. "You know about horses. What do you think?"

"May God protect him from the evil eye, he's very beautiful. Even Koroghli[8] never had such a fine steed. He's entirely worthy of you," answered Khacho, walking up and petting the horses neck. "You've never had such a fine horse. Where did you find him?"

"He's a new gift to me from the vali of Erzeroum," answered the *bek*. "He loved him more than his own two eyes, yet he had him sent to me, his friend. He had received him as a gift from the sheikh of Aleppo."

"He's a beautiful horse," Khacho repeated.

Encouraged by all this praise, the *bek* prodded his horse into action once again. The fine steed galloped around the courtyard in front of Khacho's door, executing impressive turns, and, while displaying his own fine qualities, showed as well the skillful control exercised by his rider.

The *bek* dismounted and handed the reins to one of his servants, instructing him to walk the horse away since it was covered in sweat.

Khacho took his esteemed guest by the hand and led him into the guest room which had been freshly decorated and put in order.

The floor was covered with precious Persian rugs. Pillows were piled along the walls to relax on, and a special divan of pillows had been prepared as a seat for the *bek*.

Inviting his guest to take his seat, the old host now pronounced the civilities that were traditional in this region:

"My house is your house. You are most esteemed in my eyes and my heart. I am your humble servant. My sons are at your command, and the women of my household are your attendants. Welcome, and a thousand times welcome! Whatever I have is at your bidding. Please take your seat."

The *bek* conveyed his thanks, and one of Khacho's sons approached and took off his red shoes, then led him to his place of honor at the guest-seat. Nearest the *bek* sat a couple of his brother's sons and a few other close relatives who were his intimates. The rest of his party left to take care of the hounds and horses and benefit from the ample provisions of Khacho's barn. The *bek* and all his men were fully armed, not parting with their swords, shields, revolvers, rifles and spears, though they were in a friendly home. A Kurd, whether inside or outside, whether in peace or in war, will never part with his weapons. A weapon is like an inseparable part of his body to him.

Khacho's sons had just come in from the fields and were going in and out fulfilling their father's instructions. But they carried no weapons. To begin, they served coffee without sugar in delicate china cups.

"Where is Stepanig? I haven't seen him yet. I'm accustomed to having him serve me coffee when I visit," said the *bek*.

The old father, hiding his discomfort, gave orders for Stepanig to be called.

Stepanig arrived with an innocent smile on his face. He approached the guest and kissed his hand (this being a form of respect expected by Kurdish chieftains). Touching the young man's silken hair, the guest asked, "Do you know about the surprise I brought for you?"

"Yes," responded Stepanig, flushing a little, "it's a cute little roe deer. I offered him some hay, but he wouldn't eat."

"So you see, he already has his gift," said the *bek* turning toward Khacho.

"I knew he was for me, so I took him," Stepanig interjected.

"Well, then, go along and play with your little roe deer," said the *bek*. The young man nodded his head and left.

"He's a very good boy. He seemed disappointed that I never brought him anything on my previous visits," said the *bek*.

"He means well. He's not used to getting anything from you," said the old man with an involuntary smile.

"Ah, how wonderful your mountains are here, Godfather," said the *bek*, changing the subject. "You encounter game with every step—roe, stags, great herds of deer. The partridge and wild dove are countless. That roe deer I captured for Stepanig was caught alive by my hounds. If you could only see how fine they are! I just got a couple of them from the leader of the Tselants people. I traded them for a couple of mules. We got the mules from some Persian pilgrims to Mecca. (Keep that to yourself, though). But those hounds are truly amazing. They fly faster than a thought!"

The *bek*'s talk focused totally on his hounds and hunting, and he went on at great length in this vein. Old Khacho found this "nonsense" quite boring, but nevertheless listened patiently and interjected a few appreciative remarks.

It was already meal time. The table was set with great containers of pilaf and entire roasted lambs. Bowls with various flavors of sherbet and yoghurt drinks were set out and served in large saucers. No alcohol was served. Everyone began to eat and drink.

"You haven't sent your sheep out to pasture yet?" asked the *bek*.

"No, we haven't," answered Khacho. "You can't be sure of the weather this time of year. April is unpredictable here, so we're waiting until it's over."

"Heat and cold are in God's hands, Godfather Khacho. What will be, will be," the *bek* answered. "Our sheep were sent to pasture a week ago. But do you know how soon our provisions ran out this year? For quite a few days our shepherds have had no bread to eat."

"Well, isn't our food your food? Just say how much flour you need, and it is yours," said Khacho, understanding the true import of the *bek*'s words.

"May your house be always protected!" said the *bek*. "Who could ever come between us? What's mine is yours, and what's yours is mine, isn't that so, Godfather Khacho?"

"With God as my witness, it is so. How much do you want?"

"For now, ten oxen loads will do. If we use it up, we can always get more from your stores, since you're in no danger of running out."

A forced smile crossed the old man's sad countenance as he nodded in agreement.

When dinner was finished, Stepanig brought water for everyone to wash their hands, then made and served the coffee. The *bek*'s attendants, who had been standing by during the meal, were now told by the *bek* to go outside and eat with their fellows at a special table set out for them on carpets in the courtyard. The *bek* and a number of his relatives remained inside with Khacho. The conversation now turned to the horse which the vali in Erzeroum had sent as a gift to the *bek*. The *bek* explained the fine line of breeding from which his steed had come, and stated that its precursors went back to the time of the famous Antar[9] and was of the purest Arabian stock.

"But this gift weighs very heavily upon me," the *bek* said, concluding his account.

"How so?" asked Khacho.

"Because, don't you see? I have to pay the vali's servant a hundred pieces of gold for bringing it to me."

With this, Khacho understood what the *bek*'s "belly-ache" was and the real purpose behind his visit. Yet, as they say, "choosing his words carefully," the old man replied, "For such a fine horse, you should give whatever you have. Even a hundred pieces of gold is not too much."

"Who ever gave a Kurd that kind of money?" said the *bek* irritably. "This accursed metal can only be found among Armenians!"

The *bek*'s relatives, having remained silent up to this point, now joined the conversation. One of them said, "Why should you worry about money, *bek*? Has Khacho ever let you down when you really needed it?"

"With God as a witness, that's so," said another.

"Godfather Khacho is a very good man. He has no equal among the Armenians," added a third.

The old man saw that, against his will, a demand for a hundred pieces of gold was being hung around his neck.

"I can't see the *bek*'s heart broken for lack of a hundred pieces of gold," said Khacho.

"May your house be preserved!" the Kurds cried in unison.

The old man stood up and walked out of the guest room. He called to his oldest son and told him to go to the hayloft without being noticed and bring back one hundred pieces of gold.

"What for?" his son asked.

"Don't you see? These bandits came; they ate and drank their fill, and now it's time to pay their levy," his father answered.

"May God cut off your root, you accursed people!" said his son, and picked up a basket and made as if he were going to get hay.

This was a levy routinely exacted from Armenians any time Kurds paid a visit to them. Refusal to pay would assuredly result in a beating. In our day, although this practice has somewhat abated, gold is still exacted, but by more civil methods.

While the old man was out, the Kurds were engaged in the following conversation:

"If the old fellow doesn't bring the gold, I'll soon enough have his house burned down," the *bek* said vehemently.

"That won't be necessary," said one of his relatives to calm him down. "Khacho's a good Armenian. You don't need to harm him. His door has always been open to us, and we took whatever we wanted. He's a good man, and we can't forget his hospitality."

Just then, Khacho came back in. "As God is my witness, this money was for my soul, to make a pilgrimage to Jerusalem..." he said, presenting the pouch of gold to the *bek*.

"Don't lie Khacho. I know you have plenty and then some," said the *bek* as he picked up the pouch and put it in his pocket without counting it.

The cool of the evening was already setting in, and the *bek* ordered the horses to be prepared to leave. He left the guest house and, while the horses were being readied, walked around the courtyard with his host. He saw Stepanig playing with the fawn, and went up to him.

"He's a good little fellow, isn't he?"

"Yes, he's good, but he has a dog bite on his leg. I'll take care of him, though. That seems to be the reason he hasn't accepted any food," answered the youth as he bound up the wound.

"Stepanig, I see that you're fond of animals, so I'll send one of my colts for you."

"I don't care for horses."

"Well, what do you like?"

"I like deer like this one, or partridge."

"Well, then, after my next hunt if any remain uninjured, I'll send one for you."

The *bek*'s servants informed him that the horses were ready. He thanked his host and left the house. His fine horse stood waiting for him outside the door. Old Khacho held the stirrups for the *bek* as he mounted. This was an important gesture of subordination to his respected guest. Now mounted, the *bek* took up his spear, and saying goodbye, rode off. The old man stood motionless for a long time, looking after him. Once more he watched as the *bek* prodded his horse to leap over the culvert, disdaining to use the bridge, which, from his point of view, was only for the use of the weak and lazy. He saw the *bek* give chase to a rabbit among the bushes, and, pursuing it with the speed of an eagle, pierce the body of the unfortunate animal with his spear.

And as he looked, he thought, "Why is it the judgement of heaven and earth, that the Kurd, having no bread of his own to eat, the Armenian works and plants and provides for him? The Kurd receives a beautiful steed as a gift; he rides it; he enjoys himself and steals the earth itself with every step he takes, and still the Armenian pays him money... the Armenian who doesn't have the right to mount anything but a donkey."

CHAPTER 8

That evening, all of Khacho's sons had returned from their labor in the fields. An oil lamp in one corner cast its feeble light around the room. His sons took their places around the table and sat eating silently. Only their father spoke from time to time. The sweet springtime air flowed through the house. The bellowing of the sheep newly returned from pasture could be heard outside. In the kitchen, the daughters-in-law were making dinner for the shepherds and field workers; these men hadn't eaten yet, and had to be served before the daughters-in-law themselves could sit down to dinner with their girls. The little children, worn out from playing, had long since gone to bed without anything to eat.

After the meal, Khacho's sons returned to their chores. Much remained to be done: caring for the animals, irrigating the fields (since it was their turn to do so), and going to the mill to grind flour. In short, there were a thousand and one things that still needed to be done.

The table was cleared, and only Khacho remained sitting. His eldest son stayed and prepared his pipe for him. A deep silence prevailed. It seemed the black-winged demon of sadness sat upon the heart of this peaceable household.

After taking a few puffs on his pipe, Khacho asked his son, "How much flour did the Kurds take?"

"Exactly twelve loads worth," his son answered in a troubled tone.

"The *bek* only asked for ten."

"They brought their own extra large sacks with them and filled them right to the top. You'd think they had ordered and paid for the flour in advance, the bastards!"

"Whose oxen did they use to carry it?"

"Ours, and thanks be to God if they come back on their own. I'm afraid the Kurds will eat the oxen along with the flour."

"The *bek* wouldn't do such a disgraceful thing."

"Where would a Kurd acquire such decency? Is it unheard of for them to eat sumpter animals like ours? To tell the truth, what really bothers me is not so much giving away the hundred pieces of gold. What really bothers me is that after we served them our own food, we had to give away our flour to be carried off on our own oxen so they could take it home and enjoy it. What kind of punishment from God is that? How long will those Kurds go on plundering us? They come, they take and take, and you can never get anything back. They demand more and more, and they have no shame or conscience. It seems God created us just to feed them."

"Are you surprised at that?" old Khacho responded, now puffing harder on his pipe as if trying to quench his own anger. "What can we do, son? If we don't willingly let them have what they want, they'll just take it by force. It's better that they steal from us under the guise of civility and friendliness."

"It was we, ourselves, who got them used to such robbery," said his son. "We could refuse to give them anything, and then they'd be forced to plant and sweat for their own bread. We're the ones who taught them to be lazy and live at our expense."

"That's true," his father responded sadly, "But a pattern handed down to us by our forefathers can't be undone in one day. We're forced to reap the bitter fruit of their stupidity. Listen, son, I know your heart is brimming with hatred. I know that subservience is odious to you. But if we don't give them what they want, they'll become hostile. You saw how they stole a whole flock of sheep from the mountains. And whom can we complain to? Who will listen? Everyone in a position to punish wrongdoing and defend justice is a bandit, from the vali and the pasha, right down to the lowest moutir and kaimakam. Bandits are brothers, and, as they say, 'a dog runs with a dog, and both of them come from the same house.' You can see for yourself that instead of sending chains to arrest and hang this great bandit, Fattah-Bek, the vali sends him the gift of a beautiful horse; this criminal who has filled the whole province with blood and tears. If the vali himself, the governor of this entire region, conducts himself in this way, whom can we complain to? Only God is left, and it seems that even God doesn't hear us because of our many sins..."

His son was silent, and Khacho spoke on:

"We are Armenians, and God's curse is upon us. It's we who have ruined our own home. Disunity, dissension, jealousy, and enmity, these and a thousand and one other similar evils have poisoned our hearts for too long. It's the burden of these sins that we are carrying. That's not the Kurd's fault. If we were unified and brave, what could the Kurd do, the simple-minded and lazy Kurd?"

He asked his son to light his pipe again. His son gave him a light, then said, "There are six of us brothers, father. With just one word from you, we could easily throw out Fattah-Bek and his thirty men so that never again would they set foot here and dare perpetrate these indignities."

"I know you could. But what good would that do? You might kill two or three, but you can be sure their entire tribe would descend on us and level us all to the ground. And what Armenian would come to our defense? Not one. In fact, many might well be glad. That's the way Armenians are. But not so the Kurds; if you kill one of them, the entire tribe will avenge his blood; they have unity. The blood of one is seen as the blood of the entire tribe, as if they all belonged to one household. Do we have that kind of unity? No. Each man has his own cares, and he worries only about himself. Whatever happens to someone else, so be it. What does he care, so long as he is comfortable and unmolested? Ignorant people like this have no notion of 'one for all, and all for one.'"

Though not an educated man, old Khacho had learned a great deal from life, from experience, and the world. His native intelligence had undergone such development through life's vicissitudes that at times a degree of truth emerged from his judgements as is usually available only to persons who have engaged in deep study of human existence. He spoke again:

"We've been placed by circumstances in a position where we have no other way of surviving except by working to feed our enemy. There is no alternative. We have to get along with those who rob us. It's true that Fattah-Bek robs us, but we can't reject his friendliness no matter how false it is."

"Why?" asked his son.

"Because, by being on good terms with a big robber, one gains freedom from little ones; they're all tied together. Other Kurds will keep their hands off our sheep and crops, knowing that we're on good terms with Fattah-Bek, and that if they steal from us, he'll find what they stole and get it back for us."

"What good does that do? None," responded his son. "Fattah-Bek brings us an egg and takes an ox. He won't let another Kurd steal our sheep, but when he needs them, he takes them by the hundreds. We're his milk-cow, kept and protected for his own use alone."

"That's all quite true, son, and I understand what you mean. But you have to recognize that this is how Armenians learned to survive ages ago. I certainly haven't seen it myself in books, but once there was a monk at the monastery of Uch-Kilisah who explained to me that in the past, whenever an enemy invaded our land, Armenians met them with precious gifts and chests full of gold instead of meeting them with sword and fire. It was they who taught us to bribe rather than punish our enemy; they are the ones who taught us to give away our possessions to save our necks."

"But we shouldn't go on forever perpetuating the same mistake our forefathers made," his son interjected.

"It's very hard to rectify such an old mistake all at once. This is something that has gone on for centuries, and it will take centuries to correct. Let me see you try to convince people that there's any other way to deal with the enemy; that the enemy is simply a man like us; that his body isn't made of iron, and that when he comes to rob us with weapons in his hand, we can respond in kind. Harangue the people with this—and more. Do you think they'll understand? They'll take you for a fool and laugh at your stupidity. But their attitude is nothing new; it was inherited from their forefathers."

His son had no reply to this, finding all his father had said irrefutable; yet he couldn't help considering what it would take to change the outlook of the people, and he asked, "Granted that this is how our ancestors did things and that we have simply gone on following their pattern—aren't we compelled to change our way, seeing that it is leading to doom? Isn't it necessary to get the people to understand how badly they're being abused?"

"It's necessary, but who can do it? That's a job for the kind of people who have responsibility for informing people and showing them the way. It's a task that calls for every priest and vartabed. But all they preach is 'turn the other cheek.' It's a job for the teachers who instruct our children, but there isn't one real teacher in our entire province."

"I can't go along with everything you say, father. The Kurds don't have priests or vartabeds or teachers, and yet they know how to deal with people. Who taught them that an unarmed man is no better than a blind chicken, at everyone's mercy?"

"True, the Kurd has no vartabeds or teachers, but he has a sheikh; and though the sheikh is a spiritual leader, he bears arms and joins in with the people in looting and pillaging. He never preaches against these things. Now, what do our priests preach?"

His son remained silent as Khacho continued. "Out of all this misfortune there's one consolation: As much as they loot and rob us, our stores remain full and they never have enough to eat."

"Have you heard that saying, Father, 'The thief, unable to make a house of his own, destroys another's house'? The Kurd, who neither labors, nor plants, nor brings in a harvest, stays hungry; but when he steals bread from a toiling Armenian, he leaves him starving too. Don't take our home for an example; look at how many Armenians have been reduced to poverty and hunger because of the Kurds?"

"That's true, son, but there's something else you have to consider. Look at how many sheep are slaughtered; and yet they grow, they multiply, and turn into great flocks. The wolf who pounces on them and eats them stays hungry and scarcely multiplies at all. Have you ever seen wolves in great numbers? The wolf is a beast; now he pounces on a sheep, he eats it, he fills himself up, then he doesn't know where his next meal will come from. He's forced to hunt, but prey doesn't come along every day. A predator is full one day and starving the next. So—the Kurd is the wolf, and we are the sheep."

"The way I look at it, father, if it weren't for the shepherd, the wolves wouldn't leave one sheep; then you wouldn't find any flocks. It's true we're the sheep, but we're sheep without shepherds. In that situation, the only alternative is to have fangs and claws like the wolf."

CHAPTER 9

The road from Erzeroum to Bayazid is the only caravan route between Trebizond and Persia; it was beside this road that a tribe of Kurds had pitched their tents in a beautiful green vale. One could see from the number of tents, which filled most of the vale, that this was a large tribe. Herds of horses and cows and flocks of sheep were spread out in the mountains, evidence of the well-endowed existence of these people.

It was completely dark by the time Fattah-Bek returned from Khacho's house to this encampment which was under his sole authority and rule as chieftain. Fires for heating milk and cooking supper were still burning in front of various tents, and a lovely light spread itself about him and his men as they entered the camp. Dogs raised a chorus of barking, and shepherds voiced signals that horsemen were approaching. Their signals were answered in kind by the *bek*'s horsemen and, without seeing them, the shepherds knew who the horsemen were. The *bek* made his way straight to the tent where his guest was staying, the servant who had delivered the new horse as a gift from the vali at Erzeroum.

This man was a veteran Turkish official, implicated in every sort of misconduct and corruption. He had at one time held the post of moutir in Van, but had to be dismissed after getting involved in outrageous bribery.

"You've certainly kept me waiting long enough, *bek*. I was planning to leave this evening," he said, standing up as the *bek* walked in.

"I swear by the sheikh's head, you're a most impatient man," said the *bek*, laughing. "It's amazing you waited the full nine months to come out of your mother's belly! We haven't seen enough of each other yet. What's your hurry? Could it be you're bored here in my tent?"

"Certainly not, your hospitality is very satisfying. If some day I go to paradise (for which I have no high hopes), I'd wish to be placed in your tent. Nevertheless, I'd be much obliged if you'd see me off tomorrow morning."

"Of course, of course, I know how the Ottomans are: they've grown accustomed, in their crowded cities, to lounging on delicate cushions from morning till night, smoking *nargilehs*, drinking coffee... And what is there for you to do here, in this wilderness? Frankly, I regret not entertaining you as I should have. But you don't care for hunting or riding horses; here, in these mountains of ours, that's the only sport we have."

The moutir replied with Turkish-style compliments. "The light of your face is worth more to me than any games, and I count it a blessing to be worthy of seeing you. But understand, *bek*, that I, your servant, am not a free man. The vali allowed me no more than ten days for this trip."

"I'll send the vali a letter telling him I delayed you. You know how much he respects my word."

"How well I know. He thinks very highly of you, and your words are like pearls to him. He lets everyone know that you're the bravest and most loyal of all the *bek*s we have, and, because of that, he's recommended you for the highest military decoration, the Majitia."[10]

"I have no use for such decorations. They're nothing but women's trinkets," the *bek* replied with a contemptuous smile on his virile face.

"What is it you like then?"

"I like things made of gold."

"Well, you'll get that too, *bek*. The vali is very well-disposed toward you. You know that he's given you high rank because of your great services in protecting the frontier and keeping the peace in this province. He's agreed with your proposal that there be no more moutir or kaimakam assigned here, and that all administration be placed in your hands. He's gone along with your wishes on all these points and he's never let you down."

"For that, I'm obliged to him."

While this conversation was taking place, the *bek*'s servants were sitting about on the ground outside his tent, passing their time engaged in a conversation of a very different sort. Each was recounting his own exploits in robbery, murder, chasing women, and so on:

"Osman stole as many sheep as he has hairs on his head," said Omar.

"And what about you, Omar? You're not such a fine fellow yourself," said Osman in response. "You went after as many Armenian women as I have sheep."

"Shapan doesn't like Armenian girls. He says they cry too easily," said one of the other servants, joining the conversation.

"That's no lie," said Shapan. "Those bitches are so sensitive, they fall to pieces like lilies as soon as you touch them. But, by God, our women are like stone. You can scratch them with the claws of a wild beast, and they still don't cry. I can't take it when women cry. It seems they have a knack for it."

(What barbarity, that the tears of an Armenian woman would occasion anger in a Kurd.)

"And there's something else, too," said a man who was older than the rest, "Those infidels will never let go of their damned religion. As you know, I have three of them, and to tell you the truth, I never beat them, even though I catch them praying in secret. But they work like oxen and don't sleep all the time the way our women do."

A young Kurd spoke up with considerable animation. "But Khacho has some cute daughters-in-law. If the *bek* and Khacho weren't friends, I'd take one of them for myself."

The barking of dogs interrupted this conversation. Again, the warning signals of the shepherds could be heard in the distance. A few of the servants grabbed their weapons and ran toward the sounds. As they moved out into the darkness, they heard sighs. "For the love of God, lead us to the *bek*. We have a grievance to present." Had it not been for the timely arrival of the servants on the scene, the dogs would have soon attacked this pitiful group. It is only at the greatest risk that one approaches a Kurdish camp at night; in a flash, one could find oneself pierced by a spear.

The small group of strangers was escorted to the tent where the *bek* sat entertaining his guest. In the light of the lanterns it could be seen that they were traveling merchants. They bore fresh, crudely bandaged wounds on various parts of their bodies, and one had a cut on his head.

Hearing all this commotion, the *bek* called out to one of his servants, "What has happened?"

"Some merchants say they have a grievance to bring up with you. They say their caravan has been robbed."

An uncomfortable look passed over the *bek*'s face, but he soon composed himself and ordered the group to be sent in.

"This is really astonishing," he said turning toward the moutir. "Nothing like this has ever happened in my territory. How could their caravan have been robbed?"

The *bek* had a habit of calling whatever area his clan was living in "my territory," though Kurds never owned a shred of land and went from place to place like gypsies.

"Banditry can happen anywhere. No country has ever been entirely free of it," the moutir responded calmly. "Devils have even shown up in heaven. In Erzeroum, a day doesn't go by that the vali doesn't hear grievances like this."

Encouraged by such ingratiating comments, the *bek* said, "I swear by the sheikh, not even a bird flies over my territory without my knowledge. I wonder what sort of devil could have robbed these poor people."

The bloodied, wounded merchants approached.

"We have come to kiss the dust of your feet, *bek*. Up above, we honor God, and here below, we honor you. For the love of the prophets, help us; we are humble merchants. Our caravan was robbed and many of our brethren were killed. Before your benevolent eyes, you see those who survived wounded and close to death. Everything we had was taken. Nothing was left."

Some of the wounded, too weak to stand, sat down on the ground.

The others remained standing.

"Where did this happen?" the *bek* asked.

"Right in this vicinity, in the nearby mountains. They forced our caravan off the road and into an isolated vale. They robbed us, then stuck us in a gully and disappeared with everything."

"What time of day was it?"

"In the middle of the day. We stayed tied up in that gully until evening, when, by the mercy of God, one of our number was able to untie himself and set us all free. But for that, we would have starved to death there and been eaten by wild beasts."

"Where are you from? Where did your caravan start and where are you going?" the *bek* asked, continuing his interrogation.

"We, your servants, are Persian merchants. We picked up our wares in Trebizond, and they had been shipped there from Constantinople. Everything went well on our way from Erzeroum to this area. Our next stop was to be Bayazid, and then on to Persia. But then this calamity befell us. Our caravan was loaded with highly valuable goods, but they left nothing. They picked what they wanted and burned the rest."

"With the sheikh as my witness, I have never before heard of such a thing," the *bek* said, addressing himself to the moutir who had been closely following the merchants' story.

"Could you tell who the bandits were?" the moutir asked, taking up his own interrogation.

"How could we tell?" responded the spokesman for merchants. "Their faces were all covered. We could only see their eyes. As soon as they got hold of us, they blindfolded us; then they started going through our goods. But we saw enough to know that they were Kurds."

"How many?"

"Around fifty."

"Which direction did they go?"

"We couldn't tell. As I said, we were blind-folded and stuck in a gully with our hands and feet tied."

"That's enough! I get the picture," said the *bek*, irritably breaking in on the moutir's interrogation.

The *bek* then turned to the merchants and said, "Go now and rest. If the bandits happen to be Kurds from this area, I will surely find them out, and you won't lose anything. If they are from somewhere else, I will find that out, too. Rest assured, I won't tolerate such crime in my territory."

The merchants bowed their heads and invoked blessings on the *bek*'s life.

"Grbo, take these men to your tent and treat them as befits a guest of God," said the *bek* to one of his servants. "Call the physician immediately so he can take care of their wounds. I'm placing them in your care; if they have any complaints, I'll hold you responsible."

Once again, the merchants invoked blessings on the *bek*, then departed.

When they were gone, the *bek* turned to his guest, saying, "Now do you see what has happened here, esteemed moutir? You tell me what devil made off with their goods! I'm sure the bandits couldn't have been Kurds from here. I mete out strong punishment to bandits. I am feared in this area, and no one would dare do such a thing. But frequently, such people come from elsewhere, mostly from Persia, and carry out their banditry here. If Persians put on Kurdish clothing, who can tell who they really are? This has occurred many times and has caused us many headaches. But I'll have to do something about it. Perhaps I'll succeed in catching them."

"Ahmeh," he said, turning to one of his nephews who had been sitting quietly by, "I want you to go quickly and gather twenty of our bravest horsemen. Go to the spot where the robbery took place and search for clues. Ask the shepherds in the area what they saw. In short, do everything possible to find out who the outlaws were who committed this crime in my territory. I don't have to waste words. You know what to do. Such robbery in my territory brings dishonor to my name, and I won't tolerate it."

Ahmeh set forth into the night to carry out the *bek*'s orders.

"Ahmeh has keen senses. If the bandits aren't far off, he'll surely find them," the *bek* said to his guest.

"That's obvious," said the moutir in a knowing tone.

It was already well into the night, and the *bek* called for supper to be served. After eating and drinking together, the *bek* bid good night to his guest and wished him a good rest, then left for his own tent to go to sleep.

But the *moutir* had something on his mind, and didn't fall asleep for a long time.

CHAPTER 10

Fattah-Bek's tent was divided into two parts, one of which was the women's quarters and the other his living room. His tent was plain in design like those of Kurdish shepherds, made entirely of black sackcloth sewn together by his wives and attendants. The *bek* entered his living room and ordered the servant who was accompanying him to lower the curtains and then leave. Sitting there, he seemed to be waiting for someone. The lamps suspended from the ceiling poles flickered dimly. In the women's quarters, it seemed everyone was asleep, as there was not a sound.

Grbo appeared, the same servant to whom the *bek* had entrusted the care of the merchants who had been robbed.

"Are your guests comfortable?" the *bek* asked in a special tone, looking directly into his servant's eyes.

"Thanks to my gracious master, they are at rest," responded the wily Kurd. "They ate, they drank, and they went to sleep. Perhaps they are dreaming they're about to find their lost merchandise."

"No dead person has ever returned from hell," said the *bek* sarcastically. "Where did you put the merchandise?"

"In our village, in lame Alo's house."

"Is it good?"

"Never before has God dropped such good a haul into our hands, *bek*. There's gold, silver, the very finest goods. In short, whatever you'd want, you'll find."

"Did anyone see you when you entered the town?"

"Who could have seen us? There was no one there. They had all taken their animals to pasture. There were only a few Armenian families left, and as soon as it got dark they locked themselves up in their houses like a bunch of blind chickens. They kept their heads down and went to sleep without ever looking out again."

"Where did you store the goods?"

"In Alo's house, as I said. That old wolf's house has hundreds of places to hide things in. We filled one of them with the merchandise and locked the doors. The devil himself couldn't find the stuff. I brought the keys with me," he said, handing the *bek* two keys.

"That's fine. Alo is dependable. This won't be the first time he's helped us like this."

Having finished his account of the arrangements that had been made, Grbo began describing the manner in which the attack on the caravan had been carried out, the details of the robbery, and the various feats of valor of specific individuals, etc.

"May you have a long life, Grbo. I've always recognized your courage," the *bek* responded. "As soon as that bastard is gone (he referred to the moutir), I'll divide the stuff up, and everyone will get his due."

Grbo nodded without saying anything.

"But one thing still bothers me," said the *bek* "I just wish this whole thing hadn't happened while he was here."

"You mean the moutir?"

"Yes. The moutir."

"That's not a big problem," Grbo said with a smile. "We'll send the moutir off with all due respect and loaded with gifts, and he'll go away a happy man. But two of our horsemen can follow along behind him, and before he makes it to Erzeroum, they'll chop off his head and take back the gifts we gave him. So the moutir will never get close enough to the vali to say a word. Isn't that a good plan?"

The *bek* made no immediate reply and deeply pondered the matter.

"Needless to say, he will be killed far outside our region, in the area around Erzeroum, so that no one could suspect us," Grbo added.

"That won't be necessary," the *bek* said after some moments of reflection. "If the vali gets any word of this, I'll find a way to keep him satisfied, and he won't say a thing."

As if suddenly remembering something, Grbo put his hand to his broad chest and pulled out a silver case wrapped in a handkerchief and covered with beautiful embossed designs. He handed it to the *bek*. "I didn't want to leave this in Alo's house. It's too small and could have got lost," he said.

The *bek* opened the case and found an assortment of women's adornments each in its own special recess—rings, bracelets, necklaces, all made of gold and mounted with precious gems.

"These belonged to a Jew; he had them made in Constantinople for a Persian prince due to get married this summer," said Grbo in an amused tone. "The poor bride will have to go without her adornments. The Jew murmured for me to give them back, but I put a stop to that and laid him to rest."

In Grbo's language, laying to rest meant killing.

"You can go now, Grbo. Treat your guests with respect. We'll see what can be done tomorrow," the *bek* said.

The bandit leader nodded and left.

The reader will note that this man, Grbo, who played host to the aggrieved merchants was the very same Grbo who had led the attack on them; and that the leader of this entire gang of bandits was Fattah-Bek himself, the man to whom the robbed merchants now came with their grievance, the man who had sole responsibility for law and order and defense of the borders in this district.

After Grbo's departure, the *bek* sat for a long while looking over the beautiful jewelry. He himself didn't understand what it was about these gleaming gems that was so fascinating to him. "I'll send this case to the vali in Erzeroum. There could be no better gift for him," he mused. Suddenly another idea came to him, as if remembering a creature more dear to him than anyone in the world. "No, that beautiful necklace must adorn *her* lovely neck. Only *her* stunning arms are worthy of these bracelets, and *her* wondrous fingers were made to wear these rings," he said with deep feeling.

Under the influence of love, this half-civilized man changed, becoming finer and more sympathetic. Wild beasts become crazed in love, but men become more tender, and it was this that now distinguished the *bek* from beasts.

"I have to keep this jewelry for *her* and no one but *her*."

He had lost himself so deep in thought, these last words were quite audible, and he was totally unaware that someone, having lifted the curtain of the women's quarter, approached him and now stood as silently as a statue, closely observing him in his trance. It was his wife, the youth Khourshid, distinguished in her beauty. But only death itself could be as pale and as driven as this lovely woman at this moment.

Standing behind him, she seemed on the verge of tearing his soul from his youthful body when, suddenly, he looked back and was astonished to see her. They looked at each other silently for several moments, like two combatants considering where to strike the next blow.

The jewelry box with its glittering contents was still open before him. His wife gave it a sidelong glance, then went and seated herself on a pillow at the side of the tent. These jewels, which would have had any woman beside herself to possess—especially a Kurdish wife, bewitched like a child by any little thing that glitters—these jewels were to her like broken glass, the slivers of which had the power to pierce her heart like a lance.

"Why are you angry? Some of them are for you," said the *bek* on seeing how upset she seemed.

"All I need is bandages, nothing else!" she said, her voice quivering.

The feeble lantern light fell directly on her pallid face, which, in this agitated state, was even more beautiful, like the face of a maddened angel.

"What's going on, Khourshid? Did you have a bad dream?" the *bek* asked solicitously.

"I had no dream. With my own eyes I see what's going on."

The *bek* had no reason to believe that his criminal conduct, the banditry and stupendous bloodletting he carried out with his own hands, would be upsetting to his wife; he knew that his wife, like any other Kurdish wife, would give her man no rest if he ceased his banditry. So it had to be something else that was upsetting her.

Khourshid was the *bek*'s only wife, and though as a Mohammedan he was allowed to have several wives, there were two reasons he did not, one being the custom of the Kurds to have few wives, and one other more significant reason: Khourshid was the daughter of a Kurdish sheikh, a powerful man whose spiritual authority extended to every tribe and from whom just one word could strip even the most eminent tribal chief of his position. And the *bek*, being this man's only son-in-law, owed his position to him. Adding another wife would be an affront to Khourshid's nobility. These were the thoughts that went through the *bek*'s mind as he looked at his wife's anxious and distraught face.

He viewed the emotions that filled his heart now from a purely practical and mundane point of view, without any further psychological dimension. He concluded that since his wife was the daughter of a sheikh, it was no use trying to replace her with another. And yet when his eyes fell again on the gleaming jewelry before him, he pictured once more that lovely creature to whom just a few moments before he was planning to give them.

He understood the reason his wife was distressed, but his heart was now ruled by the very same madness that strikes a wild animal when it is in love.

"Khourshid," he said with emotion, "What do you want of me?"

"I want our marriage to be annulled," she said calmly. "From now on, I am not your wife. In the morning, I'm going to get on a horse and return to my father's home."

"What for?"

"I can't tolerate my womanly dignity as the daughter of a sheikh being shared with a filthy Armenian girl."

"She will be kept as your attendant."

"I have more than enough attendants."

"But I love her."

"Love her as much as you wish, but that love will cost you."

"What are you going to do?"

"That's for me to know."

"So, you're threatening me, are you, you fool! Well, I could crush you under my foot right now like a clay dish."

"Don't move. Take a look," said his wife showing a small pistol gripped in her hand.

She was on her feet now.

The *bek* was taken aback. He had never expected such a decisive act from his wife. Not quite knowing what to do, he remained still, though he put his hand to the dagger in his belt.

Just at that moment, from the women's quarters, came the sound of a crying baby who had just woken up. It was a pacifying sound and seemed to soften the couple's rage. Maternal love overcame womanly jealousy, and Khourshid hurried toward her crying child with just these parting words:

"I'll get my revenge, yet!"

CHAPTER 11

Following the birth of their last child, Stepanig, old Khacho's wife had died. Though it was unusual for a peasant of Khacho's age to be without a wife, he had never married again. His wife's role in directing household affairs was taken over by his eldest daughter-in-law, Sara, known throughout the village as a prudent and capable housewife. She often gave advice to old Khacho, and all the other daughters-in-law acknowledged her authority.

One morning when all in the household were busy with their daily tasks, a servant girl, returning from the spring with a jug of water on her shoulder, had a message for Sara. She informed Sara that a Kurdish girl was outside looking for her.

"Tell her to come here. You can see that I'm busy."

"She won't come in. She says she has something very important to tell you," the servant girl replied.

Sara went out and found the girl standing near the door.

She was thin and tall, with a striking face.

"Let's go somewhere where people won't walk by," the girl said, pointing toward some trees in the distance.

Taking a look at the girl's animated eyes, Sara was struck with doubt about her intentions. Why did she want to take her to those distant trees, away from everyone? What did she want with her?

"Come inside," Sara said, taking hold of her hand. "There are plenty of places inside where we can talk in private if that's what you're concerned about."

The young stranger agreed to go in without the slightest resistance. Sara led her in to a part of the grounds that were shaded by willow trees.

"We'll sit here, since you are so fond of trees," Sara said, and they sat down on the thick grass near a garden bed.

"Now," said Sara taking the girl's hand in a confidential manner, "What have you come to tell me?"

"Chavo was sent to you by Mistress Khourshid. You must know who she is. She is Chavo's mistress. Chavo thanks God every day for such a mistress. She doesn't beat Chavo, and she gives Chavo her old dresses, and says, 'Wear these, Chavo, you're a good girl.' But who could tell they've been used? Look how new it is! And all of it from mistress! She just wears it for one day, and then it's too old for her."

And, indeed, it's true that Kurdish girls are dressed very well and attractively. But Sara learned little from Chavo's incoherent words, speaking about herself in the third person, as she did. All Sara understood was that her name was Chavo and that she was the maidservant to Khourshid, her mistress. Sara had already heard of Khourshid, since she was the wife of Fattah-Bek, an accustomed guest at Khacho's house. But she still had no idea why Khourshid had sent this scatter-brained girl to see her. Being familiar with the uncultured nature of Kurdish girls, she allowed Chavo to reveal the purpose of her visit in her own time.

"So your name is Chavo. What a pretty name!"

"My mother called me Chavahir, but my mistress likes to call me Chavo because she says Chavahir is too long."

"Well, I will call you Chavo, the way your mistress does. Now, Chavo, what did your mistress say to you when she sent you off to see me?"

But the girl was easily distracted from giving a direct answer, apparently due to the jumble of thoughts in her mind, the challenge of putting them in some kind of order, and not knowing where to begin.

"Chavo's mistress had a fight with her husband last night," she replied. "Don't look at me like that. Chavo is no child; she's quite a little devil. Chavo heard everything from behind the curtain when they had their argument. Oh, how angry my mistress was! She tore at her hair and ripped up her dress. Too bad about the dress; it could have been mine to wear."

"Chavo must know how to sew. She can patch it up and then wear it," said Sara, seeing how concerned the simple girl was about clothing.

"Of course I can sew! Look at these fingers," she said, displaying the fingers of her left hand. "You can see how often Chavo's mother pierced her fingers with a needle, saying, 'If it's the last thing you do, you'll learn to sew!'"

"I can see that you're a nice girl. Please tell me what they argued about."

"He said he was going to bring another woman home, and she said, 'No you won't! If you try, I'll strangle you!' Isn't that awful? Khourshid has no equal. Why would he want someone new?"

Little by little the riddle became clearer to Sara. "No one can compare with Khourshid, that's for sure," she replied, "but who is this new woman her husband wants?"

"Chavo's mistress will die if he brings in another woman, and Chavo will die soon after," the servant-girl said with her eyes full of tears.

"Well, who is this woman he plans to bring home?" Sara asked, her patience running out at last,

"First, ask Chavo why her lady sent her to you, and then Chavo will tell you who it is."

"All right then, why did she send you here?"

"The morning after their big fight, my lady said, 'Chavo, go to our friend Khacho's house. Give Sara a big greeting, and ask her how she is, and then say'… Oh, no! I forgot to ask how you are!"

"I'm very well, but what did your mistress say?"

"She said, 'Take Sara to a private spot and tell her'… (that's why I asked to go to the trees, to be alone there)."

"It's just as private right here; there's no one around. What did she say?"

"She said that you should get Stepanig away from here as soon as possible. She said if you can't spare anyone to escort him, she will provide someone herself, and Stepanig will be taken wherever you want. She told me all this before daylight. 'Go, now, Chavo, and don't say a word to anyone,' she said, then Chavo left."

The girl went on to describe her lady's various warnings about secrecy. She added that she herself had reason to fear her mistress, since she knew she was capable of killing, as Chavo had seen her do when she killed a servant girl, though Chavo did not divulge the reason for the incident… But Sara didn't hear any of this. At the mention of Stepanig's name, it was as if she were struck by lightning. She became faint and would have fallen to the ground, if it hadn't been for the support of the Kurdish girl's strong arms.

This naïve country girl could hardly comprehend the reasons for Sara's pathetic reaction, but she felt sorry for her and offered her words of comfort.

"Don't worry, as long as my mistress lives, she won't permit any girls to be taken from your home."

"What girls do you mean? There aren't any girls of age in this household," Sara said, somewhat regaining her presence of mind.

"The *bek* knows that Stepanig is a girl."

All this time, Stepanig was out in the yard feeding the roe deer the *bek* had brought as a gift a few days earlier. The sunlight fell on the young man's beautiful face, and, at a distance, one could see the comeliness of youth in his features.

"Look, there's Stepanig," said Sara, pointing into the yard. "Now, you tell me, who says that he's a girl? Who told the *bek* such a lie?"

"One of your Kurdish servant girls did—Hilo's wife, and my mistress said, 'I'll kill that scamp!'"

"Hilo's wife was lying. She stole from us and we got rid of her. Because of that, she made up a lie."

Except for her innocent loyalty to her mistress, which is normal in Kurdish girls, Sara could see that Chavo wasn't as dull-witted as she thought at first, and she decided to entrust her with a message. She told Chavo to greet her mistress warmly and to ask after her well-being, as well. She told her to thank her mistress for the information she had conveyed. Her mistress should be told that though she was entirely wrong in believing Stepanig was a girl, her wishes would be followed and Stepanig would be sent away. She added that she would like very much to have a personal meeting with Chavo's mistress to discuss the matter further, and that she would leave arrangements for a secret meeting up to her.

At last, Sara said, "Now, my bright little Chavo, can you remember all that?"

"Chavo has a sharp mind. Chavo won't forget," she said and kept repeating what Sara had told her, though here and there she made errors or changed the order around. Sara would correct her errors, then she would continue repeating her lesson.

"Now Chavo can say it just like Sara did," she said. "On the way back, Chavo will keep saying it so she doesn't forget."

"But someone might overhear it."

"Chavo is not that stupid! Chavo will say it to herself in her mind."

The girl looked at the sun, and seeing it was not far from sunset, stood up and said she had to be on her way since it was a long way back to her lord's tents.

"Wait a moment, Chavo. I have something to give you, you're such a nice girl," said Sara, and she went inside.

Meanwhile, Stepanig, who had been occupied with the roe deer, saw the girl standing alone and approached.

"Are you leaving now?" Stepanig asked.

"Yes. Don't you see the sun? It will soon be dark," she said, with a gesture toward the sky.

"But you came to our house and didn't have anything to eat yet," said Stepanig.

"Oh, that's right! Chavo hasn't had a thing to eat all day. Chavo is famished."

"I'm going to get something for you to eat," said Stepanig.

The Kurdish girl, struck by the boy's kindness, hugged and kissed him. Stepanig hurried into the house and returned with honey and butter rolled up in lavash.[11]

"Now, sit down and eat," said Stepanig.

"Chavo will have to eat it on the way."

Just then, Sara returned with a beautiful red scarf made of silk, the kind that Kurdish women prize the most as adornments for their heads. On catching sight of it, Chavo was so thrilled she forgot all the rules of politeness and snatched it from Sara's hand. She lost no time wrapping the lovely scarf around her pretty head, and looked at Sara and Stepanig as into a mirror.

"Isn't Chavo pretty now?" she asked them.

"Yes. She is pretty," they both agreed.

"Well then, give Chavo a kiss."

Sara hugged and kissed her.

"You, too, Stepanig," she said, and Stepanig followed suit.

After giving each of them a kiss, the simple Kurdish girl set out on the road back to the *bek*'s tents.

CHAPTER 12

It was only after Chavo had been gone for a while that the full import of the news she had brought struck Sara. Stepanig was still nearby, totally unaware of what awaited him.

"What makes those Kurdish girls so simple-minded?" he asked, putting his hand on Sara's shoulder like a child.

"They aren't simple-minded, my child. They've grown up in the mountains like the wild animals who live there."

"Like my roe deer. I've given him food and water for days now. I hold him in my arms and kiss him, but he still doesn't like me. He still runs off when I come near."

As he spoke, Sara took a look at this tender-hearted youth and her eyes filled with tears. Until this moment, she had never looked as closely at the charm and delicacy of his expression, shining with the fullness of youth. She turned her head away to wipe her tears so he wouldn't notice.

But Stepanig's thoughts were still on the Kurdish girl.

"She was starving, Sara. She said she hadn't eaten all day, so I gave her some bread with butter and honey. I told her to sit down and eat, but she said she would eat it on the way. She must have been in a hurry."

"Yes, she was. She has a long way to go."

"How far?"

"As far as the blue mountains."

"But it's already getting dark. How will she make it through the mountains on foot, without a companion. Won't she be afraid, Sara?"

"She won't be afraid. That's the way her people are. What would a wolf cub have to fear?"

Just then, their conversation was interrupted by someone calling for Sara.

The poor woman was absorbed in bitter worry all day. Acting like someone who is drunk, or whose attention and thoughts are dispersed, she didn't know what she was doing. Instead of picking up what she wanted, she picked up some other object; instead of going where she meant to go, she ended up in some other spot. She made repeated mistakes and was constantly beside herself. Following the death of her mother-in-law, Stepanig had become Sara's dear one; nourished at her breast; taken care of by her hands. Now, a terrible fate was in store for him. With whom could she share what Chavo had told her? She knew if old Khacho ever got word of the *bek*'s plan, he would be unable to withstand the shock of it. The old man already carried an unhealing wound in his heart... Yet, thought Sara, keeping it a secret would be not only impossible but dangerous. Something had to be done immediately to counteract the misfortune that threatened Stepanig. But whom could she talk to about it? All day long, this was the question she grappled with, yet found no satisfactory answer.

That evening when she was finally alone with her husband, Hairabed, he said to her, "Sara, you don't seem yourself today. Are you feeling sick?"

"I do have a bit of a headache, but it's nothing. It will go away."

"Have you tried rubbing some vinegar on your forehead?"

"I've tried everything..."

Gradually preparing her husband for the news, she still didn't quite know how to bring it up, when he himself presented the opportunity. "Who was that Kurdish girl who visited here today?" he asked her.

"She was the maidservant to Khourshid, Fattah-Bek's wife."

"Every time that scoundrel or his people come around, there's some kind of bad news. When will we ever be left alone by those damned people?" said Hairabed bitterly.

"Whatever harm they do us we have to see as God's providence..." his wife said mysteriously.

Seeing that Hairabed was taken aback by these words, she added, "There is some purpose in every misfortune. We have to patiently accept whatever suffering God sends us..."

These humble people found some kind of consolation in any misfortune, ascribing every tribulation in the world to God, and God alone, as if God were the author of every affliction.

"What's going on? What happened?" Hairabed asked with a start.

Sara began recounting what she had heard from the Kurdish girl, and, while she spoke, Hairabed's face turned colors and registered a whole succession of emotions—shock, hatred, fury, and profound sadness, one after the other.

"I've been expecting something like this for a long time," he said, regaining his composure somewhat after the onslaught of emotions he had experienced. "Poor father will die if he hears about this."

"That's exactly what I've had on my mind all day. It will kill him for sure," Sara said.

A complete silence prevailed as they sat thinking about what to do.

"We don't have to tell him," said Hairabed, breaking the silence at last.

"But we can't keep it from your brothers."

"I'll let them know."

"Then we don't have a moment to lose. They have to know as soon as possible. Whatever you decide on has to be carried out right away. Who knows what may happen next?"

Some of Hairabed's brothers were already home, but the others hadn't returned from the fields yet. He stood up and told his wife to keep the matter secret from all her sisters-in-law. He then went to call together the brothers who were home, and, leading them away from the house, told them that when all the brothers were together in one place, there was an urgent matter to be discussed.

As a meeting place, Hairabed chose a spot in the little forest where the family watermill was located, to insure that no one would disturb them, and to keep their father from encountering them and asking questions about what they were discussing.

When all the brothers were present, Hairabed let them know everything Sara had told him. They all just sat as if petrified for a long time; no one could think of a word to say. Their situation was like a scene in a forest, when, in the cool of the evening, thousands of sparrows fill the branches of the trees, their bellies full after a long day's work, chirping away in the branches, filling the entire forest with their lively clamor, when suddenly a hawk glides over-head, and their chorus falls silent. It was this same effect that rendered the brothers mute on hearing the mere mention of Fattah-Bek's name, let alone the news of his evil intentions.

"So much for friendship with a Kurd," one of them said at last. "The *bek* is godfather to our children, yet has forgotten our generosity."

"What kind of friendship can there be between a wolf and a sheep, between a fox and a chicken?" said Hairabed indignantly. "But we are even worse off than sheep and chickens... At least a sheep has horns to defend itself, and a chicken has its claws... But we have nothing... We are a blot on mankind that needs to be washed away, the scum of the earth."

He uttered these words with such complete bitterness, his brothers were aghast. He continued in the same vein:

"What are we? We are diligent, hard-working tillers of the earth... that is what we take pride in... yet the donkey, the horse, the ox, and the buffalo are stronger than we are... and they do more work... We, like them, are nothing more than beasts of burden... The Kurd accomplishes more with his spear than we do with our plow... We do the work, and the Kurd gets the food... We raise beautiful daughters, and they take them away and enjoy them... Whatever is beautiful or desirable is not meant for us... Only what is ugly is left for us, because that's all we deserve..."

"A few days ago I had a talk with father," he went on. "He tried to convince me that our situation isn't so bad, after all, and pointed out the wealth we're surrounded with here, enough to withstand one visit by a band of Kurds. But see, everything is depleted. Now, go ask Father, if they come to take your dear child away from home, are you just going to stand by with your eyes wide open and not dare to speak up? Can that be called a good situation? This is the kind of situation that only an Armenian will put up with, the shameless and demeaned Armenian! Just try taking a tiger cub from its den and you'll see what happens; you'll be torn to shreds in front of its den. The Kurds are like that too. But what are we? We are nothing..."

Hairabed's words had such a powerful impact that some of his brothers resolved to protect Stepanig from Fattah-Bek, even at the cost of their own lives.

"But that would be a waste," Hairabed responded, prudent and experienced as he was. "After killing us, they would still take Stepanig away..."

"At least if we were dead we wouldn't have to witness our sister's humiliation, and we could rest in peace..." said Abo.

But some of the brothers opposed this idea.

"What good will it do to leave our children fatherless for the sake of a girl? I'll have nothing to do with that. We have just one sister. If we lose her, so be it. Why should we risk our lives?" said Ohan.

Another brother, Hago, took a more calculated and practical view of the matter: "That wouldn't be such a great loss, and, in fact, there might be some advantages to it. With Fattah-Bek for a brother-in-law, we will be feared by all the other Armenians. For example, look at our neighbor Mrgo. He's a nobody, and he doesn't even have enough food to eat, but because his daughter is married to a Kurd, we're all afraid of him. We won't even talk to him for fear that any little thing we say may get back to his Kurdish son-in-law and all the Kurds will descend on us one night and slaughter us. Would it be so bad to have a brother-in-law like that?"

But for Abo, who had argued in favor of a life and death fight to save their sister's honor, this was too much: "Jesus Christ as my witness, you've lost your senses, Hago! Even a madman doesn't talk like that. Are we to abandon our light-giving religion, and turn our sister over to a lawless, unbelieving man just to get other Armenians to fear and respect us? Who needs that kind of respect? And consider this, that people can show you respect to your face, but curse you in their hearts. Mrgo gave his daughter to a Kurd, but who likes him? As for being afraid of him, people are afraid of dogs, and wolves, too, and many are afraid of..."

One of the brothers who had been silent up to this point, engrossed in pondering his own religious philosophy, now joined the discussion to oppose Abo. He argued that it was impossible to change what God had ordained; that what will be will be; that God had made the Kurd a Kurd and the Armenian an Armenian; that He had given a weapon to the Kurd, and a hoe to the Armenian; that the two could not trade places, and that God had done this with His own hands. He cited the following as an example:

"The crow wishes it had peacock feathers, but it can't have them. God made each with its own nature."

"But, brother, you're overlooking the fact that the crow and the peacock are two different kinds of birds, whereas the Kurd and the Armenian are both human beings," said Abo in response. "The Kurd isn't born with a weapon in his hands. He is born naked and weak just like us. Why blame everything on God? Did God give weapons to the Kurd to come and drag our daughters away from home? Are we so abject and cowardly because that's the way God created us? No. God has nothing to do with it. He gave us a mind to choose what is best for us. If you go and throw yourself into the river over there, do you think God will take your hand and save you? No. You will perish on your own..."

The oldest son, Hairabed, who had been listening to this exchange in deep silence, came close to rising and planting a kiss on Abo's forehead, but he didn't want to engender jealousy among his brothers.

"You see? Here we are, six brothers gathered together, yet we don't understand each other and can't reach any agreement," he said gravely. "How much harder would it be to achieve unity as a people or a nation!... As long as we are like this, our condition will never change. They will give us blows to the head, they will spit in our face and take our daughters, our possessions, and our land away; and we will be forced to bear every indignity and torment with patience, and work like miserable pack animals so that our enemy can enjoy a prosperous existence. And after all that, we are supposed to thank God that we're permitted to live and crawl on the earth like reptiles..."

Having finished his speech on a deeply sad note, Hairabed went on to set forth a plan of action. He proposed that Stepanig be sent away to the monastery of Saint Hovhaness and kept there until such time as safe passage to Russian territory could be arranged.

Even this plan was unacceptable to Ohan and Hago. They argued this would simply be another form of resistance to the *bek* and only provoke him to greater anger and revenge. They repeated the notion that whatever God willed would be, and that no man could alter it.

Some of the brothers insisted that their father should be notified, as head of the household, and that the decision on what to do should be left with him. The debate went on and on in this vein without reaching any agreement.

Suddenly, the cry of an owl pierced the forest air—the repugnant owl, bearer of bad tidings. All the brothers heard its portentous call emanating from the branches above, and a shudder went through all of them.

"Listen! We were right!" Ohan and Hago cried out. "The owl confirms what we said. Things will turn out badly if we try to hide Stepanig."

But Hairabed and Abo remained unswayed in their position, and the meeting adjourned without any clear decision being reached.

CHAPTER 13

But what sort of riddle was this? Stepanig at first a boy, and now a girl?

The riddle will be explained in full, but its key is hidden in a sad little story:

In a remote spot on Khacho's property there was a grave shaded by a few poplar trees. It had no cross, or grave-marker, nor a single letter written on it. The old man might often be seen on his way to this inauspicious spot, and, in the silence of the night, spending many a moment there with tears flowing from his eyes. Other members of the household paid visits here too; from their deep sadness it could be seen that the happiness of the whole family was bound up with the person buried there.

At one time, Khacho had a daughter named Sona whom Stepanig greatly resembled. When she had turned sixteen years old, proposals came for her hand in marriage from all sides, not only because she belonged to a wealthy family, but also because she was very pretty. Her father gave a great deal of thought to choosing a husband for her, but couldn't decide on one. Then a tragic event put an end to Sona's happiness. One day she went into the fields to pick herbs, but she never came back again. There was much talk about her disappearance. Some said that wild animals had attacked her; some made the superstitious claim that she had been carried off by evil spirits; others said she had been abducted by Kurds. Which story was true was difficult to ascertain. People looked high and low for her, yet despite her father's offer of a sizable reward for reliable information about her disappearance, all efforts to find her failed.

Several weeks passed by.

One day a Kurd showed up at Khacho's house leading a mule with a casket tied to its back. Sona's body was inside.

From the account the Kurd gave, it seemed that a Kurdish nobleman had abducted her from the field. Although this man didn't come from a very distinguished background, he had distinguished himself within his tribe as an outstanding criminal. Finding no other way to escape this despicable man, Sona removed some coins from her cap[12] and paid an old Kurdish woman to procure poison for her. The old woman did as she was told. Sona took the poison and died. The Kurds refused to bury her in their graveyard because, until the very end, she would say, "I am a Christian and will not change my faith," and her body remained unburied. The Kurd who now delivered her remains to Khacho's house had found out the kind of family she came from and had seen an opportunity for personal gain.

There are many instances of this sort of refusal to bury in the Armenian Church, as well, and it has shown fanaticism in the way it has treated those who died in untoward circumstances, citing various circumstances, such as suicide, or death at the hands of impure persons, not having confessed, or not having received Holy Communion, as justifications for priests to refuse burial in the Armenian cemetery.[13] This was why Sona was buried at home. Rejected by the church, she was accepted by her family.

The grief thus visited upon Khacho's home is self-evident. But there were yet more painful consequences to follow. Following Stepanig's birth, her mother, Rehan, unable to bear the grief of losing Sona, began to waste away and eventually died. Sona's tragedy had an extraordinary effect on Stepanig's life, as well, for though dressing as a boy, Stepanig was, in reality, a girl. Lala was the name given to her at baptism. But why was she raised in disguise?

Sona's death was such a shock to Khacho that when Stepanig was born he was seized with foreboding that his new daughter would meet the same fate. This fear was not without foundation, for he knew of hundreds of cases in which girls had been abducted by Mohammedans, something that had become an everyday event in this province. Because of this, Khacho decided to raise his new daughter in the guise of a boy until she had come of age. His poor wife concurred, but died soon after without being able to raise her child. This was the household secret. Only three people outside the home knew of the child's true identity: the village priest, her god-father, and her grand-mother, who was long since dead.

Lala (for that was Stepanig's true name and the one we will use henceforth) was now sixteen years old, an age after which village girls did not long remain at home. Her father was considering a husband for her, but having raised her disguised as a boy, this was a difficult matter, and no proposals for her hand had been offered. In addition, he hoped for a husband from someplace far away. Lala could be taken there, and his fellow villagers would never find out the subterfuge he had engaged in all those years to protect her, though this was common practice in the province. Given these circumstances, where should he look for the right man?

He had his mind set on one particular individual whose name was Tomas Effendi—a deceitful, roly-poly, talkative fellow who was anything but a true human being. No one really knew his origins, but by his own account he was from Bolis[14] where many of his family were *amirahs*. Lala's brothers hated this monster, not only because of his odd-looking face, but also because he was a heartless troublemaker. He always kept his distance from the Armenian community; he always spoke Turkish; and he could always be seen in the company of moutirs, kaimakams, and Kurdish *bek*s. He boasted of his friendship with them and dropped their names to intimidate the Armenian peasants. Tomas Effendi was the moultezim, that is, the official tax collector for the Sultan's court. In the mind of the peasant, the moultezim occupies the same place as an angel of death, or a devil, or Satan in the mind of a non-believer—a being that inspires fear and trembling.

But to peasants the source of greatest fear is also the object of greatest respect. If the devil appeared among them, he wouldn't be met with hatred, but rather flattery. This is how humankind has always been and always will be. People in their primitive stage always honor good and evil equally and offer sacrifices to each. But the remarkable fact is that evil has been offered the majority of these sacrifices. "The good is already ours," thought the primitive, "but evil has to be warded off with sacrifices."

This being so, it is easy to see why Tomas Effendi was received as an honored guest at Khacho's house. As elective headman and official representative of the village, old Khacho had frequent dealings with the tax collector concerning the various types of taxes: tributes, annual levies, tithes on farm produce, etc. Under these circumstances, Tomas Effendi came and went as he wished at Khacho's house, sometimes staying for weeks at a time in the course of doing his job.

The traditional "inn" maintained by the village headman in regional villages like this was always perfectly suited for such visitors: the kaimakam, moutir, moultezim, the vartabed gathering his "spiritual fruit," the ordinary policeman, and even the lowliest of beggars—all sought shelter there, each a very different sort of person.

The morning after the brothers' secret meeting in the forest, Tomas Effendi showed up in the village of O... accompanied by his inseparable cohorts, two Turkish policemen. He had come to select sheep and other animals for taxation, since it was springtime and the villagers would soon be leading their herds away to graze in distant pastures, protected from the fierce summer heat. Having finished up his work, Tomas Effendi was walking home with Khacho.

The Sultan himself, on his way through Bolis to attend morning prayers in the mosque of Ayia Sophia, could not have put on greater airs than this little man, Tomas Effendi, as he made his way through the village of O... With his little pot belly sticking out and his nose in the air, he looked around constantly to see how many villagers bowed their head toward him in respect. On this day he was wearing a sort of uniform emblazoned with an array of yellow buttons, as if he were on his way to a meeting with the vizier.

No sooner had he entered the guest room at Khacho's house than he ordered coffee to be served and started issuing orders on what should be made for supper. The tax collector is master of any house he enters, and if the residents are slack in ministering to his needs, he has his ways of forcing them to comply...

Having sat down together, Khacho addressed himself to the tax collector. "Effendi, it wasn't necessary to beat that peasant the way you did today."

"You're wrong about that, Khacho. 'If you don't beat the donkey, it won't carry the load,'" he replied in his cat-like voice.

"But the man didn't do anything wrong."

"It doesn't matter if he did or he didn't. He may have done nothing wrong today, but tomorrow he might. Haven't you heard that story about Nasreddin Khodja? One of his donkeys got loose and ran off, but instead of catching up with him and punishing him, he beat one of the donkeys that was tied up and quietly standing in his place. They asked him, 'Why are you beating that donkey?' The Khodja replied, 'You just don't know how fast he'd run off if he got the chance!'"

"But the villager wasn't lying. I know very well the Kurds ran off with most of his sheep," said Khacho, with the conviction that it was wrong to beat the well-behaved, innocent donkey instead of the one that broke away.

"I already knew the Kurds had got some of his sheep," the Effendi said gravely. "But if I start making allowances for things like that, then, 'The water will pour down and wash away the mill,' and I'll have to pay the court out of my own pocket. During last year's inventory, that peasant declared one hundred sheep. Now if some Kurds ran off with fifty or sixty of them, how can I be responsible? They steal all the time. True men would keep them from stealing."

"But you have to have a conscience in what you say, Effendi. You only have the right to tax the man on the sheep he actually has. He shouldn't have to pay on sheep that got lost, or were stolen, or died."

"How am I to know if they were stolen?" the Effendi said irritably. "A peasant can hide his sheep and say they are lost or stolen or dead, and make a thousand other such excuses."

Khacho remained silent.

"Haven't you seen the new Decree the Sultan sent me? If only you knew what was in it, you wouldn't be talking like that, Khacho!" and, so saying, the Effendi produced a large packet. Opening it, he drew out a stack of papers and started leafing through them attentively. At last he pulled out a very large, red poster, printed with large letters in a variety of scripts.

"Here, read it," he said, handing it to Khacho.

Khacho took it and looked with wonder at the large print (whatever is big or grand occasions awe in simple folk) and, if he had been able to read Turkish, he would have seen that this enormous red poster was nothing more than an advertisement for a benefit for a famous actress.

But Tomas Effendi was studying him closely and said, "Khacho, you don't handle a Decree from the Sultan in such an uncivilized manner. When you take it in your hands, first you kiss it; then you read it."

The old man humbly kissed the Decree and handed it back to the Effendi.

"No matter how many times you tell these peasants that now the law is such and so—that the taxes have gone up—they still don't understand and keep asserting what they think is true," the Effendi said with particular consternation. "I am a man, too! I lose my patience and beat them. A donkey that gets stuck in the mud won't get near the same spot again no matter what you do, yet these peasants don't even have the sense of a donkey!" (Tomas Effendi had a habit of drawing his key examples and metaphors from the life of donkeys).

"Listen, let me tell you a story, Khacho. You know very well that I have jurisdiction over many villages here in Alashgert. Well, one day a peasant brought in his harvest. He had it threshed, then piled up the clean wheat and called for me to measure it for the tithe before he had it milled. I demanded that he pay the tithe in money instead of wheat. He answered that he couldn't pay in money and that I should take my payment in wheat, since that was within my rights to do. (I can't bear it when these peasant asses start talking about rights!). So I said to myself, 'Curses on you, then! I'll show you what rights are!' and the wheat just lay where it was. The rains came and the wheat got wet; it sprouted, then it got scorched by the sun and turned into nothing. After that, I came back and said to him, 'I won't violate what is right. Pay me in wheat.' But how could he pay? His wheat had turned into a useless powder. So I said, 'Then pay me in money instead.' But he had no money to pay, so I gave him a good beating. After that, I had all of his oxen sold and took the money. That same villager is now so careful in everything he does, he carries a whole load of eggs without breaking a single one. And if he sees me from far away, he humbly bows his head in my direction. Now, that's the way to deal with people!"

"But does that show a good conscience?" old Khacho asked softly, as if afraid of being heard.

"What is conscience?" the Effendi said contemptuously. "Governing is one thing, conscience another. Even though you've governed this village for the last forty years, you still don't understand what it is to govern. You've already heard the story about Nasreddin Khodja's donkeys, but I'll give you another example. A certain pasha was appointed governor of a district. The first thing he did after taking over was to have some innocent people arrested and thrown in jail, as if they were guilty of something. One even had his head chopped off. Though they were innocent, the pasha needed to sacrifice their lives to frighten people. That's what it takes to govern! The people must always be kept in fear. If I hadn't dealt with that peasant's crop the way I did, all the other peasants would think I wasn't a man and wouldn't give me what I need from them."

Thus, Tomas Effendi spoke about his dealings with the Armenian peasants in the same routine tone as used by the Kurds when boasting of their criminal exploits. And what difference was there, indeed, between this Armenian and Fattah-Bek? Only this: that one was a base and wily robber, while the other was a bold, big-hearted bandit.

And so, it was with one of these two men that Lala's fate was to be bound. Yet, neither of them had asked her whom it was she loved...

CHAPTER 14

Tomas Effendi needed to stay at Khacho's house for a few more days; he still had some work to do in the village of O...

Another annual guest at Khacho's house was a young man from Ararat province. He came to the village to buy sheep, oxen, wool, cheese, and oil from the villagers for transport to Alexandropol or Yerevan where they would be sold. With him he brought many goods not available in this province; for instance, various tools for making clothes, and cotton, linen, woolen fabric, tea, sugar, coffee, and many other articles. This type of small merchant was very important to isolated villages like the village of O... and would keep them supplied with whatever they lacked. In turn, these merchants took products from the peasants that they had no way of transporting to distant markets on their own, especially given the many dangers posed to transport in this region, for there were no well-traveled caravan roads here, and contact with the outside world had been entirely cut off for fear of bandits.

The arrival of this young man was an occasion of great joy for everyone in Khacho's home. So welcome was he that everyone carried on with him as if he were a member of the family. On arriving at the village of O... with his small caravan, he would head straight for Khacho's house. He would unload the goods from his few pack animals, stay for weeks at a time until his business was concluded, then take to the road once again.

He arrived one day after Tomas Effendi, and, as he was unloading his animals in the yard, he caught sight of the Effendi standing in the doorway of Khacho's house.

"Ah, so you're here too," the young man said, crossing himself over and over again as he approached the Effendi. "Ach! I have seen the face of a devil and now all my work will fail... in the name of the Father and the Son and..."

Smiling with great delight, the Effendi took hold of the young man's hand and looked him straight in the face.

"You're crazy, truly crazy; I've said it a thousand times, and I'll say it again, you're crazy," said the Effendi. "Now tell me truly, did you bring some rum for me?"

"I brought you some poison to drink so these poor peasants can be rid of you," the young man said, also smiling.

Some of the peasants who had been helping Vartan (for this was the young man's name) unload his wares stood nearby. The Effendi, realizing it was unwise to be seen joking with the foolish young man, started to leave, saying he had work to do in the village and that he and the young merchant would meet again at dinner.

"To eat with you is a sin," was the young man's reply.

"To be sure, a donkey's tail gets neither longer nor shorter, and it's the same way with your judgement. 'Taking a donkey to Jerusalem will never turn it into a pilgrim,'" the Effendi said.

"Oh goodness! Once you get going with your donkey sayings, there's no end to it!" the young man said, turning away.

The Effendi left.

Everyone in Khacho's home, from the oldest to the youngest, had by now got word of Vartan's arrival and could hardly wait for him to begin unpacking his goods. Each and every member of the household had asked Vartan to bring them something special. He carried his wares inside and set them down, and the whole household gathered around. One asked, "Did you bring the shoes I asked for?" Another asked, "Did you bring the hat I wanted?" In a word, voices came from all around asking for one article or another. Even the little children tugged on his clothes, clamoring for various things.

"I brought it, I brought it. Whatever you asked for, I brought."

"Give it to us, give it to us!" they all cried.

"Oh, you little devils, give me a chance to rest, then I'll open everything up. You'll all get what you asked for," Vartan said.

"Now! Now!" everyone shouted.

They were all so familiar with Vartan that they paid him no heed and set to opening the packages themselves. Everything was torn open and spread out on the floor, and everyone grabbed what they wanted. Vartan just stood back with an affectionate smile on his face. "May your house be protected, even the Kurds couldn't plunder a merchant's goods like that!" he said.

But there was one member of the household alone who didn't approach the wares, and that was Stepanig, or Lala, as we call her now. She stood apart, smiling occasionally.

Vartan went up to her and asked, "Why aren't you taking anything?"

"What should I take?" she asked, blushing.

And, indeed, what should she take? So long burdened with the role of playing a boy, she had difficulty settling on something appropriate for a girl. Vartan understood. "I brought something very nice for you," he said to her in a low voice.

"What could that be?" she asked in an equally low voice.

"I'll give it to you later. But no one should see..."

Lala smiled again, then left.

Vartan was a young man of twenty-five; he was tall, with a solid build, and broadly drawn features that could not, truly speaking, be seen as beautiful. His large black eyes had a quite piratical look to them, and a distinct sarcasm could be discerned in the rather tight set of his lips. His bold, agile movement gave signs of unusual physical strength. As for where he was from, no one here had any idea. He was regarded as a foot-loose man with a checkered past, in and out of all kinds of dark dealings. Once, he had been a deacon and a monk in a monastery; at another time, a teacher. But as to why he had left monastery and school, no one knew. Stories told about his monastery and school days depicted a man of brash temperament.

But one thing could be said with certainty about Vartan: he had a reputation as a smuggler among the locals, and, indeed, displayed all the qualities one would associate with this trade—virility, cleverness, and satanic intelligence. Constant exposure to danger and adventure had fostered a steady, fearless, and brave spirit within him.

And there was one more thing: Tomas Effendi wasn't the only one who regarded Vartan as crazy. In the village, as well as in its environs, Vartan was known as "the fool," as if the term was his surname. Of what did his madness consist, since Vartan was not a stupid young man? He was well read and well-rounded in knowledge about human affairs; and despite his youth, he was well-seasoned and had known many trials at the hands of others. In what way was he a fool, then? Only in this, that he engaged in no hypocrisy and ran counter to people's biases. His heart was totally resolute, and he frankly stated whatever unpleasantness needed to be acknowledged. Even in regard to his own mistakes, he covered up nothing and would freely address them. A person like this is regarded as a fool by people. What people demand is that an individual be one person on the outside and a different person on the inside; and they bear an intense hatred towards anyone who states the truth.

People have always regarded the old philosophers as mad, even the eminent Bahloul[15] and Nasreddin Khodja,[16] those in whose madness can be found an exceptional wisdom. But Vartan was no philosopher or prophet, and in the eyes of the common folk his way of assessing and understanding things, his way of thinking, as well as his strange comportment, seemed suspicious and excessive.

In promising Lala that he had brought something special for her and letting her know that he could only give it to her in secret—in this circumstance, Vartan was forced to depart from his usual straightforwardness. It seemed some special feeling obliged him to be secretive. It seemed something sacred was hidden in his heart and needed to be kept inaccessible to outsiders. As he was looking for some way to meet with her secretly, the opportunity presented itself quite naturally.

I totally forgot to describe the lay-out of the yard at old Khacho's house. Most of this great area was so densely filled with mature trees and shrubs of various kinds, it would have been impossible to see anyone from a distance of a few feet. Having put all his wares in order, Vartan stepped out into the garden to find some rest in the coolness of the shade. His heart was in great turmoil… and his soul was beset with sweet agitation… In moments such as these, trees and flowers and the rustle of leaves speak with greater consolation to one in love than any words uttered in the language of ordinary people. Lying down on the tender grass, he looked up for a long time at the blue sky visible through the leafy boughs and followed the movement of white cloud fragments. They flew through the air, jostled each other, piled up, then turned into a single black mass, presaging a storm—like Vartan's heart. It was as if, deep in his heart, indistinct and formless passions had been all at once thrown together and taken the form of that feeling psychologists call love…

Vartan had long known that Stepanig was a girl and even knew why her parents were forced to dress her, name her, and raise her as a boy. It was the knowledge of these circumstances that drew this sensitive young man's attention to this unfortunate girl and filled his heart with the heroic aspiration to liberate her from this unnatural state. Then compassion was succeeded by love, but until that day it was a love unspoken that he carried in his heart. Until that day, not once had he confided his love, nor in any way indicated to her his knowledge that she was a girl. Although Stepanig was quite comfortable around him, there comes a time when nature demands its own, and, despite all her caution, she could not hide the distinctive qualities that appear in a girl who has come of age.

Vartan lay for a long time in the garden, restlessly turning from side to side. Suddenly, his ears caught a rustling sound. He turned to look and saw Stepanig approaching. The poor young man's heart began to pound; his steely heart had never before palpitated like this.

Stepanig walked toward him, then timidly stopped a few feet away.

"Dinner is ready and my father is calling for you to come."

"Is the Effendi going to be there, too?" Vartan asked, as he stood up from where he had been lying. He sat down in a little bower enclosed by climbing plants. Stepanig, with a frown of displeasure crossing her pretty face, responded.

"Well yes, damn him. He's going to be there."

"So, you too have no use for the Effendi, Stepanig."

"Why should I when no one else does?"

Vartan saw that this was an opportune moment to present her with the special gift he had brought, and asked her to wait in the garden until he came back. He went inside to the guest room where his wares were stored and returned with a package a few moments later. He stepped into the bower and asked Stepanig to join him.

"But my father is waiting for you," she said.

"We won't be late. Sit down, Stepanig. It's not dinner time yet. Now, here's the gift I brought for you."

Delighted at this, Stepanig sat down beside Vartan as he began opening the package. He took out a small box made of black wood and decorated with beautiful pictures. Taking a key out of his pocket, he opened the box. Inside it, beautifully placed, each in its own place, was a set of tools for women's work: scissors, thimbles, a needle case, etc., all made of silver. A small mirror was tucked on one side and, in the bottom was a music box which began to play when Vartan wound it up. Stepanig looked on with wonder, for this was the first time she had seen anything so beautiful.

"Isn't it beautiful?" Vartan asked, looking directly into her eyes. "Here, take it. It's for you."

Though she was at first delighted by the gift, Stepanig suddenly became sad, as if remembering something, as if it was something difficult to accept. She drew back in confusion.

"What am I going to do with scissors, and thimbles, and embroidery needles? You should have brought something else for me. I'm not a girl."

She uttered these words in such a trembling voice that it seemed they burned her rose-colored lips. Vartan had never expected this level of secrecy from her and was totally at a loss. Yet, unable to hold his inner turmoil in check, he said, "But you *are* a girl, Lala!"

"Oh no! How do you know my name?" she cried out, and fell against his chest.

He held her fast to keep her from falling down; and Lala, her heart in the throes of deep anguish, softly and tearfully murmured, "I am a girl... yes... I am a girl..."

This was the first time this confession had escaped her lips, sealed for so many years; this confession, given to a young man she barely knew, but whom she loved though never having dared to express it.

But the two of them, in their rapture, were unaware that a pair of eyes was watching them through the trees and brightened with happiness. This was Sara, drawn by the sound of the music box.

"At last! Lala will be saved!" she thought, and went away.

CHAPTER 15

Dinner was ready at Khacho's table. Khacho and Tomas Effendi were waiting for Vartan. Also seated at the table were the two policemen assigned by the government to accompany Tomas Effendi, two scoundrels who assisted the Effendi in all his dirty work. No one else was present; Khacho's sons would never come to dinner when such important guests were on hand.

"He'll be here soon enough. He'll be barking so much, he'll desecrate our food," the Effendi said, referring to Vartan.

"His jokes are sometimes stinging, but he has a good heart, really," commented Khacho.

"Oh, I know very well how good-hearted he is, Khacho, but in his mouth he carries the poison of a snake. You can't just joke around with anyone that way. When I cough, people tremble. One has to know and appreciate who Tomas Effendi is. You, yourself, saw the Decree from the Sultan. And I'll say just one more thing. The vali of Erzeroum and I have always been very close. If you don't believe it, ask them," he said, indicating his two policemen.

"When asked to testify, the fox pointed at his own tail." Thus, these two loyal and willing tricksters could be depended upon to back up the Effendi in any of his fraudulent claims.

"How should I not believe you?" said Khacho in response.

Tomas Effendi was bothered by Vartan not just because of his effrontery that morning, but because whenever the two of them had crossed paths in the past, Vartan had the habit of accosting him in the same rude manner.

"If I really wanted to," said Tomas Effendi, "I could turn the world upside down in an instant and let that scoundrel know just who Tomas Effendi is!"

"You don't have to weigh every word he says, he's just a youngster. And besides, he's not as bad as you think," said Khacho sympathetically.

At this moment, Vartan entered looking pale, preoccupied, and taciturn. Tomas Effendi, who just a few moments ago was speaking such ill of him, as they say, "tucked in his tail," and assumed his typical flattering tone.

"Good Lord, you've kept me waiting long enough! You know very well that Tomas Effendi won't lift a morsel of food to his lips without your being present."

"I know," Vartan said and, without saying anything further, found his spot at the table and sat down.

During dinner, he spoke hardly at all. He seemed melancholy and acted as if he was either sick or in pain. His ever-affable personality now seemed shrouded like a cloudy sky. Love, which in most people imparts joy and contentment and causes some people to lose their heads and feel sacred emotions; love, which relieves the bitterness of life with its sweetness, brought nothing but sadness to this man. At the dinner table, he drank far more than he ate, as if trying to quench the fire in his heart.

Tomas Effendi was very talkative, as usual, and went on and on about himself, his life, his past. Everything he said indicated that he was a prominent man; that the great patriarch Nerses always referred to him as "my son"; that he didn't care for Khrimian[17] because he was common and allowed himself to be drawn into talks with the *hamals* from Moush and Van. That Nubar Pasha[18] always addressed letters to him as, "my noble friend"; that he owned a palace on the shores of the Bosporus which he had rented out to some Englishmen; that his ancestors had donated such an enormous sum of money to the church in Jerusalem that every day in the monastery of St. Hagop, the monks said mass in honor of his entire family; that there had been a falling-out between him and Odian[19] because Odian had offered the Effendi his daughter's hand in marriage, and that he, the Effendi, had refused, and a thousand and one other such tales. But while Vartan was barely paying any attention to him, Khacho, the simple-minded host, listened with rapt attention, thinking, "How fortunate Lala will be to marry a man like this, a man who even refused Odian's daughter and owns a palace on the shores of the Bosporus."

Then the Effendi started talking politics. Great troubles were taking place in the Balkan Peninsula at this time; the Slavic peoples were shedding their blood in a struggle for freedom. A high diplomatic conference was being held in Constantinople to find a solution to the conflict and, Midhat,[20] that great diplomatic juggler, had promulgated the Ottoman constitution. Tomas Effendi, seated there in the midst of a peasant home, had something of his own to say about the future of the Armenian people.

Concerning the "foolishness" of the Slavs in daring to rise in revolt against such a righteous nation as Turkey, Tomas Effendi began to assail the Armenians, making it clear that such "fools" existed among them, as well; people who found the Turkish yoke onerous and had their minds set on freedom and self-government. He made the point that without the

Turks, the Armenians were a hopeless people, unable to govern themselves.

However, this was too much for Vartan, and he said, "It's people like you—moultezims and tax-collectors—who get to suck the blood of the Armenians because of the lawless Turkish government. You will always be supported by the unjust, criminal government. People like you snatch fish out of murky waters, because thieves love the darkness."

"Sir!" the Effendi spoke up, "Consider that two law officers are seated close-by!"

"Take your policemen and try to frighten the poor peasants with them, those who are stupid enough to believe you have palaces on the Bosporus, or that you refused Odian's daughter, or that mass is offered daily for your soul in the church of St. Hagop... Curses! That's all people like you deserve... You are the ones who destroy the Armenian home, from the lowliest country moultezim, whose agent you are, to those great *amirahs* at the Sublime Porte who trade the interests of their own people for personal gain..."

Tomas Effendi did not usually get angry, or rather, did so only when he saw that his opponent was truly strong and able to get his way; but, in Vartan's case, the Effendi had known him for a long time, and, wishing to use Vartan's indiscretion to his own advantage, he took it as a joke.

"It seems the wine is too strong for you. Good Lord, why do you drink more than you can handle?"

Vartan looked daggers at the Effendi, but said nothing. His expression conveyed nothing but contempt for this vulgar sycophant.

Khacho remained silent, too, for he knew that Vartan had stated the truth; at the same time, he didn't approve of his brashness, and found it imprudent to speak to an official in this manner. When dinner was finished, Khacho was relieved, and he expected no more disturbances.

In keeping with the local custom, coffee without sugar was served immediately following dinner. Thomas Effendi had commanded that whenever he was a guest in Danouder Khacho's house and it came time to have a smoke following coffee, his chipoukh must be prepared and brought to him by Stepanig, because, as he would say, "A chipoukh prepared with Stepanig's hands tastes the best." Here lay a remarkable puzzle in the poor youth's destiny, for whenever Fattah-Bek was a guest in the house, he would similarly insist on receiving his coffee from Stepanig, because "it tastes the best." The Kurdish chieftain, for one, was aware that Stepanig was a girl and loved her. But could it be that the Armenian effendi also knew her secret and loved her? When Stepanig appeared with the long Turkish chipoukh and was about to offer it to the Effendi, Vartan exploded in rage, well aware of the unseemly significance of this Turkish custom. He pulled the chipoukh out of Stepanig's hands and flung it out the window.

"Get out of here, Stepanig!" he said to her, and she left in confusion.

The pipe might as well have struck the Effendi on his head. He was very angry.

"I don't care for jokes like that. You're being disrespectful to me."

"People like you have no right to talk about respect."

"I? I, who am the moultezim for this entire province?" the tax collector said.

The Effendi started fidgeting about as if he wished to leave the table.

"Stay where you are or I'll kill you like a dog," Vartan said, passing his hand to his sword.

One of the policeman spoke up. "You're getting angry for nothing, sir. The Effendi didn't say anything wrong."

Without paying him any attention, Vartan addressed himself to the Effendi again.

"You shameless scoundrel! Just like the Turks, you've learned how to get yourself inside any Armenian's home, lap up his food, quaff his wine and put his daughters-in-law, his daughters, or his young sons to work serving your vulgar needs. Shameless!"

Old Khacho just sat there petrified, his mouth stuck shut, crossing himself at times and muttering God's name in the hope of warding off evil.

But no matter how boastful or blustery or full of inflated threats the Effendi was, he was to the same degree a coward, like the timid fox. As far as the young Russian subject was concerned, the Effendi knew he couldn't simply deal with him as he did with the peasants of Alashgert. Vartan was armed with a sword and was a subject of the Russian emperor. Therefore, taking all of this into account, the Effendi answered in the mildest possible tone.

"I don't follow the ways of the Turks. You're slandering me for no good reason, Vartan."

"I am slandering you? You who bow down in prayer with the Turks, then sponsor mass at the Armenian church to win the sympathy of the common folk? You, who tell all the Turks that the Armenians are *gavours*, and then when you find yourself among Armenians, you curse them. You who betray every decent Armenian concerned with the welfare of his people to the Turkish government? You who keep company with robbers, then bear false witness in court against Armenians, saying they are dishonest in their protests over their plundered possessions? You who have taken women and married them in ten different places, then abandoned them to come here looking for yet another wife? And you say that you don't follow Turkish ways! I only have this to say: a Turk is a thousand times better than an Armenian like you who is neither an Armenian nor a Turk!"

These latter words about the Effendi's taking several wives in different places, then coming here to look for a new one—these words struck poor old Khacho like a lightning-bolt. He wanted very much to give Lala to this man whose relatives were *amirahs* in Bolis, this man who had a palace on the Bosporus and had even refused the hand of Odian's daughter. "No, no," he thought, "Vartan is slandering him. Tomas Effendi is not an impostor."

Having poured out all his passion, Vartan left, and it was only then that the Effendi opened his mouth again.

"I will most definitely write to the Sultan about him," he said with great emphasis. "I will also definitely write to the Russian king and get that scoundrel sent to Siberia. No one can fool with Tomas Effendi like this. 'Unless you give the donkey a thrashing, he doesn't know his place.'"

Tomas Effendi habitually used the names of prominent men when issuing his threats, thereby making a show of his relations with them to achieve his purpose. Old Khacho was not totally stupid; and yet, after having suffered so greatly at the hands of minor officials like this, all peasants came to believe these men could do whatever they wished. And so, on hearing what the Effendi had just said, he sprang to his feet and begged him with tears in his eyes, "For the love of God, don't have him sent to Siberia. Have a little respect for my white hair. You know he's crazy."

After a few moments of reflection, the Effendi responded.

"Because I have been a guest at your table, I will respect your wishes."

CHAPTER 16

The well-being of even the most peaceable of households can be darkened when tribulation comes, piling upon tribulation. Khacho's home was beset by misfortune on every side, threatened from every quarter by an array of dangers.

Vartan's quarrel with Tomas Effendi had a strong impact on the entire household. Some laughed and took note of the Effendi's meekness, taking pride in Vartan's boldness, while others put the blame on Vartan, saying he was crazy and didn't know when to hold his tongue. Of the latter opinion were two of Khacho's sons, Ohan and Hago. They were the most outraged at Vartan's behavior and said, "How can you expect to play around with a government official like that?" It was inconceivable to them to oppose such a person, not only during the execution of his official duties, but at any juncture in life, since, for them, the man always retained his stature as an official.

Although Khacho didn't blame Vartan, he was very uneasy with what had happened. Vartan had reason for what he had said; and yet, it wasn't necessary for him to act as he did. Khacho was quite familiar with the Effendi, and knew he would do all in his power to injure Vartan. Failing that, he would take out his anger on the entire household; he had ample grounds for betraying Khacho to the authorities, for Khacho had offered hospitality to a known smuggler.

Beyond that, Khacho had been deprived of one great hope: from the moment Vartan declared that Tomas Effendi had married and abandoned several wives, Khacho's mental torment knew no bounds, and now all his hopes were dashed. Yet, how could one be sure about such matters? Although Khacho knew that Vartan wouldn't make up lies, were not statements made in the heat of an altercation always subject to doubt?

What power, then, did this loathsome and shameless official have over Khacho's mind that he could still consider turning his daughter over to him? Khacho knew well that he was a vulgar, evil, and unscrupulous robber; a man who held nothing sacred and would sacrifice anything for his own gain. Yet, in the presence of official authority, the old man forgot all of this. He willingly humbled himself in accordance with a long-established predisposition. From his viewpoint, every sort of indecency vanished and became as nothing, disappearing beneath the mantel of authority worn by this petty official, this representative of the Court Moultezim. His official position purged him of his faults.

Having the Effendi for a son-in-law was something Khacho had every reason to find attractive. Such a son-in-law would be someone who stood out from the common run of humanity, a person before whom everyone would bow. As simple and fair minded a man as Khacho was, in his role as *danouder*—as leader of an entire household—he had a certain pride. He wouldn't readily agree to give his daughter's hand to a common peasant, especially in view of the abnormal circumstances of her upbringing. And there was one other reason for settling on Tomas Effendi as a son-in-law, a practical one: as *danouder*, Khacho frequently had dealings with the provincial government; the Effendi would be useful in smoothing out many difficulties. Now, all those hopes were dashed.

If, on top of all this, he had known the fate that Fattah-Bek was preparing for Lala, the grave alone would put an end to his afflictions. So far, none of his sons had breathed a word to him about the matter. But the agonizing secret oppressed them and gnawed at their entrails, especially Hairabed and Abo. Since that ill-fated meeting in the forest with their brothers, they had no idea how to prevent the loss of their sister. What would become of her if she was dragged away from her father's home by the Kurdish chief? Would she turn into a Mohammedan wife; or end her suffering with suicide like her sister Sona?

The brothers endured all this anguish just to allow their sister a brief moment to feel secure and happy. From the time her beloved Vartan had given her the mysterious black box, her boyish clothes seemed to scorch her body. She was a girl... she wanted to dress like a girl... she wanted to be a woman... The feel of Vartan's kiss still lingered on her lips, and his tender words still sounded in her ears. From the moment she had witnessed his mastery over Tomas Effendi—a man before whom the entire province trembled—his esteem had risen in her eyes. I don't know why it is, but women love to see extraordinary greatness, superiority, and power in men. They are awestruck at seeing a power in men that exceeds their own. And so, on crushing the proud Effendi into nothingness—this man whom Lala hated with all her heart—Vartan had gained her respect. She had many times been forced to put up with the Effendi's disgraceful behavior. Whenever he appeared for a visit to her father's house, she would run away and hide. But, since the Effendi had so often made the point that a pipe prepared with her hands tasted the best, her father would have her located and call for her to come and prepare the Effendi's pipe for him.

Lala told Hairabed, her oldest brother, about how Vartan had dealt with the Effendi.

"He did well," Hairabed responded. "He should have given the bastard a beating. The Effendi is used to having a completely free hand when he tortures the poor villagers. He thinks everyone will be like them."

Lala was close to throwing her arms around Hairabed and baring her heart to him about her love for Vartan and how she had loved him for a long time. But Hairabed was in a hurry; some important matter required his attention outside the house.

This was the day there was to be a meeting between Hairabed's wife and Khourshid, Fattah-Bek's wife. Chavo had appeared early that morning to notify Sara that Khourshid would be coming to the village of O…under the pretext of making a pilgrimage to a nearby chapel where she would present an offering for her little son, who had a cough; she would meet Sara there. This was a chapel venerated by both Kurds and Armenians. Sara was delighted when she learned Khourshid had accepted her proposal.

On leaving the house, Hairabed was anxious to find out what had come of this meeting. He left the village and sat down in the shade of an enormous boulder some distance down the road. Sara would have to cross this spot on her way back from the chapel.

A most interesting view presented itself from this vantage point: the foot of a mountain strewn with broken rock and rubble worked loose from the mountainside by the ravages of time. This area was bordered by wild thickets and many kinds of bushes, surmounted here and there by trees. Hairabed's attention was drawn to an apple tree whose trunk was wrapped by a parasitic, climbing plant, and whose upper branches were already dried out and leafless. The plant grew up into the tree and, serpent-like, sent its twisting creepers in every direction as if its goal was to weigh the tree down with its mass, to stifle, and crush, and then, all at once, to engulf the poor apple tree. There are moments in life when ordinary people become philosophical, and thus Hairabed thought, "Now, there's a perfect example: a weed which has made no effort of its own, done no work, nor sent roots of its own into mother earth, yet with its clinging tentacles engulfs a more cultivated and fruit-bearing plant, feeds on its juices, uses up its life energy and then, finally, kills it. Isn't this exactly the way the Kurd has dealt with us? Isn't he just like that parasitic plant, living at the expense of the poor Armenian?"

Hairabed was a man of sensitivity and clear understanding. Where did this understanding come from? It is certain that if he had never ventured beyond the horizons of his native land, he would have grown up and developed with the same narrow attitudes as his fellow countrymen. But fate had something else in store for him. In his youth, he had spent time in foreign lands. When still at a tender age, there had been some sort of misunderstanding between him and his father, and, as so often happens in the provinces, he left home to wander from country to country, and the workings of fate brought him to Bolis, which is regarded as the place where Europe and Asia meet.

Here, he came into contact with various circles in the life of the city, and though not learning anything fundamental, he absorbed many of the enlightened ideas which are beyond the cognizance of any ordinary peasant.

He sat in the shade of the boulder and waited for his wife. The sun had almost set, and its last lovely rays illuminated the mountaintops.

At last, Sara appeared on the road. Even from a distance, Hairabed could tell from the bright look on her face that she brought good news.

"Is it a boy or a girl?" Hairabed asked from where he sat.

"It's a boy," she said, and being very tired, sat down beside her husband.

This colloquial exchange about the gender of a new-born baby expressed the belief of the peasant that a boy betokened happiness, and a girl sadness.

After wiping her brow, catching her breath, and resting a few moments, Sara began recounting her meeting with Khourshid. The substance of her account was as follows:

Khourshid revealed that the *bek* was no longer greatly preoccupied with Stepanig because of new, pressing concerns; that, for the moment, he had forgotten about her. She said that Fattah-Bek had received orders from the vali of Erzeroum which he was busy executing: taking a count of all the men in his tribe, passing out weapons to them, giving them money to buy horses, clothing, etc. She had no idea what it was all about. On the other hand, she still advised that Stepanig be sent far away, or married to someone, because she knew for certain that, sooner or later, the *bek* would carry out his plan for the poor girl. Khourshid also added that she had told her father about the *bek*'s plan and that her father promised to do something to bring the *bek*'s passions under control. Even so, Khourshid had said, it might eventually be necessary for her to part with her husband entirely.

Hairabed listened intently to every word of Sara's report.

"Then we can't say the danger is over yet," he said when she had finished. "The only good that comes of this is that the *bek*'s plan is delayed, and that gives us a chance to do something for Lala."

"That's what I was thinking, too," said Sara.

"But what can we do?" asked Hairabed. "The only possibility is to marry her to someone, but even that won't guarantee her freedom. The *bek* has the power to take a woman right out of her husband's arms."

"She has to be married to a man who doesn't live here and can take Lala away with him," Sara said.

"That's a fine idea, but where do we find such a man? You know there's not a peasant anywhere who would take responsibility for such a marriage. The *bek* could have his house burned down and his entire family put to the sword if he found out. What man would take on a responsibility like that?"

"That man is waiting," said Sara happily.

"Who?"

"Vartan."

Hairabed's anxious expression was transformed by happiness as Sara began telling him what she had learned that day among the trees in the garden; how Vartan and Lala had held each other and kissed; how they had pledged eternal love to each other.

"That's good. Vartan is the only man who can save her," he said.

The sun was set by now. The couple rose and hurried off toward home. On the way, Hairabed pondered what it could be that was occupying the *bek*'s attention and required the distribution of weapons. Were these not preparations for some terrible undertaking?

CHAPTER 17

It was completely dark by the time Hairabed and Sara reached home. They heard that Tomas Effendi had left in a huff after his clash with Vartan and that Khacho was worried he might set some mischief afoot against them all.

But, despite his easily provoked and excitable temperament, Vartan was not so uncultured as to show disrespect to a person without good reason. In his eyes, the Effendi was a disgusting individual who, as a tool in the hands of the Turkish government, sucked the blood of his own people; robbed them, and left them destitute. Furthermore, he was familiar with the Effendi's past. This outrageous swindler had done his work in many different parts of Armenia, and, it is true, married women and abandoned them, driving many innocent girls to madness. Now he was trying to do the same with Lala, taking advantage of her father's naïveté to play his evil game. This was something impossible for Vartan to tolerate, especially as it involved the girl he loved.

But it wasn't simply an aversion to seeing Vartan again that prompted the Effendi away from Khacho's house so soon after their confrontation; the Effendi was patient with such outbursts and had long ago learned how to wait quietly until they went beyond certain bounds. On this particular day, he had received special orders by messenger directing him to gather all the Court's wheat and barley together into certain storehouses and under no circumstances to put it up for sale, because the government required it. Evidently, secret preparations were being made: here, concentration of provisions, and there, in Fattah-Bek's camp, the distribution of weapons...

Whenever a guest stayed at Khacho's house, Khacho spent the whole time with him, never leaving his side. As for Vartan, he wasn't actually regarded as a guest, but rather more as a member of the family. But one other guest arrived after Tomas Effendi, a slender young man who had the look of one who had spent long years in school, seated on the student's bench, wasting away and growing pale. His occupation or calling was unclear, and it was only known that he was a Bolsetsi and an Armenian; therefore Khacho felt an obligation to honor him, being, as he was, an Armenian who came from the great capital city.

The new guest arrived with nothing but his traveling bag; his worn European clothing indicated he must be poor. The caravan driver who had brought him here simply dropped him off at the village and continued on his way. The young man was walking about, looking for a place to spend the night when he encountered Vartan. They say there is a bond between certain hearts, and after exchanging just a few words together these two men who had never met before took to each other like brothers in the same sect. Vartan took him by his hand and led him to Khacho's house.

The new guest identified himself as Mikayel Tutukjian, a name which accorded with the tradition in Turkish Armenia of basing most family names on the livelihood of one's father or grandfather. Mikayel's name derived from the fact that his father's trade was the manufacture of duduks, that is to say, a kind of pennywhistle[21] for children to play.

In keeping with the village custom, dinner was served immediately after the evening lamps were lit. Since Tomas Effendi was gone and there were no other important guests present, Khacho's six sons came to the dinner table. Vartan was simply regarded as one of their own; and, as for the new guest, they just regarded him as someone who should be grateful for a place to eat this evening. Old Khacho actually had considerable trouble with the young man's name and found it difficult to pronounce;

he was no less troubled by Mr. Tutukjian's sickly and pale appearance, the restlessness of his gleaming, feverish eyes, and his dark, mysterious personality, which immediately aroused suspicion. But Vartan had reassured Khacho, "He's a good man. Once you know him, you'll like him."

On entering Khacho's house for the first time, Mr. Tutukjian just had one question for Vartan.

"Can I trust these people?

"You can…" was Vartan's reply.

A mood of sadness hung over the dinner table. Vartan and the new guest spoke hardly at all. Hairabed was preoccupied with the problem of the Kurdish chief and Lala, mulling over what Sara had told him and what could be accomplished the next day. Lala's lovely image wandered through Vartan's mind. And, as for the new guest, only God knew what he was thinking…

After the table was cleared, Stepanig brought water for the guests to clean their hands and poured it out for them. Each of them washed his hands, voiced his appreciation, and gave thanks to God. Khacho began smoking his long pipe, and Tutukjian, for his part, produced a beautiful cigar box which was wholly out of keeping with his worn-out clothing. He took out an expensive cigar, pinched the end off with his long fingernails and lit up. The small room was soon filled with the pleasing, sweet smell of tobacco. It would appear that Mr. Tutukjian had been no stranger to the finer things of life at one time, though now he found himself in the midst of highly irregular circumstances.

After dinner, the conversation settled on Tomas Effendi. Vartan had already told Mr. Tutukjian a great deal about the Effendi so that he was already quite familiar with the subject of conversation. Khacho, in a circumspect manner, voiced his observation to Vartan that he had conducted himself in a disrespectful manner toward the Effendi. The old man had a practice of citing his seven sons as support for what he said, though Vartan had long known that Stepanig was a girl.

"Let the sun of my seven sons bear witness that I speak the truth. You, too, are one of my sons, and my house is your house. You can come and go as you wish; you can stay as long as you want. My door is always open to you, but you have to realize that this isn't a place like other places. Men like Tomas Effendi carry a great deal of weight around here—a great deal. For that reason, one has no choice but to show them respect and keep quiet about whatever it is they do or say… What choice do we have? As the saying goes, 'If you can't cut off the evil-doer's hand, then kiss it and submit.' It may be that the Effendi can do you no great harm, since you are from another country, but we may suffer in your place. As the saying goes, 'Afraid to beat the donkey, he struck the load.'"

The old man's words provoked the fool's demons once more, and he replied, "Where I come from, the Armenians have an apt saying about the Turks. They say, 'Unless you beat a Turk, he won't become your friend.' I see no difference between Tomas Effendi and the Turks, and my only regret is that I didn't give him a good beating, though having him for a friend would be distasteful to me."

Old Khacho's brow wrinkled up at this, clearly showing his difficulty in hearing such a response from Vartan. But Stepanig's face lit up with a bright smile, and Vartan couldn't help but notice... She was still standing and, as the youngest member of the family, waiting on the guests. Vartan looked at her admiringly, and, as he did so, he thought, "That is the only person in this household who sees this man as I do, because she is the only one who knows how completely shameless and immoral he is..."

Now Vartan went on with even greater vehemence than before:

"You permit yourselves to be oppressed like this by these vile, immoral miscreants because you keep your eyes shut tight in the face of all the evil they do. I acknowledge that the Turk and Kurd rob and oppress the Armenian, and, after taking every ounce of life-force from him, kill him in the end. That I understand, and, what's more, I consider it natural, because that's the way they've dealt with the Armenian for centuries, and that's what they will always do. This has become a necessity of life for them, and they can barely live without it. But when an Armenian is even more evil in dealing with his fellow Armenian than the Turk or the Kurd, that can't be tolerated. I said all of this to the Effendi's face, and he had no reply."

"I could say even worse things to him," Hairabed broke in. "But my father has always counseled us to remain quiet, to be cautious. He says we will be free some day, that we have to be patient. But I don't know how much longer we can wait."

"Until The Second Coming of Christ!" said Vartan sarcastically. "But then it will be too late, because by then there won't be any Armenians left to save; they will all have become Turks or Kurds."

"Patience is life," Khacho intoned in a homiletic voice. "That is what our priests and vartabeds have always preached. Certainly some day, God will remember his lost sheep... We have to be patient, my children... Patience is life."

"Patience is death!" responded Mr. Tutukjian who had listened to the debate in silence up to this point. The young man's wan face went completely pale now, and his thin lips, equally colorless, began to tremble.

"Patience is death," he repeated in an agitated voice. "Patience can only be learned in the grave ... This kind of Jewish patience we have is carrying us toward irreversible loss. The Jews showed the greatest patience of anyone, undergoing every persecution the world could offer, waiting for a messiah to come and renew Jerusalem and restore its ancient glory... And they are still waiting... But we don't even have that kind of hope, to the point that I don't know what it is we are waiting for..."

"Our priests and vartabeds preach patience..." he continued in the same bitter tone. "But clearly, they are the ones who have brought ruin on our house and reduced us to this subjugated position. There is only one thing that can save an oppressed and down-trodden people, and that is protest by whatever means necessary. A feeling of discontent, a sense of grievance, a desire for something better—these are the redemptive impulses that can propel us to freedom from oppression. But patience is the death of such noble impulses..."

Khacho made no reply. Vartan and Hairabed warmly grasped Mr. Tutukjian's hand. Khacho's other sons understood none of this and only thought, "Yet another fool."

Khacho ordered the beds made for his guests then stood up from the table with his sons, wished everyone good-night, and left. One of the daughters-in-law, her face covered, came in and prepared the beds.

The lamp in the guest room was still burning. The two guests remained awake for a long time in their beds. Mr. Tutukjian lit what remained of his cigar and began smoking again. Vartan was looking at him.

"My friend, your language is incomprehensible. You'll hardly be able to accomplish anything around here... To talk to the people, you have to be familiar with hundreds of parables and proverbs... Christ accomplished more with his parables than with high-flown sermons."

"Yes. I never did learn to speak the language of the people..." Mr. Tutukjian responded, then fell silent.

CHAPTER 18

The feeble light of the oil lamp still cast itself about the guest room, and Vartan remained awake for a long time. The evening's discussion had struck a nerve in him. He had taken note of the cold indifference of Khacho's sons toward his own and the new guest's "preachments." He was upset by the suspicion with which they regarded this inspired and noble young man. In addition, his heart was divided between two loves, each similar in nature: on the one hand, his love for the oppressed peasant, and on the other, his love for Lala, for she was equally a victim of moral oppression.

He took a look at the newcomer and saw that he was asleep. In the faint light of the lamp, he could see great integrity reflected in this pallid, anxious face. Mr. Tutukjian was sleeping uneasily, in a tormented delirium. His parched lips moved from time to time, muttering fragmentary phrases in French and Armenian:

"Peasants... the time has come... you'll buy it with your blood... your liberation... the present... the future... belongs to us... show what you can do... brave ones... who from the Turk... the iron rod... hasn't completely killed... the life that's in you... and... freedom's... feeling... of fire... in which... we are going to find... our salvation... forward... brave ones..."

"Poor fellow," said Vartan, shaking his head. "He's read too many books. Here he is, asleep in an Armenian peasant's home, and he imagines he is talking with his friends in Paris... Poor fellow."

Just then the soft sound of a song struck Vartan's ear, the sadness of its melody clear in the still of the night. He recognized whose voice it was and went outside.

Vartan hadn't been the only person in Khacho's house who found it difficult to fall asleep that night and lay tossing and turning in bed. All around, everyone was lost in deep slumber, for there is no such thing as wakefulness in the limbs of the tired, hard-working peasant. But Lala had found no rest. She dressed herself and quietly left the house. Even a cat could not have moved more carefully and quietly than this young lady as she made her way out. A dog, noticing her, began to bark. "Shush," she whispered to it almost inaudibly, and the dog stopped barking. It was a tranquil springtime night. The air was chilly but invigorating, and soothing to her fevered face. She made her way to the garden and went beneath the trees. Here the darkness was the deepest, and no one would see her. She sat down on the velvety grass, and, putting her hand to her chin, looked up at the sky. The moon had not yet appeared. "Where is it? It must be asleep," she thought. A deep silence reigned around her; not even a leaf was stirring in the trees. Everything was at rest; the breeze that so often rocked the branches, as well as the river whose flowing sound she had always heard in the still of the night. Everything was at rest. She remembered a song she had learned from her grandmother, and its sweet phrases unconsciously escaped her lips:

> In the depth of the sky, the moon is asleep,
> In its tender nest, the bird is asleep,
> Not a leaf is moving, the wind is asleep,
> There's no sound from the river, the river's asleep.
>
> Oh, Mother dearest, why can't I sleep,
> My eyes won't shut, yet I need to sleep,
> Oh, Mother dearest, what's troubling me,
> This fire in my heart, what can it be?

She finished her song, put her head down on her knees and, covering her feverish face with both hands, began to sob. The tears flowed in a torrent from her lovely eyes. She herself didn't know why she was crying. Could it be the thought of her beloved mother whom she had never seen nor heard any endearing words from? What was it that made her cry? What inexpressible feeling produced such turmoil in the maidenly innocence of her heart?

She felt somewhat better after crying and, raising her head to look around her, her gaze fell on the grave of her sister, Sona, in the shelter of four poplar trees not far away. She had never seen Sona but had heard the story of her tragedy many times. Among the common folk of the village, Sona had assumed the status of a martyr, and, on many occasions, they brought their sick to visit her grave. In keeping with Khacho's orders, an oil lamp was lit at her grave on the eve of every Sunday. Tonight, the lamp still flickered and bobbed and illumined the white plaster surface of the grave. Lala looked at it with dread. In her inflamed imagination, her sister's painful story became real. Then, after focusing on the grave, she saw a black Kurdish tent standing in a remote mountain vale. Sona was sitting inside with a frightful, despondent look on her face. She held a cup of poison in her hand and brought it to her lips, then put it down again. She contended with life and death for a long time. And behold, the Kurdish nobleman was approaching her tent, the man who had abducted her. Once again, she raised the cup of poison to her lips, crossed herself and drank...

The scene changed again, and Lala once again saw the grave in front of her. Then in her imagination she pictured two individuals: one, Tomas Effendi, with his sly, repulsive face; the other, Fattah-Bek, the Kurdish chieftain with his wild, bestial look. A shudder went through her entire body. Could she know or see the kind of traps these very two men were setting for her? She didn't know; she only sensed... "No!" she cried out in a terrible voice. "I won't join Sona. I'm afraid of the grave..."

Just then, someone softly placed a hand on her shoulder and called her name.

"Lala..."

But she heard nothing.

"Lala," the voice called once again, "I won't let you join Sona. I will save you..."

She turned around to look and saw Vartan standing there.

"Yes! Save me!" she said as Vartan sat down beside her. For many moments they were silent, not knowing what to say. Lala, not wholly free from her frightful vision, continued to see its images in her mind. Vartan wondered why this young, inexperienced girl begged to be taken far from her father's home where everyone loved her; why she wished to be taken to a faraway, foreign land. Perhaps it was her love for him that had deluded her so. Yet, for her love was still something ill-defined and obscure. Vartan asked, "What makes it so bad here?"

"It's bad, very bad," she said with great sadness in her voice. "Do you see that grave there?" she said, pointing to it.

"Do you know who is buried there?"

"I do."

"Do you know how she died."

"I do."

"I don't want to die like Sona, Vartan. Poison frightens me... the grave frightens me," she said, her eyes filling with tears once more.

"Why are you afraid you'll meet the same fate as Sona?" Vartan asked, taking her hand in his. "That was terrible, but it's not every girl's fate. What makes you think the same could happen to you?"

"That's what I've always thought ... That's what I've always expected... from the first day I learned why they dressed me like a boy... To be a girl here is a punishment from God... It's something bad... especially to be a pretty girl... Listen, Vartan, there was a girl I knew whom I liked a great deal. She was very nice and was a neighbor of ours.

Her mother would slap her every day, angry at her that she was born a pretty child and every day became prettier. Her mother would say to her, 'You will bring a scourge upon us' and the girl would cry. Her name was Narkis. Her mother wouldn't let her wash her face, or brush her hair, and kept her in tattered clothes. Then the Kurds came and took her away. I saw her a few days ago, and, oh, how ugly she had become… She wasn't pretty anymore… She said to me, 'Stepanig, being a Kurd's wife is harsh,' and then she started to cry."

Then, Lala herself began to cry. When she felt a little better, she asked, "Vartan, you're going to take me away from here, aren't you?"

"Yes, I will. Rest assured."

"Do it soon. Take me right now if you will. I'll go with you wherever you go."

"Just wait a few days until I have a chance to speak with your father."

And so, sitting together, they talked long into the dark night until their sadness gave way to the joyous feelings of love.

CHAPTER 19

Vartan awoke very late the next morning; he had been awake most of the night. A secret happiness shone in his rather pallid face. He noticed that Mr. Tutukjian was gone and had left his traveling bag in one corner of the room. Where could he have gone? From the first day they met, Vartan could see that he was a young man unseasoned in the ways of the world and who, as such, needed to be watched over and protected.

Everyone in the house was engaged in the various tasks of the day. Khacho's sons had already left the house and gone to the fields for their day's work. Khacho went out to check on what they were doing. His daughters-in-law were busy with their household chores; there wasn't an idle moment. Only Hairabed remained inside. He considered this the best opportunity to approach Vartan and elicit what his position was in relation to Lala. With the exception of Abo, his other brothers had all but forgotten the danger posed by Fattah-Bek. They had abandoned Lala to her fate, with the fatalistic conviction that whatever God willed would be. Khacho had so far heard nothing about the matter. He was preoccupied with verifying the past of his prospective son-in-law, Tomas Effendi.

When Hairabed came into the guest room, Vartan asked him, "Where did my friend go?"

Hairabed knew whom he meant and replied. "That new friend of yours is an amazing fellow. He got up early in the morning, put on his boots, and left the house carrying his big walking-stick. He didn't wash, or brush his hair, or have breakfast. We asked him where he was going, but he didn't answer. He just nodded and left."

"Where did he go?" asked Vartan impatiently.

"I don't know. I saw him in the village talking to a half-naked, barefoot girl who had gone to the river for water. 'Why are you dressed like this?' he asked her. 'It's not decent for a girl your age to be dressed like this.' The girl answered that her parents were poor. He took a gold coin out of his bag and gave it to her. I suspect that was the last of his money, Vartan."

"That's very likely," Vartan said with concern. "But where did he go after that?"

"He went up to a group of villagers who had just come out of church and were standing near the church doors discussing the apportionment of taxes. He joined in on the discussion and began explaining to them that they were paying the government too much and neglecting their own everyday needs. He talked about schools for girls and boys which our villagers don't have. He talked about mutual assistance to improve their economic situation. He said they should have a common treasury from which to borrow at low interest in their time of need. This was the sort of thing he was talking about."

"And what response did the villagers give?" Vartan asked with keen interest.

"The villagers laughed and... and didn't answer him. One of them said, 'This man is a fool.'"

"Praise God, I'm not the only one!" Vartan said with a laugh. "I thought I was alone in being seen as a fool. What happened next?"

"One of the villagers invited him into the tavern for a drink of *aragh*, and he accepted. There was a very drunk crowd there. He drank little himself but paid for everyone else. Then he began preaching again about progress for the peasants and explaining the reason for their troubles. He spoke in a heated and inspired manner. For the first time, I realized just how powerful words can be. But the peasants listened to him with contempt. One of them asked, 'What sort of office do you hold or what do you do, anyway?' When he replied that he wasn't employed, the peasant said to him very rudely, 'Well, what are you talking about, then?'"

"Naturally. To have any effect on a crowd like that you'd definitely have to be a moutir or kaimakam or moultezim like Tomas Effendi.

What significance could an ordinary intellectual have in their eyes?" Vartan said with profound sadness. "But go on, Hairabed. This is most interesting."

"I took him by the hand and pulled him out of the tavern almost forcibly. I was afraid there was going to be a disturbance. Once outside, he said to me, 'It's easier to get acquainted with the people in places like this. When they get drunk, they tell you what they really think.' We went on our way through the village. He was carrying a bag on his shoulder full of various pamphlets and he would hand them out to the peasants he encountered. Some refused, saying they didn't know how to read. I asked one of them who took one, 'What are you going to do with it now that you've taken it?' 'It's paper,' he said. 'It will be useful at home. My mother takes snuff and she can use it as a wrapper.'"

Vartan's face now took on an even sadder expression, as if something was hurting him from the inside.

"Do you have some of the pamphlets?" he asked.

"Yes. I have a couple."

Vartan opened up the pamphlets and gave them a quick reading.

"Passing out pamphlets like these to backward people is stupid. After that, where did he go?"

"We left the village together, and then he asked me to leave him. He took the first road he came to and went in the direction of the next village visible in the distance. I stood for a long time watching him, and he was in such a hurry, you would have thought someone was expecting him there. It was clear he had no idea where he was going. He kept wandering around and leaving the road." Hairabed made the last statement with a touch of humor in his voice.

"My dear Hairabed, Mr. Tutukjian isn't familiar with every twist and turn in your country road here in the valley," said Vartan, "but be assured that on the road of life he is a skillful guide."

"I recognize that quality in him, as well. He seems to be well-read," responded Hairabed, repenting of his facetiousness.

"Aside from being well-read, he's a very decent and noble person."

But Hairabed's main concern wasn't the young stranger; he was looking for a chance to have a talk with Vartan about his sister.

Ever since Sara had informed him about the bond of love that existed between Vartan and Lala, he was waiting for Vartan to address the matter; there was no one in the household except Hairabed that Vartan could speak to about it. But, at this point, it seemed that Vartan had forgotten about Lala. On hearing what Hairabed told him about Mr. Tutukjian, he became very anxious. He stood up to go outside.

"Where are you going?" Hairabed asked.

"I'm going to look for Mr. Tutukjian. You shouldn't have let him get away from you like that, Hairabed. He's very inexperienced."

They walked out of the house together.

"Let's go to the barn. I haven't checked on the horses for several days," Vartan said.

On the way to the barn, Vartan saw Lala sitting and washing herself at the brook which flowed through the garden. She appeared to have just woken up.

"Good morning, Stepanig," Vartan called to her from a distance.

Lala said nothing in reply, but nodded in acknowledgement and gave him a meaningful smile.

Vartan's three powerful horses were tethered in the barn. One of them was his mount, and the other two were for Sako and Yegho, his two strapping companions who were at his side wherever he went.

"Sako, the horses have to be shoed and prepared for travel. We won't be staying here much longer."

He went up to the horses, stroked their lovely necks, and looked at them silently, assessing whether they had rested enough to undertake a journey of several days in the course of one night.

Then he ordered his horse to be saddled. When it was ready, he mounted and asked Hairabed, "Which way did Mr. Tutukjian go."

Hairabed pointed out the direction, and Vartan rode off.

When he was gone, Hairabed succumbed to a host of anxieties: Why did Vartan order the horses shoed? Where was he going? Was he just going to leave without addressing himself to Lala's plight, without freeing her? And why, after all, did he become so worried about Mr. Tutukjian's "childish behavior?" So overwhelmed was he with all these thoughts that he ended up in a state of total bewilderment.

On returning to the house, he encountered Sara, coming from the sheepfold with a large pan of milk.

"Didn't Vartan say anything?" she asked, setting the milk pan down.

"Nothing. He's become quite secretive," said Hairabed sadly.

"I can explain it," said Sara cheerily. "Sit down, and I'll tell you."

They sat down on a sled that had been left in the yard.

Sara told her husband how Lala confided in her that while everyone else was asleep the night before, she had met with Vartan secretly in the garden. She held nothing back. Vartan told her he would talk to her father and that if he didn't give permission for her to leave, he would just take her away, regardless.

"So that's why he had the horses prepared to travel," he said, biting his finger. "That's fine. Let him take her away. So much the better; then that lawless Kurd won't get her," said Sara.

"I'm not against it… but…" was Hairabed's response.

These poor people; under any other circumstances they would have beaten or killed a girl like this who had met secretly with a young man not her husband, yet now they were forced to yield in the face of bitter necessity.

CHAPTER 20

Vartan rode his horse all day through various villages, looking everywhere for Mr. Tutukjian. The only answer he got to his inquiries was to the effect that, yes, a young man had been seen; he wore boots, had European clothing and a wide-brimmed hat, and walked with a thick cane and a satchel of pamphlets slung over his shoulder; and from everyone came the same comment, namely, that the man was crazy.

In the evening, Vartan returned to Khacho's house without having found his friend.

One of Khacho's shepherds, a Kurdish youth, told Vartan he had seen Mr. Tutukjian in a neighboring village. There, the Turkish villagers had surrounded him and beaten him up. The young shepherd recognized Mr. Tutukjian as one his master's guests, and freed him from the villagers.

"I was expecting something like this…" Vartan said to himself, and then turning to the shepherd he asked, "Why did they beat him?"

"I don't know. I wanted to put him on a donkey and bring him back, but he refused. He said he could get back on his own. But how could he have made it? Every bone in his body had been beaten."

This made Vartan very sad. He knew all too well the kind of beating Turkish villagers could mete out, especially to a poor Armenian.

"Where did you leave him?"

"Partway down the road. He was staggering."

The evening lamps had just been lit in the guest room when, suddenly, Mr. Tutukjian appeared, exhausted and soiled from head to foot with mud. Vartan expected him to begin immediately recounting his experience with the village thugs, but he didn't say a word. His face only conveyed a mixture of profound despair and hatred. He walked by and sank down on a pillow against the wall.

"Could you spare a little tobacco? Mine is used up," he asked.

"Of course," Vartan said and handed him a box of tobacco. Mr. Tutukjian took it with trembling hands, rolled himself a cigarette, and started to smoke.

"Those people are just like the Sphinx; they're a complete riddle," he said to himself. "Try as hard as you can to figure them out, and you still can't do it. They have no sense of history; or, if they do, it's just some distorted and odd impression…"

He then fell silent and blew out an unbroken stream of smoke from his lips. Vartan was silent as well, and he looked down with concern on his ardent young friend, at this moment seeming to him like a moth at play with a lamp, trying through the beating of its fragile wings to quell the flame…

Khacho came in at this point, and within a few moments he was joined at the dinner table by his sons in accord with the normal evening pattern. Although it had been only an hour since sunset, dinner was promptly served; being farmers, they had to eat and get to bed as soon as possible so they could rise early the next morning.

Mr. Tutukjian had quite a bit to drink during dinner, and his somewhat melancholy mood gave way to better spirits. He even sang, Oh Lord, Preserve the Armenians, the famous hymn by Taghyatiantz.[22] After the table was cleared, he turned to Khacho and said, "Have all the doors shut so that no one interrupts us. I have something very important to say."

Khacho was amazed that his guest had something so special to say and ordered one of his sons to have the doors closed. There was complete silence as everyone waited to hear what Mr. Tutukjian was going to say.

"Very soon, a war between Russia and Turkey will be declared. Have you heard about it?" Tutukjian asked.

"We've heard nothing about it," answered Khacho and his sons.

"I've heard about it," said Vartan. "Where I come from, the Russians have been engaged in all kinds of preparations."

This news of war struck old Khacho like a thundrbolt. Having been a witness to several wars between Russia and Turkey in his long lifetime, the horrible consequences they had brought for the Armenians were still a vivid memory to him. For Hairabed, the mystery behind all the preparations of Fattah-Bek and his men was now solved.

"Yes, there's definitely going to be a war," said Vartan, his voice tinged with sarcasm. "The horse and mule are going to fight, and, caught between them, the donkey will be killed.'"

"That's right," said Hairabed. "The Armenians here will bear the brunt of it, and they'll lose everything they have."

"I know only too well," said old Khacho, his voice choking with the grief that filled his heart.

"Listen," Mr. Tutukjian said, trying tonight to speak in a plainer, more comprehensible language, "This won't be like any of the other wars the Russians and Turks have fought; it has a very different cause. You don't read newspapers here, so naturally you have no way of knowing what is happening in a distant part of the world called the Balkan Peninsula. There are Christian nations there, too, and they have also suffered under Turkish barbarism for centuries. But, unlike the Armenians, they got fed up and revolted to throw off the Turkish yoke. They won some victories, but finally, after suffering heavy losses, they were beaten. Then the Russians involved themselves and stepped forward to defend them in the name of liberty for the Christians. European diplomats called a great conference in Bolis to see what could be done to secure a few rights for these oppressed Christian nations, but no agreement was arrived at, and nothing came of it. It was at that point the Russians decided to force Turkey to go along with liberty for its Christian subject peoples by making war against it."

Though word of these events had reached the farthest corners of the world, it was total news to these peasants, and they listened with astonishment to what Mr. Tutukjian had to say. Only vaguely had they heard the Turks were at war with someone, but with whom or for what reason, they had no idea. The only sign they had that the Turks were at war was the steady rise in taxes, much heavier than before and always taken from them with the refrain, "The government is at war, and you have to help."

"The Russians are declaring this war to liberate oppressed Christian subjects," Mr. Tutukjian went on, "But understand this, that of all the Christian subject peoples ruled by the Turks, by far the most tormented and oppressed are the Armenians. You can see this quite clearly in your own experience, because you have had every kind of Turkish barbarity inflicted on you. Therefore, the moment has arrived for the Armenians to think about what is in their best interest."

"What's there to think about?" said Khacho in response. "You're the one who said the Russians are going to war to save the Christians. May God grant them success so they'll be able to come and save us."

"That's right," said Vartan, joining in on the discussion, "But you have to remember one thing, 'Unless the baby cries, its mother won't offer her breast.' Nothing will come of silence and patience and waiting full of hope. Armenians must protest."

"Yes, they have to protest," echoed Mr. Tutukjian, "and that protest has to be carried out just the way it was by the other Christian peoples."

"Are you saying the Armenians will have to fight?" asked Khacho, breaking in.

"Yes, that's what I'm saying. The way the world is now, and the way it has always been, whoever doesn't know how to spill blood and slaughter people will be told they have no right to be free. If the Armenians want to gain anything, if they want freedom, they have to prove they don't lack courage and that they still know how to kill; and this is the very time to show it."

"Good Lord! How are the Armenians supposed to prove their courage? The Turks haven't even left us a knife to cut a chicken's neck when the time comes," said old Khacho, a bitter smile playing over the crevices of his face.

Mr. Tutukjian was somewhat at a loss, but Vartan answered for him.

"I can give you whatever weapons you want, provided you're fighters. You all know very well what I do. I'm a smuggler. I know all the mountain passes and all the secret roads where weapons are hidden."

"But weapons aren't enough," prudent old Khacho responded. "Can you inspire Armenians here with that same spirit of courage those other Christian people show in their fight for freedom? What good will weapons do in the hands of such a down-trodden people?"

"You can't so quickly pass judgement on the people, Danouder Khacho," Mr. Tutukjian said. "Our people haven't lost all their spirit, their courage, or their desire for freedom. They just need an impetus; the right moment. The Russians are going to war against the Turks. It's time for the Armenians to stand up and be counted. I know the Russians will do everything they can to help us."

Khacho's sons sat in silence. They had no comments to make. Among them was Hago who, a week earlier during the meeting in the forest about Lala's plight, had expressed the view it would be just as well to give Lala up to the Kurdish chieftain and enjoy the benefits of his power and protection. After a long period of listening with distaste to this discussion between his father and the guests, Hago finally addressed himself to Mr. Tutukjian:

"Brother, there is the smell of blood about you," said Hago "We don't want anything to do with you—whether it's good or bad. The best thing for you to do is to leave this house as soon as you get up in the morning. Otherwise, you will bring calamity down upon us."

Khacho told his son to be quiet, then had something of his own to say to Mr. Tutukjian:

"Don't mind my son, he doesn't know what he's talking about. But listen to me. I haven't had an education and I don't know much about people in other countries. But as a farmer there's one thing I know: we villagers never go out and start sowing until we've given the earth a good plowing and softened it up to receive the seed. Otherwise we know that the seed will never turn green and root itself; it'll just sprout and dry up. Christ says the same in the Holy Gospel, and I've heard it many times in church. My boy, the soil isn't ready yet—by that I mean the people. Preparing the soil should have begun years ago—twenty, thirty, even fifty years ago. If so, your seed would be falling on fertile soil now. It would grow and ripen and yield a hundredfold or thousandfold harvest. Nothing can come of just one day. We farmers know that our crops have to endure many seasons—some hot, some cold—before they ripen and are ready for the harvest. They have to withstand all the extremes of the weather: they're sometimes lashed by storms; they're sometimes beaten by hail or covered in freezing snow; they're sometimes warmed by the life-giving rays of the sun. In a word, only after passing through all those trials is the seed that was planted finally ready to fulfill the sower's wish... In the same way, the seed planted in the hearts of the people has to endure many seasons, some peaceful and some stormy, before the harvest can be reaped."

"That's an excellent way of putting it, and I totally agree," Mr. Tutukjian said. "But you're forgetting one thing. I'll speak to you in your own language now; in the language of farmers whose job it is to care for animals and till the earth. That will make it clearer to you. What would happen if you let your fields go without doing a thorough *kagh-han*?[23] You'd see weeds grow and multiply and eventually smother the crop you had planted and take its place. Everything you planted would be lost. Isn't that war, in a sense, where the weak is destroyed by the strong? This war can be seen throughout the world of plants, where one kind of plant struggles to overwhelm and annihilate another to ensure its own existence; and any plant that lacks that power to struggle and fight back will be deprived of its life. In other words, this is the capacity for self-defense, and its teacher is nature itself. To every being that has the power to grow and multiply, nature has also given the power to fight back against its enemies. One may have a little of this power, another may have more; it is a power found in trees, grasses, animals, and human beings. Only rocks, or wood, or dead bodies just lie where they are, unconscious of self-defense, because they have no life in them. But wherever there is life, you will find that natural struggle.

"So now you should understand what I'm saying," he continued. "What is true in the world of plants and animals is no less true in the life of mankind. There, that same fight goes on, only in a fiercer and many-sided way. Each nation develops weapons according to its knowledge and ability. (When I say weapons, I don't just mean swords and rifles. The trades and sciences are weapons, too, used by one people to compete against another.) With wild and uncivilized people, that fight is just physical—with the sword. That is the sort of weapon that is used against us by the Kurd and the Turk. It is the law of self-defense to respond to your enemy with the same weapon, the very same weapon, he uses to bring you down and kill you. It would be stupid of me to expect anything more of the people than that, more than they have to give. It isn't my intention to say we have to raise the sword and destroy the Kurds just because we want to go on living on the land we inherited from our forefathers. What I am saying is that we have to learn to defend ourselves before we are destroyed by the Kurds and the Turks. There is a great difference between those two statements."

Khacho had something to say and broke in on Mr. Tutukjian's discourse: "I understand, I understand everything you're saying, but I have to repeat what I said a moment ago. A great change like that in which people overcome their meekness and grasp the meaning of self-defense can't take place overnight. You Bolsetsis should have begun working on that years ago. If you had, then today, while Christian nations are at war, the seed you had sown would bear a rich harvest. But you did nothing to prepare us. You all just sat there silent in Bolis, and now you come and urge us to raise the sword against the Kurd and Turk in self-defense. How can you expect to convince the people to do that, now?"

"You're right. We Bolsetsis fell short; we were negligent in preparing you," Mr. Tutukjian responded without rancor. "But my point is not that the Armenians here have lost their finer qualities. Those qualities depend on a certain level of culture and development, which we Bolsetsis had an obligation to provide. But what I'm talking about is simply self-defense.

For that, one doesn't need a great deal of culture and education. As I was just saying, it's so natural you'll find it in the world of plants and animals and uncivilized people. Is the Armenian so much lower than the animals that he feels nothing, as if he is wood or rock?"

CHAPTER 21

Vartan and Mr. Tutukjian remained alone together after Khacho and his sons left.

"He is right. The soil hasn't been prepared yet," Vartan observed, looking at the extremely pale and dejected Bolsetsi.

"Who is to blame?" Mr. Tutukjian asked, seeming to be overwhelmed by anguish. "The old man is very smart, smarter than us foolish Bolsetsi paper-shufflers. There was great truth in his point that we Bolsetsis should have set to work long ago preparing the people. And what did we do? Nothing! Because we weren't really concerned with all the terrible afflictions Armenia was suffering; we were only dazzled by the glory of ancient Armenia. We didn't even know what Armenia really was, and we did nothing to find out. Our only familiarity with it was based on a few traditional stories, and we imagined that titans like Dickran, Aram, Vahakn, Vartan, and Nerses The Great still inhabited the land. We conjured up its populous towns where Armenian crafts and commerce flourished and contributed to the general wealth of the country; we pictured the buildings they had built with their own hands, the fields they cultivated, their granaries filled with every gift of God. We thought the Armenians made up the majority of people in the country and lived out their lives in peace and prosperity, secure in the possession of their ancestral property. Yet we didn't know that all the Armenian areas had been emptied of Armenians, either through impoverishment or forced religious conversion. We didn't know that instead of real, live Armenians, all that we would find there was either the living-dead or vast cemeteries. We weren't aware that religion, that mainstay of the nation, had been smashed and that all that was left of it was the ruins of once magnificent monasteries and churches. We didn't know that our language, that sacred national legacy, was no longer to be found on Armenian lips, because everyone spoke either Kurdish or Turkish. We had no idea that, just fifty or a hundred years ago, the great majority of today's brave Kurds, who are now God's scourge on the Armenians and a great plague, were our brothers, related to us by blood, and spoke our language and prayed in our churches. In short, we knew nothing. The only information we had about Armenia was vague and uncertain. We didn't realize yet that those dispersed remnants of the Armenians—ending up here and there due to tragic events and crushed beneath the harsh yoke of oppression—had changed into something very different, had lost their finer qualities, and had acquired a low, dull, timid, and shifty nature..."

Vartan listened attentively, and Mr. Tutukjian continued:

"But we Bolsetsis had so much at our disposal, we could have done a great deal. We had the patriarch there, the head of the people, yet he was aloof from the body of the people. We had the national parliament, but it was only preoccupied with minor matters and useless questions. We had our educated youth, who, on the anniversary of the national constitution, made the shores of the Bosporus ring with their songs, all the while ignorant of the blood and tears that were flowing in Armenia. There was the press, which paid no attention to what was happening in the Fatherland and was more interested in the lives of foreigners. We had schools which never sent one teacher to Armenia. We had the theatre which not even once performed a play having to do with the plight of the Armenians, content instead to entertain people with French kitchen vulgarities. We had the leading lights of the nation, and they spent all their time lavishing praise and flattery on the officials of the Porte. And we had material power—money—which was only spent on beautifying the palaces of the *amirahs*, while not one cent was spent to improve conditions in Armenia. In short, we were at the helm of national advancement, yet, it seemed, we occupied that position only to lead the nation astray and bring it to destruction.

"As for me and my comrades," he went on, "I have no choice but to view our goals as purely quixotic. What could anyone expect from us? We were completely idle in Bolis; we didn't examine what life was like in Armenia; we didn't study the country to acquaint ourselves with the living conditions and the needs of the people to prepare them for a better future. Then, suddenly to appear in their midst and thrust weapons into their hands for self-defense, such a thing could hardly be accepted. Yet, I don't waver. My faith is still intact, because even if I and my comrades fall, that will open up a way for those who follow, and they will move forward over our bodies..."

On hearing this last statement from Mr. Tutukjian, Vartan was deeply moved and embraced him.

"Yes, success in that kind of undertaking will demand the sacrifice of life. All praise and honor to him who is willing to be the first."

It was already the middle of the night. It had been hours since their beds were prepared for them, yet sleep still eluded the two young men.

Mr. Tutukjian went on to speak with unsparing criticism of the idealistic youth of Bolis. Of the clergy, he said, "If just one tenth of the monasteries and churches had been converted to schools, Armenia would already have been saved."

Suddenly they heard a soft knocking at the door. Vartan got up and opened it. Standing there were Hairabed and Abo, those two of Khacho's sons who were so distinguished in character from their other brothers.

"We came at this unusual hour so that we wouldn't be seen," Hairabed said as he and his brother sat down. "We must have disturbed you."

"Not at all," said Vartan. "We couldn't get to sleep and were still talking. I assume everyone in your house is asleep."

"Everyone except my father," said Abo. "He's been lying in bed, coughing over and over again. When he coughs like that, it's a sign he has something on his mind."

Vartan and Mr. Tutukjian already suspected the two brothers had not come without good reason to see them at this unusual hour and were waiting for them to reveal what it was.

"We couldn't speak at all with our father or our other brothers," said Hairabed gravely. "We had to let you know as soon as possible that we're in total agreement with your views, and we're ready to do whatever you think is best to help you in your work."

Mr. Tutukjian's grim countenance was suddenly transformed by a glimmer of happiness—the happiness of a missionary who has just found two converts and believes they are the first members of a flock that will soon number in the thousands.

"It's entirely untrue that the Armenians here are dead of heart and soul to all the higher impulses, but there's one general fault among Armenians," said Hairabed. "If left to himself, every Armenian is cautious and fretful and unsure of himself. He doesn't have a will of his own and always waits for someone else to set the example for him. An example makes a big impression on him, especially if it's successful, but only under certain conditions. He doesn't care how people in other countries live or work. What I mean is this: the Armenian won't follow an outsider's example; he waits for one of his own to set the example. For that reason, I think it's up to us to set that example, and then many will follow. I know our people well. They've been so tormented, if they find a way they're already prepared to eat the flesh and drink the blood of the Turks and Kurds. They bear a deep hatred in their hearts, but it is covered up."

Vartan and Mr. Tutukjian listened happily as Hairabed spoke, hearing in his words the voice of the people.

"Blessed is the people that knows how to hate!" the Bolsetsi exclaimed with singular fervor. "Whoever doesn't know how to hate knows nothing about love, either..."

"My father said the soil isn't ready," Hairabed said. "He is actually very wise, and he has many good ideas in his heart, but his prudent counsel and caution have gone too far. We've been numbed by his patience and left in a petrified state, unable to act. As I see it, in a situation like this more can be accomplished by a certain boldness and self-confidence, and even an extreme of madness, than by the sober and earnest thoughts of philosophers."

"Yes," said Vartan, smiling, "*While the prudent stand and ponder, the fool has already crossed the river.*"

"That's so true," said Mr. Tutukjian. "The wise are often misled by their own wisdom, and they only find out they've been made fools of when their plans end in misfortune... There was a time in Bolis when our intelligentsia considered an uncultured, anarchic Turkish government better for the Armenians than an orderly and civilized one. Their logic was that a government with a high degree of culture would have absorbed and put an end to the Armenians, whereas by exploiting Turkish backwardness, Armenians could compete and win in the struggle for existence. That idea makes sense in theory, but there are times when the truest of philosophical theories is proven wrong in practice. History takes its own turns. If a large, advanced nation can absorb smaller peoples, a large, backward nation can similarly put an end to its smaller subject peoples. The only difference is in the ways and means used. One kills through barbarism, the other with culture.

"I will make things even plainer," continued Mr. Tutukjian. "With childish short-sightedness, every one of us repeated the same refrain, 'Our future is with Turkey.' We only looked at the surface of the abuses, the various disorders and barbarities; what we didn't see was the hellish mechanism hidden within them all. All we saw was the oppression and killing and forced religious conversions carried out by neighboring peoples. We thought they were just abnormalities and incidental events, unaware that the encouragement of highly placed individuals was behind them all. We just blamed the government for being excessively lax and unconcerned, powerless to control its more unruly subjects. We failed to understand that it was government officials who were instigating these barbarities against the Armenians with the purpose of wiping out the Christian element. You ask me why?

"Because Turkey knows full well that if it someday loses its territories in Europe and Asia, this will be on account of the Christian populations who live there. It understands that the presence of Christian subjects under its rule provides an excuse for interference in its affairs by Christian rulers and threatens a renewal of the Eastern Question.[24] So, to hang onto its territories and prevent interference from Christian nations, Turkey has every reason to annihilate its Christian population. Because of Christians, it has lost many of its territories in Europe and is close to losing the rest because of them. Of its Asian territories, the only one it still has possession of in its entirety is Asia Minor, and in this area the Christian population that presents the greatest danger of breaking away is the Armenian one. And so, to silence the European governments, the Turkish government has to show that there are no longer any Armenians in Armenia; and to execute this undertaking, they have chosen the very best of executioners—the Kurds and the Circassians.

"If we consider what has happened over the past twenty, thirty, or fifty years, we will see that all of this is quite accurate. We will see that all the violence and oppression, all the persecution and rapine—in one word, every barbarity—was not some incidental outbreak, but rather the working out of a deliberate plan; to weaken and exhaust and, finally, destroy the Armenians. I'll cite you a few examples: to prevent any kind of self-defense from developing among the Armenians, the first thing the Turks did was take away any weapons they had, tie and shackle them, then hand their weapons over to their enemies. But they saw this wasn't enough to weaken the Armenians. They saw that this people—hard-working and economically capable—was still able to compete with its rivals and maintain its existence on the basis of its material strength and wealth. Therefore it became necessary for Turkey to use every means at its disposal to impoverish the Armenians and destroy them economically. Their taxes got heavier. Their currency was devalued without any prior warning. In short, they put every kind of financial trickery into practice to ensure that whatever money the Armenians had left would be worthless and they wouldn't be able to pay their taxes. This then gave the government the excuse to demand their most basic property as payment for taxes, the kind of things that were essential to their way of life. But even this wasn't enough to satisfy their designs. The people endured. If it was impossible to make a living on the land of their fathers, they emigrated to foreign countries to make money, then bring it back to fill the government treasury. So, what was Turkey to do given that situation? It decided to dry up the livelihood of the Armenians. It started applying its most unjust laws on land ownership. Armenian land was turned over to Kurds, and Derebeys, and Circassians; to Muftis, and kadis, and various wild Eshirats. These people became the owners, and the Armenian, the industrious and productive Armenian, became a slave and a menial on his own land. The countless legal disputes over land ownership between Armenians and Mohammedans have either gone unresolved because the government ignores them; or if they're resolved, they're always settled in favor of the Mohammedans. There are thousands of such cases. Just a close look at any one of them will be enough to prove the government has no intention of leaving any land at all to the Armenians. It rather wishes to strip them of the land they inherited from their fathers and put increasing pressure on them to emigrate, thus emptying Armenia of Armenians, and letting the Kurds and Circassians take their place.

"Now do you see the common thread that runs through all these evil policies?" Mr. Tutukjian went on. "Do you see the secret hellish intention that lies hidden in them all? It seems to me unnecessary to cite specific instances and show how local authorities have often used artificial devices to induce famine in the provinces where Armenians are most heavily concentrated, thereby ensuring that whatever Armenians have survived the sword of the Kurds and Circassians will be finished off by starvation. This is the monstrous kind of killing that only the brutal and merciless Turk is capable of. Crushing the people with poverty, bankrupting their economy, stripping them of every means of making a living—these are the main weapons the Turk is now using to wipe out the Armenian populace. He knows that no other weapons can so effectively destroy a people whose strength is based on their industriousness and material capability. The Armenians of Zeitoun have nowhere to plant their crops. The main basis of their livelihood and productivity are their iron mines from which they manufacture all sorts of tools, or take the raw iron to neighboring provinces and trade it for whatever they need. Turkey has tried to take these mines away from them many times; but these brave mountaineers resisted fiercely, and they were able to protect their main source of wealth. The burning of Van is a precise example of that kind of policy. The Armenians of Van were very prosperous. Overnight, all their shops were burned. Despite their repeated protests, the local government did nothing to investigate what happened and find out who was responsible, because that would have involved investigating itself."[25] "To this day we wonder why Turkey has been so solicitous with the Kurdish and Circassian chieftains and has engaged in flattering the spiritual leaders of these people whose unruliness has caused them so many problems. These people often pay no taxes at all, then they engage in raiding one district or another. Did it ever occur to us that if it really wanted to, the government could control these outlaws? Now we can see clearly; Turkey needed them to serve as tools in its hands. Their purpose? It's now quite clear."

It seemed that, tonight, Mr. Tutukjian was pouring out all the bitterness that had weighed down his heart. The extreme suffering of the people, their miserable condition, their bleak future as he pictured it in sombre tones before his mind's eye, all this had filled his heart with righteous indignation.

"The circumstances and conditions of life have forced men to deal with others as they have been dealt with, by answering evil with evil," Mr. Tutukjian went on. "There's no other way. Of all creatures, only man exceeds the wild beasts in the pitiless and cruel manner with which he treats his fellows. At least wild beasts kill their victims all at once, and then their suffering is over. But man is systematic; he tortures and torments his victim; he exhausts him morally and spiritually; he saps his life force from him little by little. That is a horrible way to die, and it is only man who is capable of killing like that. This same kind of murder is inflicted not just on individuals, but on entire nations, as well, and this is the kind of murder we face now. Isn't it just this that lies behind the way we've been treated by the Turks, the Kurds, and the Circassians? Isn't that why the greater part of Armenia has been emptied of Armenians?"

Vartan listened to Mr. Tutukjian's lengthy exposition with deep sympathy. When he responded, it was with a bitterly ironic smile on his face:

"The Armenians are a truly remarkable people. While I won't claim that killing them is impossible, I must say, it's not all that easy. They are that legendary dragon, Hydra, whose every chopped-off head is replaced by a new and stronger one. In the course of the centuries, the Armenian has been so beaten and tormented and hewn down that he has acquired the strength of iron. Cutting him down is no easy matter. He is strong... The Armenian has persevered; he has withstood the barbarities of the greatest Mongols, those compared to whom the present-day Mongols are like flies. Mankou Khan, Tamerlane, Genghiz Khan, Houlavouni, and all their like, passed through Armenia like a flood and storm. They slaughtered and were slaughtered in turn, and finally withdrew; but the Armenian remained. Today Mongolian Turkey has set out to destroy the industrious Armenians who keep the government coffers full and, in so doing, is killing itself. This is the reason for its present bankruptcy. The Turkey of old had a better appreciation of how important the Armenians were to the government's stability. Not only did they pay attention to ensuring the comfort of the industrious Armenian peasant, but turned over the entire administration of the government treasury to Armenian capitalists. And our Sarafs have many times rescued the government from financial crisis."

It was nearly sunrise, and our hot-headed intellectuals were still talking. The ensuing discussion had to do with plans and preparations.

When they had finished conferring, Mr. Tutukjian reached into his breast pocket and pulled out three travel documents and, handing them to his friends, said, "Now that I totally trust you, I can tell you who I really am."

Mr. Levon Salman's father, Toros Chelebi,[26] had been an Armenian Catholic converted to Mohammedanism. The circumstances surrounding this event make quite a long story. Suffice it to say, he was accused of having an affair with a beautiful Turkish woman named Fatimah and was forced to marry her to keep his life. Fatimah died after Levon's birth, and little Levon remained in the care of his father, now terribly upset at the prospect that his son would be raised and trapped within an alien religion that had become repugnant to him. Salman (that is, the Mohammedanized Toros Chelebi) left his native land, Ankouriah,[27] and moved to Bolis where no one knew who he was. He turned his son over to an order of Catholic brothers, then left. Little Levon grew up in a Catholic convent until the age of twelve, and after that was sent to Italy. He received his earliest education from monks and spent his first few years in the monastery of San Lazzaro in Venice. He then left for the Mekhitarist monastery of Vienna, but never received a truly complete education anywhere. Then the love of a woman drew him away from the monastery, and he ended up involved in the Paris cause. Here, for a while, he lived a carefree, idle life, going from one political party to another and joining many different brotherhoods, but only to talk and never to act. When his sweetheart's money ran out, he was forced to look for real work and took to writing various newspaper articles on eastern affairs to make a living. But when the Eastern Question took on new life, he left Paris and his sweetheart and moved to Bolis.

CHAPTER 22

A month before Mr. Tutukjian showed up in the province of Bagrevant, a mule-driver named Haji Misak set out for Erzeroum with his caravan. He had been given the title Haji because of the two pilgrimages he had made to Holy Jerusalem, and, God willing, he would make one more to complete the mystical number. In general, he was a good Christian, his devotion sometimes bordering on superstition. Well known in every town, village, and inn, he had transported cargo with his mules to every part of Asia Minor and Armenia for over twenty years. He was a stocky, solidly built man of medium height and unusually quick in his movements. His features were obscured by a heavy growth of facial hair, except for his great Armenian nose and his fiery eyes which shone with a bright look of kindness.

The arrival of his caravan was an occasion for general rejoicing wherever he went. Everyone had requested him to bring something special: the merchant expected his wares; a woman awaited a letter from her emigrant husband; various greater or lesser officials along the road expected a particular type of food, drink, or clothing. Often, an Armenian refugee, sick and weak and fallen by the wayside, would wait for him to come by with his caravan, and, out of the kindness of his heart, pick him up and take him where he needed to go. Haji Misak's sympathetic nature and readiness to help others had won him the affection of everyone who knew him: "Haji Misak, bring me some coffee, mine is used up." "Haji Misak, deliver this Zeitouni oil to our home." He would deliver such items without charge for people, often helping them with money from his own pocket, as well. For this reason, whatever authorities he encountered along the road were lenient with him, and he passed by all the customs houses without interference.

Caravan drivers, especially the well-known ones, enjoy a great deal of prestige in the East. Transport of the most precious articles, including chests of gold and silver, is entrusted to them without benefit of vouchers or official papers, and they safely deliver them to the desired destination. Every town knew when Haji Misak would arrive; his caravan kept such a regular itinerary that, barring untoward circumstances along the way, he never strayed so much as an hour from his established schedule. But on this particular day his caravan was moving at a slower pace. Despite the rather small volume of his load, it seemed quite heavy. Most of the containers were long, rectangular cases strapped with metal bands; they had the names "Persia" and "Tehran" printed on them, in English letters.

The caravan proceeded at night most of the time. Haji Misak said he didn't want to tire his mules beneath the scorching daytime heat.

On this particular day there was one other person in the caravan with Haji Misak, a merchant who said he was an Armenian from Persia and went by the name of Melik-Mansour.

In the course of the preceding twenty or thirty years, the Persian government had made considerable advances in the development of weapons and adapting them to European design. This development opened a whole new field of business for Armenian entrepreneurs, and they became arms suppliers to the government. Melik-Mansour was one of these merchants, and the heavy cases the mules were carrying belonged to him. The customs officials paid no particular attention to these items, since they were in transit to Persia. There was nothing new about the transport of such cargo on the Trebizond-Erzeroum-Bayazid road to Persia.

Melik-Mansour was thirty-six years of age. He had a pleasant face and was always in good cheer. His sunny personality together with his ever busy tongue lent a special liveliness to his endless conversations with Hadji Missak, especially when it came to recounting his adventures in distant lands.

He spoke many languages, both eastern and western, and over the course of his life had come into contact with all kinds of people; he knew all their tricks and how one had to deal with people. For this reason, he was a different person on the inside than he seemed outwardly. Nevertheless, Haji Misak treated this rather mysterious individual with great respect, not only because he was transporting his merchandise, but because, beyond that, there was something more about the man that won his respect.

All the overseers of the various caravansaries were very fond of Melik-Mansour, since he was quite liberal with his money and handed it out right and left.

"You're spoiling them; next time we come here, the rascals won't even give us a cup of water free."

"That's fine, men are blinded by the glitter of gold," Melik-Mansour answered with a laugh.

The caravan proceeded without incident as far as Erzeroum and then, within a week, had entered the province of Bayazid. It was at this point that, gradually, certain changes began taking place in the nature of the cargo. The long wooden cases began to disappear, and the space they had occupied was taken by altogether different ware. These changes occurred whenever the caravan made a stop at one Armenian village or another. Melik-Mansour could sometimes be seen in the company of certain strangers who disappeared after conversing with him in their own language.

At last the caravan approached the Turkish-Persian border and crossed into Persia; but by this time, not one of the wooden cases bearing the inscriptions "Persia" and "Tehran" remained on the backs of Haji Misak's mules, and Melik-Mansour himself, that counterfeit merchant, had disappeared.

CHAPTER 23

The daily atmosphere of life which had prevailed of late in Khacho's home now underwent considerable changes. Mr. Salman (whom the members of the household still called Mr. Tutukjian) was often gone from the house; he and Vartan would sometimes disappear from the village of O… for several days at a time. Hairabed and Abo had turned very pensive and incommunicative. The other brothers had no use for the two guests; they regarded them as outsiders and were not enchanted with their "foolishness." As for Khacho, he was preoccupied with village problems that became more pressing with each passing day.

As a result of all this, the guest room had lost a great deal of its previous liveliness, and there was a lull in the great discussions and debates, and exchanges of opinion.

Only the life of the women went on without change. This was a routine that had been established over the course of centuries and continued so. This part of the household, separate and apart from the world of the male members, had no idea what the concerns of the men were. Nothing crossed their minds except their daily household responsibilities, and they had no awareness of what the men had been talking about in the guest room. The village guest room was still not a place that could be approached by ordinary women.

Mr. Salman had frequently stated, "That energy which is enclosed within the four walls of the women's quarters needs to be liberated and put to good use. Then our success will be assured."

"It's still too early for that. The most important thing is that they be well prepared," was Vartan's response.

"Without women's participation, there can be no renewal in a people's life. If our people have been stuck where they are, it's mainly because our women haven't taken part in the general task. We have wasted away that force—that life-giving power—inside those four walls. If we wanted to go about educating our people, our first step would necessarily be the education of our women. On this journey, I've wandered through every part of Armenia and studied Armenian women with utmost attention; what I've discovered is very encouraging. No matter how thrown off course or corrupted or out of touch with their unique Armenianness the men have become under Turkish influence, the women have maintained a high degree of moral purity. There's no evil that doesn't contain some element of good in it. Though the women were closed up within their four walls and suffered this condition for centuries; though they became dull and were denied a normal existence, on the other hand, they clung to their Armenianness in this imprisoned condition. That was a great accomplishment. While the men were losing their distinctive national identity, the women, in their part of the home, far removed from these outside influences, were preserving it. And so, unconsciously, a certain balance was struck; the women made up for what the men had lost. This can be seen in the smallest matters. The women's distaste for Mohammedanism has reached the level of fanaticism; anything Mohammedan is seen by them as indecent: the meat slaughtered by Mohammedans, the cheese or bread they make, all these they refuse to eat. But the men make no such distinctions. I have heard hundreds of stories about women and girls abducted by Mohammedans, and who, if they found no way to escape, resorted to suicide. Such feelings can scarcely be found among the men. And there's something else, as well, something very important: in many localities, especially in the towns, it's become totally normal to hear our men speaking Turkish, yet I never found a case of an Armenian woman who spoke Turkish or even knew it. In the home, it is the woman who is the preserver of the Armenian language and the one who imparts it to her children. This influence extends even to foreigners. All the Kurdish boys and girls who work in Armenian homes speak Armenian. It is the Armenian woman who has given us our language and our national identity, while at the same time protecting the moral foundations of the family. At present, she is a pure, uncorrupted and uncultivated material in our hands from which something truly marvelous can be formed."

These and similar ideas were the usual substance of Mr. Salman's discourses. Yet, despite his high opinion of women, the women in

Khacho's household didn't reciprocate his esteem. It is understandable that his intrinsic moral and intellectual worth was not apparent to them. Outwardly, Mr. Salman had many qualities that might well be attractive to any woman. Yet, women's assessment of a man's desirability is conditioned by their level of development and social class. With this in mind, it is not surprising that Vartan enjoyed greater esteem among the women of the household than Mr. Salman.

On one occasion, during the midday break in activities, the daughters-in-law were sitting and doing their handiwork. One was carding wool, another was taking it up on a spool, another was weaving a beautiful, multicolored rug on the loom, and another was sewing children's clothes. In a word, each was doing her own work. Then the conversation turned to Mr. Salman.

"Sara, what is that man doing in our village?" asked Parishan, one of Sara's young nieces.

"They say he wants to open a school," Sara answered.

"But he's not a choirmaster," said Parishan, to whose mind a choirmaster was the only teacher she had ever known.

"He's a choirmaster from Stamboul," Sara said with emphasis.

"But then why doesn't he do the services and chant the sharagans?"[28] Sara didn't know how to reply and, without thinking, said, "Well, that's the kind of choirmaster he is."

Maro, Abo's beautiful wife, spoke up.

"Abo says he's going to teach classes for the girls, too."

Maro's words sparked general laughter.

"Why would a girl learn to read? She's not going to be a priest or vartabed," they all said in response.

One of the daughters-in-law turned to little Nazlou and said, "So you see, Nazlou? You're going to go to school with them and learn your a-b-c's."

Nazlou was Hairabed's daughter, and she gave a bold response. "Why not? I'll learn everything there is to learn; I'll go to church at just the right time; I'll put on all the right vestments, and I'll sing the responses with the boys."

"There wasn't enough earth left to finish your head!" several of the poor girl's aunts and cousins derided her.

Parishan, who had begun this whole discussion, had one more question to ask. "Choirmaster Simon has been our children's teacher. Why do we need another one? Does that man know more than master Simon?"

"Certainly not. Master Simon is a well-read man, but he has one problem; he drinks too much, and then he starts to beat his pupils. Don't you remember that boy, Gaspar, from the next village? He got such a terrible beating, he was taken home all covered in blood, and he died two days later."

"That wasn't master Simon's fault. How can a child learn without taking his licks?" said one of the cousins.

This conversation was not without reason, for within the past few days Mr. Salman had been conferring with the villagers about opening two schools, one for girls, and one for boys. He promised that teachers would be sent and the children's instruction would be entirely free, including books and other necessary items. But to the peasant, whatever is free is suspect.

It therefore took a great deal of persuasion to win the peasants over, especially given their deep antipathy to the idea of education for girls. These people were only used to receiving instruction from priests and choirmasters, and they found the notion of turning over the education of their children to a man like Mr. Salman not only alien and illicit, but actually sinful; for he didn't even chant the sharagans, or celebrate the offices of the church, or keep the fasts.

Yet old Khacho, who disagreed with Mr. Salman on other important issues, agreed with him on the matter of schooling. With his standing as village elder he was able to win the villagers over, and a piece of land was designated for the new school. The work was underway, and the foundation trenches had already been dug. Suddenly one morning there was a commotion. It was discovered that some villagers had gathered during the night and filled in the foundation trenches; and that day not one villager showed up to work on the school site, though Mr. Salman had raised the rate of pay.

But what had happened?

As we learned from the women's conversation above, choirmaster Simon served also as teacher to the village children; that is to say, in winter he gathered the children together into a barn and read them psalms, the breviary, and other such books. But at the beginning of spring, he dismissed them all until the end of autumn, and by that time they had forgotten everything they had learned. Simon was the son-in-law of the village priest, Father Marouk, and an inveterate drunkard and trouble-maker. Seeing the school as a threat to his interests, he prevailed on his father-in-law to put a stop to it.

It didn't take much to incite the villagers' antipathies and put an end to the project. In a sermon devoted to Mr. Salman, Father Marouk told his congregation that the young Bolsetsi was a "freemason," that he did not believe in the God of the Armenians, and that he would destroy the children's faith. He went on to say that teaching girls was sinful, that Solomon The Wise and John The Baptist had cursed women, and that a woman had caused John The Baptist's head to be cut off. Citing cases from the scriptures, he stated that a woman was responsible for the death of Samson the prophet(?),[29] that Eve was responsible for leading Adam astray, resulting in their expulsion from Paradise. In a word, the old priest cited many examples to prove that educating girls was a dangerous matter, would lead to their learning too many things, and turn them into devils.

Besides this, choirmaster Simon carried a great deal of authority with the village women; he had inscribed various magical charms for them, and performed incantations and divinations, thus winning their confidence. The women actively pressured their husbands to help save choirmaster Simon's job.

Facing this new challenge, the old priest and his son-in-law found a major ally in Tomas Effendi, a man adamantly opposed to anything resembling schools, education, or study. On top of this, the choirmaster was the Effendi's secretary and kept the tax collector's accounts for him. At harvest time, he accompanied the Effendi and his two policemen, going from one village to the next with them to collect the tithe from the villagers.

All of this produced a great deal of trouble for Khacho, but in no way deterred Mr. Salman from his purpose. On returning to the house in the evening, Mr. Salman spoke to Vartan.

"I'm going to deal with those ignorant people the way a missionary does. Wherever a missionary goes, his first opposition comes from the literate people and clergy, but later on, those very people become his first adherents. The missionary gives them various assignments to do, or to be more precise, lets them do nothing; but he allows them various privileges. Thus, those 'Pauls' who started out persecuting the new sect become its fiercest defenders."

"That's very true," said Vartan. "What are you going to do?"

"One has to take the initiative," Mr. Salman said. "One has to know what makes an impression on people. I'd very much like to know how much that ignorant choirmaster earns from his pupils. I'll offer him the same amount to occupy a position at the school; that is to say, to do absolutely nothing. I think after hearing an offer like that, he'll show up in the morning, take a shovel or hoe, and go to work with the others to build the school."

"I agree, but you'll still have to offer the priest something to hush him up," said Vartan.

"I'll take care of that, too," said Mr. Salman.

Despite the disappointments of the day, Mr. Salman was now in a happier mood than usual. The challenges of starting the project had stimulated him, and bright prospects for the future filled his heart with joy.

"Do you realize what a great future this school promises, Vartan? It will provide everything we need. It, and it alone, can heal our centuries-old wounds and prepare the new generation for a fresh, new start in life. The indolence of our forefathers has certainly left much for us to do. They were lax in voicing the concerns we are dealing with today. But, no matter. There is still hope the future will belong to us. All that's necessary is hard work and persistence. As I see it, it's not enough just to educate the mind and cultivate the soul. The body, too, must be developed. You must have noticed for yourself, Vartan, how dull and lethargic the children are here. Their muscles have to be strengthened, their nerves have to be reinvigorated. This will require a well-designed program to teach physical fitness and foster courage in our children to fortify their sagging spirits...

"I have a very happy story to tell you, Vartan. Today I stopped to talk with some Kurds about the value of education. To my amazement, they answered that they were entirely in favor of sending their children to Armenian schools because they saw that education was so important. From what they said, it was clear they weren't happy with the prospect of their children ending up as bandits someday. And, really, how can these people be blamed that they've remained in a wild state, forced to make their living through banditry and murder? It's we who are to blame, for, to this day, we've made no effort to educate them. It was in our own interest to do something for them. If we want to be spared their wild behavior, we have to help them get used to leading a tranquil and peaceable life. Turkey is indifferent to educating the Kurds. That's understandable, since their wildness is useful to the Turks. But we have to care, because we're affected by the consequences. We won't touch their religion; we'll just educate them. After that, 'the water will find its own level.'"

CHAPTER 24

The Turkish government's preparations for war had become quite evident now, and this was particularly the case in the province of Bagrevant, since it was fairly close to the Russian border. Not only were the taxes for the current year being strictly collected, but debts from years past plus taxes for several years into the future were being collected, all at the same time. There was boundless frustration and resentment among the people. If they were unable to pay, their domestic property and their animals were taken from them by force, even the bulls and oxen, so indispensable to farming and the transport of heavy loads. But this was still not enough for the government, and all the food staples the people had stored away were taken from them: cracked wheat, vermicelli noodles, oil, cheese, rice, etc. In answer to their tears and their moans of protest, the only response the peasants received was, "The government is at war."

As a result of these disruptions, a whole new field of activity opened up for Tomas Effendi. In his capacity as Court moultezim, it was his responsibility to set aside for the army whatever commodities he had collected as taxes. Before him lay a vast harvest waiting to fall to his sharp sickle, which he now wielded with renewed fervor. Instead of an escort of just two police, he now had a standing authorization for as many as he needed. And all of this misfortune fell only on the Armenians, for the Mohammedans would be participating in the war, and nothing more would be expected of them.

Besides the loss of everything they had labored over the previous ten or twenty years to bring to completion, beyond their bitter impoverishment, the Armenian peasants faced a yet more horrendous and all-encompassing catastrophe. A bestial fury against Christians or "infidels" began to manifest itself among the Mohammedan population. That hellish word, "jihad" was heard again and again on their lips. The mullahs, the kadis, and the sheikhs were inciting the fanaticism of the rabble, provoking them, preaching religious war to them, saying that a "sanjak sherif" would soon be issued from Bolis and holy war declared; that all of Islam would raise the sword against the Christians…

All of these fanatical stirrings caused Mr. Salman a great deal of anguish. He was well aware of their true significance and the dire consequences they foretold for the Armenians.

"Very soon, they will repeat the Bulgarian atrocities[30] here. We have to move quickly to get the people ready for self-defense," he said to Vartan one morning.

"I've caught the scent of those barbarities in the air, too..." Vartan replied.

Thus engaged in conversation, the two young men left Khacho's house and headed toward father Marouk's in order to implement the plan they had discussed a few days earlier; that is, as Vartan had put it, to "hush up" the old priest by promising his son-in-law, Simon, a managerial position in the school project.

Suddenly they heard a voice. It turned out to be the call of an unfamiliar peddler passing through the village, hocking his wares, crying out the names of what he had to sell to attract customers.

"Pretty girls, rosy-cheeked brides, bring your money, for I have good needles, and thread of all colors, and thimbles made of gold."

The peddler was an enormous man, dressed in tattered clothes from head to foot. In comparison with the bulk of his body, the large container of merchandise he carried over his shoulder seemed as small as a tiny parcel would appear on a camel's back. His left leg was quite lame, and every time he rocked to his left one would think this Goliath might immediately tumble over; but he kept his balance thanks to a sturdy walking stick.

It was almost as if Mr. Salman felt an electrical shock in his heart on hearing the peddler's voice, as if suddenly he felt his heart weighed down with all the cares of the world. What tie was it that bound Mr. Salman with this vagabond? The peddler continued calling out the names of his wares, going through the middle of the village with his lopsided gait. As Mr. Salman, at a distance, crossed paths with the peddler, the two men gave each other a look. Without speaking a word, a great deal was communicated between them... But Vartan didn't notice any of this.

"What a great time to sell needles and thread to these poor villagers! They hardly have enough money for anything," said Vartan after they had gone a good distance past the peddler.

"My dear friend, like a juggler's bag, that man's box has two compartments," responded Mr. Salman. "In the lower compartment are the kinds of articles this is the best time to distribute..."

Vartan paid no particular attention to these enigmatic words. He was preoccupied with other concerns. His thoughts were on Lala. The sudden change in their relationship and its attendant worries had greatly upset him; he didn't know how to solve Lala's predicament, where to hide her, or what he could do, since, sooner or later, he might be called upon to participate in a totally different undertaking...

"The finest needles, thread of all colors, lovely beads…" the penetrating and fetching call of the peddler could again be heard in the distance.

At this point, Mr. Salman and Vartan encountered Tomas Effendi in the middle of the village. His beautiful horse had been led up, and he was about to mount. He was surrounded by a group of villagers to whom he was issuing various orders. On catching sight of Mr. Salman and Vartan he left the group of villagers behind and walked toward the two young men and called out to them from a distance:

"I've been wanting to see you for quite a while, Mr. Tutukjian (he was still unaware of Mr. Salman's true name). Ach, how lucky I am to have run into you, my dear compatriot. Apparently you didn't know that I, too, am a Bolsetsi."

Mr. Salman found the Effendi's flattery extremely offensive; they had never been introduced, and this was the first time they had seen each other. He gave no reply, and the Effendi grabbed hold of his hand.

"I hope you will allow me to embrace you, for, as a fellow Bolsetsi, I think I can expect this of you. I've been away from my native city for so long, I miss it greatly. Embracing you will put me in touch with it again."

Standing some distance away, Vartan observed this comedy in silence. Mr. Salman didn't know how to extricate himself from this tight spot. The Effendi turned to Vartan.

"Come here my crazy friend. You know that I have the heart of a child—one moment I'm upset and the next I've forgotten all about it. 'A Kurd will never call his tahn sour.' It's the same with you and me; you're one of mine. Good or bad, you're one of mine."

Vartan came close to losing his temper at this remark, but on a moment's reflection he considered that the Effendi might have some specific reason for being so friendly; he stepped forward and offered his hand.

The Effendi addressed himself again to Mr. Salman.

"I'm really very angry with you, Mr. Tutukjian," he said gravely. "Have you heard that Turkish saying, 'Call on the head of the village first, then you can rob the whole town?' Tomas Effendi is a special man in these parts. If you had checked with me before you had started all this, I could have made things much easier for you, and all these unfortunate things wouldn't have happened. Ach, youngsters, youngsters! You have good intentions, but you don't know how to get things done, isn't that so?"

"I really have no idea what you're talking about," answered Mr. Salman.

The Effendi, pretending he didn't hear this answer, turned around to look at the group of peasants who stood some distance away, waiting for him to come back.

"Ach, you asses, you asses! When will you ever learn?"

Then turning to address Mr. Salman once more, he said, "Truly, some people destroy their welfare with their own hands. That's how it is with those peasants. I just heard about what happened, and, to tell you the truth, my hair stood on end. We do everything we can to provide them with schools, to teach them so that their eyes can be opened and they won't stay blind, so they can tell the difference between good and evil, but they don't understand, and they just keep 'driving the same old donkey'…"

This "We did everything…" echoed in Mr. Salman's mind. But who was this "we" that the Effendi gave such emphasis to?

The Effendi went on.

"I was quite happy when I first heard of your plans, Mr. Tutukjian, and that's why I sought you out; to convey my special gratitude. Our people are lost in darkness and have to be brought out into the light of day. Only education can save them. Don't let those disturbances a few days ago discourage you; no worthy enterprise is without its difficulties in the beginning. You'll find me sympathetic and helpful. Just now, I have some business to do in a nearby village, but, tomorrow, when I come back, I'll call myself for the foundations to be laid. There's no one in this district who can stand up to Tomas Effendi…"

"Thank you, Effendi, but I don't want to take up your precious time; you have so much to do," replied Mr. Salman.

"It's nothing at all. I always have time for worthwhile things," the Effendi said in a tone of great liberality.

He shook hands with the two young men and left.

"Shameless one! Conniver!" Vartan said, looking after the Effendi as he went away.

"A man like him could be helpful," Mr. Salman said.

"Do you really believe he can be taken at his word? Who knows what kind of satanic plans he has afoot!"

The two young men had by now reached Father Marouk's door and knocked.

Once again, the peddler's voice resounded from one of the other streets of the village, "Beautiful needles... Thread of all colors... Fine beads..."

"Vartan, let's forget about seeing the priest today," Mr. Salman said.

"But why?"

"I have to buy a few things from that peddler..."

Vartan was amused at his friend's unusual request.

"Come on. There's something more..." said Mr. Salman in an enigmatic tone.

They left the priest's house, walked to the next street, and began following after the peddler. A crowd of children, accompanying the man, kept shouting to him, "Give us mastic! Give us mastic!"[31] He took some pieces of it and handed them out.

One villager in the street said to the man standing next to him, "I saw this same man on the road through the villages of Van the other day."

"These peddlers are everywhere," the other man said. "He has such a frightful face, Krikor. I'd hate to run into him at night with that devil's face of his."

As he made his way through the streets, the peddler would sometimes be called into one house or another and spend several hours there. At other times, people in the street would ask to see what he had; women would gather around and bargain with him at length for articles they wanted. And so, by evening he had scarcely finished his business for the day, and he left the village wrapped in darkness. He didn't take the principal road that led to the next village but made his way to a ditch which had been worn deep by the spring torrents and was now dry. Certain changes began to take place in his gait. He was still moving slowly because his load seemed quite heavy, but he no longer appeared at all lame, though he had seemed to be so all through the day. He descended into the ditch. Once at the bottom, he set down his load, then, putting the two fingers of his left hand into his mouth, he whistled a few times as a signal (the other fingers had been cut off).

Within a short time, Vartan and Salman joined him in the ditch. Mr. Salman and the peddler greeted each other with a hug and held each other for many moments.

"Now let's sit down," said Mr. Salman. "Did your business go well today?"

"Very well. I flooded the greater part of Van with my wares..." the peddler answered happily.

"And you didn't make any money on all of that, I'm sure."

"Not at all. Everything was passed out free…"

Vartan sat flabbergasted as he listened to this conversation between the two old friends and didn't in the least understand what it was they were talking about.

"Don't you see now what I mean when I say my friend's bag has two compartments?" Mr. Salman asked Vartan.

"Is there something interesting stored in the main compartment?"

"Weapons…"

Now Vartan understood who and what sort of man the peddler was, for just a few days earlier Mr. Salman had described him to Vartan. Vartan likewise embraced the peddler.

That man was Melik-Mansour.

CHAPTER 25

Even the grandest of men have great weaknesses; but though Tomas Effendi didn't belong to this highest rank of men, in the province of Alashgert he cut the figure of a giant. In places where lions don't exist, the fox can be a considerable beast. This man, too, as forceful and clever as he was, had his little weaknesses. Being occupied all day long with his official duties, he lightened his evenings with various unwholesome forms of diversion, and, following the corrupt example of Turkish officials, he drank *aragh*, called on girls and boys to dance in front of him, and surrounded himself with chalgis (musicians) of various kinds. From the moment he entered a village, every little cottage door was thrown open to him. Who could have refused to entertain such an important guest? Quite the contrary, a villager considered it an honor to be visited by Tomas Effendi; though he gained nothing from playing the host to him and would bear the cost of providing him with food and drink, he could be assured of being looked upon favorably by the Effendi after offering him such hospitality.

One evening, the kizir of the village conveyed word to a humble peasant's home that it had been chosen to host the Effendi for the night. The man of the house was the only tradesman in the district who could make and repair the various kinds of equipment and implements used by the local peasants such as ploughs, wheels, mills, etc. He was therefore away from home most of the time in search of jobs to do. He was away this evening, as well. On answering the door when the kizir knocked, the tradesman's wife responded that there was no way she could entertain the Effendi since her husband was not at home.

The kizir answered rudely, "The man isn't home, but the house is in its place!"

Such kizirs are, indeed, quite troublesome to villagers. They play the role of hunting dogs for various officials. They have keen senses and know all the paths that lead to prey…

The woman of the house was totally at a loss and didn't know what to say.

The kizir, considering his message to have been successfully delivered, added, as he made to leave, "The Effendi will arrive when the evening lamps are lit."

The woman stood dumbfounded for several moments and didn't know what to do. With her husband gone, it would be improper to entertain a stranger in her home.

She went over to her neighbor Oho's cottage and pleaded with him, "Brother Oho, the kizir just told me the Effendi is going to spend the night at our house, but my husband is gone. For the love of God, please come and deal with him."

"What kind of nonsense is this? Can't they find some other house in the village?" Oho responded irritably.

"I don't know; that's what I was told," she answered anxiously. Oho promised that he would play host to the Effendi and not leave her to deal with him on her own.

Tomas Effendi was all too familiar with the province and knew very well how to pick the best place to spend the night. His taste in this matter was well developed. His prime conditions were that the head of the household be a poor and rather simple-minded person—if not simple-minded, then with a fondness for drink (two closely associated qualities), and, of greater importance, that there be a pretty feminine face on hand to look at and delight him.

But the house that had been picked out for him this evening did not meet all his usual requirements. The head of the household, Master Bedros, was a modest and hardworking tradesman, not in the least dull of mind, nor given to drink. On the other hand, the Effendi hadn't made a poor choice, for though the man of the house was away his wife wasn't bad looking, and his sister, who was of age, was considered one of the most beautiful girls in the village.

The cottage lamps had been lit. The woman of the house, Susann, was at the oven preparing supper. Her sister-in-law, Varvareh, was frying chicken. Neighbor Oho was making various last minute arrangements to ensure that everything was in order to entertain a guest of such importance. Everything was ready by the time the Effendi arrived, led by the kizir. On this particular evening, the two policemen who usually accompanied him were absent, having found lodging in another house.

"Where's Master Bedros?" the Effendi asked, looking around the house. "I was hoping to see him. I had some very important business to talk with him about."

Neighbor Oho responded that the tradesman had gone to the next village to do some work.

"Oh, such a pity, such a great pity I couldn't see him! I had just the job for him," said the Effendi, repeating himself and going on to explain how the royal army needed a great many carts for transporting military supplies, and how he needed a permanent carpenter to repair carts that broke down along the way, and that Master Bedros was the best man he knew for the job, and that he wished to do him a "favor" by letting him benefit from this situation and have a job that would last for several continuous months.

The Effendi had a specific purpose in his choice of words. He knew full well that Master Bedros was gone to practice his trade and that he didn't require his services at all. All military supplies would be transported without compensation to the peasants with their wagons and animals. He knew very well that if any repairs were necessary on the wagons, their owners would do the repairing. Yet on hearing what the Effendi had said, the poor tradesman's wife, Susann, felt cheered by the thought of gaining something from this self-invited guest whose visit had at first seemed such an unpleasant prospect. The Effendi's intention was to raise the gullible woman's hopes so that he could carry out his purposes.

Only the Effendi took a seat. Neighbor Oho still stood, waiting for the Effendi's permission to sit down. He was finally allowed to take a seat. The kizir remained standing, ministering to the Effendi, since there were no servants or youth in the household to do the serving. The tradesman had taken his two young apprentices with him to work in the neighboring village. The lady of the house and her sister-in-law had still not appeared. They were out of sight in the other part of the cottage, separated from the main room by a partition.

But the time came for them to pay their respects to the honored guest, and both of them came out from where they had been hidden. They stood at a distance, placed their hands over their hearts and bowed their heads toward the guest, signifying, 'welcome to our home.'

"Long life to you," the Effendi said in response, giving them a side-long glance.

The face of the tradesman's wife was covered, but his sister's face was not. The two women then returned to their work of preparing the meal.

A deep silence reigned in the cottage for several minutes. No one said a word, waiting for the Effendi to utter the first word.

"What is your work these days?" the Effendi asked neighbor Oho.

"I don't have any work right now, sir," said Oho, scratching the nape of his neck. "God has punished me. All in the space of one year, I experienced several misfortunes. My oldest son was lost to evil and my animals were killed... now my plow doesn't work... I'm unemployed."

"That's terrible, really terrible!" the Effendi said with pity. "You're a good man, Oho. I know you, and I won't allow you to go without a job. I'll find something for you to do. I'll soon be needing a lot of help."

On hearing these words, Oho was beside himself with happiness.

"Just send some work my way, and you'll see how well Oho does the job!"

"'The harder it works, the more barley the donkey gets!'"

"That's so true."

The Effendi was one of those men who, wherever they find themselves, become so puffed up and proud that they "can't even pass through the palace gates," and yet, in other circumstances, can make themselves so small that they "can pass through the eye of a needle."

He simply had to offer Oho something to cling to, since he was playing the role of host, and the gullible peasant took what he had been told at face value.

"May God grant you long life, Sir. May God preserve your hand upon our heads."

Dinner was now ready. Varvareh brought in the water pitcher and bowl for hand washing, graciously setting them down before the Effendi, and he started to wash his hands. She then spread the tablecloth over the table and placed the bread on it, and then all the dinner that was ready up to that point was laid out on the table, each dish in its proper place. Throughout this process, the innocent young woman's timidity and bashfulness were quite apparent, qualities fostered in a cloistered life, isolated from contact with ordinary men.

"My child, what is your name?" the Effendi asked.

Varvareh blushed and became quite bewildered, looking all around for someone who would answer for her. Neighbor Oho told the Effendi what her name was.

"What a beautiful name! What a truly beautiful name!" the Effendi repeated in a highly appreciative manner. "I have a sister with the same name!"

On hearing these words, the hint of a smile appeared on Varvareh's face, which up to that moment had seemed so stern, and she appeared flattered that she shared her name with the sister of such an important man. In fact, the Effendi had no sister at all and simply needed some device to flatter Varvareh...

The Effendi and Oho were the only persons sitting and eating at the table. The women of this region never sit down to eat with the men.

"A mill without water will grind no flour!" the Effendi declared.

This was his way of indicating that he now wanted something to drink, and he ordered the kizir to go for *aragh*. Neighbor Oho apologized for overlooking this item and indicated that the lady of the house (who had so far been silent) would make sure that it was provided.

"No, no! That's not the way I do things. Whenever I'm a guest, I pay for the *aragh* and the wine.

And, indeed, that was so. He would simply dispatch the kizir out of this humble home to bring back drink, but the bill would be paid from the town budget. Thus, with satanic cunning, he was able to procure as much drink as he wanted.

The kizir promptly reappeared with a large jug of *aragh*.

"You can take a seat now and pour it for us," the Effendi said.

The kizir sat at the low end of the table and set the jug of *aragh* down near him. He was well aware of the Effendi's counsel, "When you stay at someone's house and you want to spend an enjoyable night, you have to loosen up the host." By this, he meant, "You have to dull the host's mind. You have to get him drunk." Therefore, the man of the house being away, Oho was in his place, and the kizir made sure the jug of *aragh* kept returning to Oho.

Neighbor Oho did have a certain fondness for drink, especially following his latest misfortunes, including the death of his son and the killing of his animals; he would give himself over to *aragh* in an effort to forget his troubles. There wasn't a drop left in his cup.

Under the influence of the alcohol, on the one hand, and all the promises of work from the Effendi, on the other, his mind had become so warmed, and he found himself filled with such gladness, that forgetting himself completely, he broke out singing various Turkish songs.

"This won't do," said the Effendi and sent the kizir to fetch the "chalgis."

The "chalgis" were a group of Armenian musicians adept at playing various asiatic instruments. They were inseparable from the Effendi and followed him on his route through the various villages, knowing he looked forward to having a good time in the evening and that money could be made playing for such occasions.

The "chalgis" soon arrived and arranged themselves around the table. The lady of the house was prevailed upon to serve them some food as well.

The Effendi deigned to ask the chalgis how they were.

"Thanks to you, we're very well," they answered.

After they had eaten and drunk their fill, Varvareh appeared from her hiding place and began clearing the table. The large pitcher of *aragh* remained where it was. It had already been emptied, taken to the tavern for more, and returned several times. It was passed around again and again until it started having its effect on the "chalgis."

"Now start playing," the Effendi commanded.

The "chalgis" struck up a tune, and now the little cottage came alive with the confused jangle of asiatic music.

The Effendi now found himself in his very favorite setting.

Within moments, the neighbor women and girls began to gather in front of the cottage and were peeking out from the windows of their houses, enjoying the sound of the music. Nothing is more pleasing to peasant women than hearing music, which they normally have the chance to hear only at weddings during the winter.

Little by little the character of the party became more excited and complicated. Reinforced by the *aragh* and the music, a general disorder began to prevail, and, as they say, "The dog could no longer recognize his own master," and everyone had lost his head. Only the Effendi remained sober and in a normal state of mind. Now, the crowd of women and girls outside made bold to start entering the cottage and, taking their seats behind the partition together with Susann and Varvareh, listened to the music with them.

"Dance! Dance! I want you to dance!" the Effendi cried, clapping his hands together.

Neighbor Oho, who by this time could barely stand on his feet, stood up and grabbed two little girls by the hands and almost forcibly pulled them into the middle of the crowd. Then the musicians struck up one of the well-known songs of the locality. The little girls were very embarrassed; they blushed and protested, but eventually began to dance.

"Shapash! Shapash!"[32] the musicians cried out, all the while playing harder.

The Effendi placed money in the dancers' hands, and they gave it over to the musicians.

As is customary, the dancing was begun by the little girls, then was taken up by the adult women. After the first pair of dancers had tired, they passed their kerchiefs to two other girls who were to take their place. And thus the dancing passed in turns to successive pairs of dancers.

The Effendi kept placing silver coins into the dancers' hands, and they then turned them over to the musicians who were now playing quite heartily.

Now it was Varvareh's turn to dance, and her dancing outdid all the others in its grace. Her every movement conveyed grace and a bewitching charm.

"Where I come from, the Armenians have a very nice custom," the Effendi said. "When the girl finishes her dancing, she goes up to the main guest, kneels before him and puts her head on his knees. She doesn't raise her head from his knees until he has given her a nice gift."[33]

"That's a very nice custom. It would be well to introduce it here, too," the musicians chimed in.

"Varvareh, you will set the example, so come here, my child," the Effendi said.

Totally embarrassed and confused, Varvareh remained where she was. She would have preferred for the earth to open up and swallow her rather than place her head on a stranger's knees. But she was urged and pestered from every side, "Go ahead. Don't be bashful. He's going to give you something," and, at last, she was led up to the Effendi and convinced to place her head down on his knees. The Effendi stroked Varvareh's lovely cheeks, then placed two gold coins in his lap.

While the Effendi was enjoying all of this, one of his policemen entered and said into his ear, "The man you were looking for has been found."

"Seize him and guard him closely until I have time to make arrangements tomorrow," the Effendi commanded in a whisper.

The policeman left.

No one had any idea who it was that all of these matters pertained to.

It was already well into the night. Master Bedros' home emptied of people little by little. The musicians were gone. Neighbor Oho had been taken home dead drunk. The crowd dispersed.

The only guests remaining in the cottage were the Effendi and the town kizir, who by this time couldn't see out of the only eye he had.

Susann prepared the Effendi's bed, turned down the lamps, and then everyone retired.

But what had taken place that night, only God knew. The next day Varvareh was deeply upset, and her cheeks remained wet with tears for many a day thereafter…

Very late that same night, in the morning hours of the new day, another tragic event occurred in the village: A young man bound in chains had been delivered to the military headquarters of an army command recently arrived in the province in preparation for the coming war.

None of the villagers had witnessed any of this; yet, in the darkness, it was Tomas Effendi who followed along behind the chained prisoner, looking after him, and saying to himself with deep, satanic satisfaction, "Go now and blow your duduk all you can!!"

That prisoner was Mr. Tutukjian, or Mr. Salman as we have come to know him.

CHAPTER 26

No one in Khacho's home had any idea what had become of Mr. Tutukjian, and everyone was worried because he hadn't returned that night. Vartan, Hairabed, and Abo were especially worried and suspected the worst. In the morning they all went out to see if they could find out something about him.

At midday, Tomas Effendi arrived quite by surprise at Khacho's house. The fact that he came alone, without a servant or his usual police escort, struck old Khacho as quite odd. He had always been accompanied by his police.

The Effendi took hold of Khacho's hand and drew him aside secretively, asking the old man in a tone half-serious and half-joking, "Did you hear that the 'duduk blower' was arrested and delivered to the bosom of Abraham?"

The shock of this news sent a shudder through old Khacho's entire body, and he almost fell to the floor, for he knew whom the Effendi was talking about.

"Get hold of yourself! This is no time to tremble. There's still more to hear."

The Effendi described to Khacho how, on the previous night, Mr. Salman had gone to a certain village and gathered a group of peasants around him. He spoke to them about "inalienable human rights," and the "labor" that farmers do. He spoke out against "oppression" and talked about how a "freer, better life" could be achieved, and other such "foolishness." He was suddenly set upon and arrested by the police. The government had been looking for this "fool" for quite a long time, having already thrown many of his comrades into prison in various parts of the country. The Effendi spared the old man no detail except one, the fact that it was he himself who had betrayed Mr. Salman to the authorities.

"Now listen to me, and listen carefully," the Effendi went on with a cynical smile on his face, as if prepared to wound the old man's heart even more deeply than before. "In a very short time, some police will arrive here to search your house. I came as a friend to warn you."

Despite the special stress the Effendi had placed on the word "friend," the old man was by now totally overwhelmed with all this talk of police and searching his house.

"There's still time for you to save yourself from all this," the Effendi went on in an even colder manner. "All you have to do is tell me if any of Mr. Tutukjian's personal effects remain in your house."

As shocked as he had been by all of this, the old man was somewhat consoled when he considered that a "friend" like this could help him in such dangerous circumstances.

"There's nothing left but his traveling bag," Khacho answered, looking nervously around him lest anyone overhear what he said.

"Come now, and let me see you pull this donkey out of the mud… So there's a traveling bag left… That's no small matter…" the Effendi said to himself.

He turned to the old man and opened wide his squinty little eyes.

"We don't have a moment to lose; let's hurry and hide the traveling bag before the police get here."

With total faith in the Effendi, Khacho led him to the guest room and pointed out Mr. Salman's traveling bag to him.

"Lock the doors," the Effendi ordered, then opened the bag and began rummaging through its contents.

Inside were several letters of recommendation with various addresses; drafts bearing different names allowing Mr. Salman to obtain money when he needed it; various instructions, plans, etc., as well as a number of pamphlets which the young propagandist passed out among the peasants—in a word, nothing but papers. The Effendi studied all these very closely, nodding his head meaningfully.

"Danouder Khacho, if just one of these papers fell into the hands of the authorities, it would be enough to send you and all your sons to the gallows and have all your property confiscated."

Khacho was totally stupefied on hearing these words and stood petrified where he was, unable to find a word to utter in response.

"These all have to be burned," the Effendi said as he stuffed the papers back into the bag.

"I don't understand any of this. I'm totally dumbfounded," said Khacho in a trembling voice, his reddened eyes welling with tears.

Suddenly, the Effendi changed his mind.

"Why burn them?" he thought to himself. "These papers have to be carefully examined. They might turn out to be useful to me... Why waste them?"

"Is there anywhere in your house we could hide this bag?" he asked Khacho.

"Yes."

Indeed, there were a number of secret places in the house that were used to hide property during times of danger, and since there was never a lack of danger in this province, all the hiding spots except one were already filled. This one could be shown to the Effendi.

They took the ill-omened traveling bag and proceeded with it toward the cellar of the house where olive oil, wine, and other such provisions were stored. The floor of this area was lined with flagstones. The old man went up to two of them and lifted them up. Underneath were two small iron doors which horizontally closed off the entry way to the secret chamber. Khacho took a key out of his pocket and placed it in the door. After moving it back and forth for a few moments, the doors sprang open on their own. The opening to the subterranean chamber was now before them, and they descended some narrow steps.

Nothing was visible in the silent void. The damp air was heavy and stifling. They deposited the traveling bag there and promptly left. Khacho locked the iron doors, positioned the flagstones where they had been, and there was once again not the slightest sign of any secret room beneath their feet.

"Give me the key, and I'll take care of it. Under these circumstances, I'm the only person you can trust," said the Effendi.

Without much reflection, the old man handed the key over to him, for he was so beset with fear he would have agreed to anything the Effendi proposed at this moment.

"I still have many things to talk to you about, Mr. Khacho, but time is getting short, and the inspectors may arrive at any moment," the Effendi said in a hurried tone. "For now, I will give you just a little advice and listen well. No one should know that I came to see you today. What we just did must be kept a secret, even from your own household. When the inspectors get here, simply act as unconcerned and undisturbed and ignorant of anything as you can. Let them go wherever they want and look around. We have already hidden the most suspicious article, and the devil himself can't find it. Don't deny that the 'duduk blower' has stayed here. Just say you're not familiar with him and that neither you nor your sons have any idea why he wandered here."

Having imparted this advice, the Effendi made to leave the cellar.

"Now show me how to get out without anyone seeing me."

The old man led the Effendi to the back of the house where there was a door used for letting the animals in and out.

"Goodbye for now. I'll be back after the inspectors are finished. Don't worry, I'll make sure they're satisfied with everything."

So saying, the Effendi left, and as he went on his way, he repeated the same words to himself again and again: "Now your soul is in my hands, old Khacho, and I will do whatever I want..."

It was an hour past midday. Vartan, Hairabed, and Abo hadn't returned yet. Khacho's other sons were still at work in the fields. The women were busy with their domestic chores, since they had to prepare lunch for the workers in the field. Most of the time, peasants have their lunch in the fields and only eat supper at home. At this point no one knew what was going on.

Old Khacho waited anxiously for the inspectors to arrive, like a condemned man who knows that death is inescapable. But he said nothing to the women of the household to avoid alarming them unnecessarily.

At last a group of police, guards, and soldiers arrived, led by a sergeant-major.

The women weren't greatly disturbed at their arrival; they had no knowledge of what had brought them here. In any case, there was nothing unusual about guests coming and staying a few days, eating and drinking their fill, then leaving. It was entirely common for Turkish soldiers to take their accommodations in Armenian homes, especially the homes of village hosts.

"I'm under orders to carry out a search of this house," the sergeant said to Khacho.

"My house lies before you, look wherever you wish," the old man said, trying to be calm.

The sergeant ordered all the doors locked, stationed guards, then began the search. He looked into every nook and cranny, starting with the guest room, then proceeded to the other rooms. He looked at every little article and found nothing suspicious. But seeing what was happening, the women realized this was no ordinary situation, that something serious had happened, and they began to cry and wail. Khacho berated them and told them to quiet down, reassuring them there was nothing to fear.

Having completed his search of the house, the sergeant began the interrogation.

"Has a young man named Mikayel Tutukjian been staying here?"

"He only stayed a few nights," answered Khacho.

"Was that the first time you had seen him?"

"Yes. I never saw him before."

"Why did you let him stay here?"

"I am the *danouder* of this village. As you know, according to our customs in this area, the *danouder*'s house is a kind of caravanserai—a kind of inn where all sorts of travelers and strangers are given lodging."

"Did he leave anything behind?"

"Nothing at all."

"Do you know why he came to this area?"

"He didn't say much to us. All I know is that he was a teacher."

"Did he meet with anyone here?"

"He talked to many people, looking for pupils."

"Do you know where he is now?"

"I have no idea."

"He is in prison."

"If he's a bad person, so much the better," responded Khacho.

Just then someone began rapping at the door.

"Don't let anyone in," the sergeant ordered the guard at the door. The guard informed him that the person knocking was Tomas Effendi.

"That man can be allowed in."

Tomas Effendi entered, and, seeing the sergeant together with all his men, acted as if he was shocked and didn't know what they were doing there.

"My goodness, what's going on here?" he asked in a concerned tone.

The sergeant explained why he was there. An affected smile passed over the Effendi's boorish face, and he seized hold of the sergeant's hand.

"I will offer my own head as bail for Danouder Khacho if it's found he did anything wrong. You don't know what a good and decent man he is!"

He led the sergeant to the guest room, but the police and the soldiers remained outside to guard all the entrances.

Addressing himself to Khacho, the Effendi said, "My good host Khacho, those men are famished. Hurry and see to it that lunch is served. And there has to be plenty of *aragh*. Do you understand?"

These last words were spoken in Armenian. Khacho was considerably relieved and left the room thinking the danger had passed.

But no, the danger wasn't over yet. The Turks wouldn't let the old man slip through their fingers so easily. It remained for him to be stuck for long months in a Turkish prison, there to be tortured and tormented and ground down to nothing. Though the search had come up empty-handed and there was nothing to charge him with, it was enough that he was an Armenian—and a rich one, at that—the sort of succulent prey that Turkish officials find irresistible.

It was Tomas Effendi, himself, who had "cooked-up this soup" and betrayed Mr. Salman to the newly arrived military commander. It was he who had instigated the search of Khacho's house, and, if he wished, he could quite easily set Khacho free from the trap he had laid. But no! To implement his satanic plan, he was still doing everything he could to make them yet more complicated.

When Khacho had left the guest room to order preparations for lunch, the sergeant addressed himself to Tomas Effendi:

"The old man seems quite innocent to me, Effendi. What do you think?"

"You should know, sir, that Tomas Effendi doesn't let people off the hook so easily," the wily Effendi replied. "There are still many questions that remain unanswered. I thought for sure that something suspicious would turn up here; some evidence of a link between the prisoner (Mr. Salman) and the men in this household and prove that they're involved in a plot together. That nothing of the sort has been found amazes me. Nevertheless, we Armenians have a secret practice that we call 'confession,' and I'll have to spend some time with these men to get them to confess. I still have suspicions about two of the old man's sons and a certain foreigner who has been a guest here."

"What foreigner?" the sergeant asked.

"A Russian subject who is a very dangerous man and an enemy of our government. He is posing as a merchant in these parts, but in reality he is a spy for the Russian government."

"His being a Russian subject would make arresting him a rather sticky matter," the sergeant responded.

"In time of war, spies can always be arrested. You know very well that there will soon be a declaration of war."

"Yes, I know…"

"I have already informed the army commandant, the Pasha Effendi, about this man. Didn't he give you any orders about him?"

"All the Pasha Effendi told me was to help you complete the work you had begun."

"Excellent!" said the Effendi with a delighted smile. "But there's just one more matter I'll have to tell you about later."

"I'm very impatient. I don't have time for these 'later matters.'"

"Well then, lend me your ear, and I'll tell you now," the Effendi said.

Even though there was no one in the room who could have heard what the Effendi was about to tell him, the sergeant leaned his ear toward the Effendi.

"The old man is quite wealthy. He should be milked," the Effendi whispered in the sergeant's ear.

Tomas Effendi was very well aware of the weaknesses of Turkish officials and knew that these greedy beasts were not so concerned with the substance or details of their formal duties as with the possibility of gaining something from the accused party. Seeking to bring his plans to the desired stage of development, he was exploiting this weakness. He was therefore delighted when he saw that the sergeant had got his point.

"How shall we go about it, then?" the sergeant asked.

"You have plenty of men with you, sergeant. Order your men to keep the old man's two sons, Hairabed and Abo, under surveillance, and, as for the Russian spy named Vartan, you will have him arrested."

The sergeant noted the three names.

"So far, today, you've just carried out a search," the Effendi continued, "But the investigation isn't over yet, and you'll continue to keep the men I mentioned under surveillance until the matter is brought to a conclusion before his eminence the Pasha Effendi."

"I understand," said the sergeant.

"And as for me, I have to go on playing the role of an intermediary and act as if I'm on the side of the accused, so that I can seek out more of their secrets. Do you understand?"

"I understand," replied the sergeant.

CHAPTER 27

While Tomas Effendi and the sergeant were thus engaged in working out the details of their satanic plan in the guest room, the soldiers outside were engaged in a very different kind of conversation.

"Mahmoud, if we spend the whole night here, which one of that Armenian's daughters-in-law are you going to choose?" one policeman asked a comrade.

"I really like the one with the rosy cheeks," Mahmoud answered with great delight.

"Well, the dark-eyed one was quite attractive to me," the first policeman answered with equal feeling.

On entering the women's quarters of the house, it would seem they paid more attention to the women than to the objects that might have concerned them in carrying out their duty. When a Mohammedan is around women, he forgets everything else.

Various expensive articles in the house had drawn the attention of a couple of the police.

"My wife has been driving me crazy to get a nice pan for her to heat milk in, and I just saw the one she wants here. I'll make sure to take it with me when we leave," an older officer said.

"Well, I saw a really beautiful rug. It would be wonderful to relax on after eating and drinking and smoke a narghileh[34] prepared by a pretty woman."

"A rug like that would be better used as a sachata[35] for prayer," responded the older officer, taking a more domestic and religious point of view.

One soldier, filled with envy and prejudice spoke up.

"It amazes me that a gavour[36] has such beautiful women and such a fine house. In our houses, our children barely have a tattered rag to sleep on at night. The gavour should be wearing such a thin, flimsy sash around his waist that it will break in ten different places when he coughs."

This saying is commonly heard on the lips of the Mohammedans. In the East, the breadth and beauty of one's sash are marks of one's status and wealth. In the view of the Mohammedan, the Armenian being a gavour, should only be wearing a thin, worn-out sash that will break in ten different places when he coughs. The Armenian has no right to beautiful women, because whatever is beautiful or desirable must belong to the Mohammedan.

Some of the soldiers went out into Khacho's beautiful garden, setting foot in it like a bear or a pig in a vegetable garden. They trampled on the beautiful flowers that the women and girls of the household had put so much work into. Instead of picking just the fruit they wanted, they yanked entire branches off the trees and ruined the whole crop. They ate the ripe fruit and threw the unripe fruit down and mashed it beneath their feet. Seeing all of this from a distance, Khacho's heart was deeply grieved. He loved those trees as if they were his own children, and he shook his wise old head sadly as he recalled the old Persian saying, "When a general snatches an apple out of the husbandman's hand without paying, his army will soon uproot everything in the farm." This is the type of barbarism for which the Turk has a facility. Whoever lacks feeling for living plants can have no feeling for people, either. The Turk eats the fruit and destroys the tree. The Turk takes what another has earned with the toil of his own hands, then kills him. The Turk, in his recklessness, has devastated the forests wherever he lives and, in the same way, has devastated the various peoples that live under his rule.

This was the barbarism that old Khacho was witnessing in his own home, but he remained silent. He went into the kitchen where the women were making lunch. The poor man. Already a prisoner in his own home, he had to render the sacred honor of hospitality to his own prison guards.

With tears in her eyes, Sara asked him, "Who are those men? What are they doing here? Why are they destroying our home?"

"Only God knows," Khacho responded and told them to hurry up with the lunch.

The women were very frightened and had withdrawn into the house to stay out of sight. They could see that something highly unusual had happened for the Turks to be behaving so disrespectfully in their house. They had seen similar guests many times in the past, but never before had the dignity of the house been violated like this.

Hairabed and Abo had gone out with Vartan that morning and had still not returned home. The other brothers hurried home as soon as they heard of the disruptions there. However, their anger was not directed at the Turks but at their innocent father, for the oppressed always lash out at the weaker side. They accepted this rapacious barbarism as natural and blamed their oppressed brethren for upsetting the Effendi. Their effrontery in scolding their father went beyond all bounds. They berated him for allowing such dangerous men as Vartan and Salman into their home, and they were prepared to go to the sergeant and tell him everything they knew about these young guests with the hope of minimizing their responsibility for the situation. "With your own hands, you have brought ruin on your house" they said to their father.

"Then let it be destroyed, since it is home to useless sons like you!" the old man said, full of vexation. "All you deserve is curses and bad luck since you no longer have any sense of self-respect, honor, or freedom left in your hearts. Those men who anger you so much are my real sons, and I don't care if I lose everything I have for them," he said in regard to Vartan and Mr. Salman.

At hearing this, his sons became even angrier than before and, fearing they might be about to do or say something careless, prudent old Khacho calmed them down by telling them there was nothing to be afraid of and that the Turkish soldiers could be placated with offers of gold. He added that Tomas Effendi had promised to do his utmost to prevent the worst from happening. This considerably mollified his sons; if Tomas Effendi had given his word, then that's the way it would be. Mentioning the names of important men always has a great effect on people like these.

Tomas Effendi appeared in the doorway of the guest room and called out, "Hurry up Danouder Khacho, those rascals have to be fed."

"It's ready, Effendi. They will be served right away," Khacho answered.

Khacho's sons prepared two tables for lunch, one in the guest room, and the other outside under the shelter of the trees. The behavior of the soldiers was now becoming more and more unbearable. In an Armenian's home under these circumstances, Turkish soldiers can become exceedingly demanding. Their taste becomes more refined, their appetites open up, and they ask for types of food and drink which they have never before seen but only heard of.

Any time the host would say, "There isn't any of that," a chorus of curses would be provoked. Although the present situation had not reached that extreme, it was all Khacho and his sons could do to meet the various demands of their shameless guests.

The sergeant and Tomas Effendi had their lunch in the guest room. Khacho didn't sit down to eat with them but stayed on his feet, serving them like a waiter. His sons were doing the same outside with the soldiers. For the time being, all the guests were occupied with the *aragh* and the various dishes from Khacho's kitchen. Khacho took advantage of this moment to communicate privately with Sara. "My child, take the keys and hide whatever there is of value in the house. You know very well where they should go."

"Yes, I know," said the poor woman, her eyes filling with tears, for this precaution was a sign of impending danger.

"Listen and maintain control of yourself," Khacho said. "We have seen this sort of trouble before many times here and, with God's help, this too will pass. We just need to be patient. After you have hidden all the valuables, send all your sisters-in-law, together with all the children, to their own parents' homes. Then take Lala with you and go to our godfather Zako's house and stay there until we see what is going to happen."

Some of Khacho's daughters-in-law were from the village, so there was little difficulty involved in their finding shelter in their parents' homes. Sara was the only daughter-in-law whose home was far away, for her parents lived in Bayazid. This was why Khacho had instructed her to go to Zako's house. He was a man Khacho trusted well.

"I have just one more thing to tell you, Sara," Khacho went on.

"Hairabed, Abo, and Vartan went out this morning to look for Mr. Tutukjian, and they have no idea what has been happening here. When they come back, they're going to end up right in the middle of all this trouble. Hurry and find someone to send out to find them and let them know they should stay away until they hear from me again."

These last words struck Sara yet more deeply in her heart, for now she realized that her dear husband was threatened with great danger as well. But what could he be guilty of? What wrong could he have done? Sara was so perceptive that no risky activities on her husband's part could possibly have been kept from her.

"Who will be willing to go look for them?" she asked, her voice full of anxiety and her troubled eyes filling with tears again.

Her perplexity was understandable, for in times of danger, brothers can betray brothers and even become enemies. When that is the case, who can one depend on? Only a short time earlier, Sara had heard with her own ears how angry Hairabed's brothers were with him.

Khacho understood the reason for her righteous indignation, and he responded sadly:

"I know there isn't anyone willing to go. How well I know that when we're faced with danger, we're deserted by everyone. But Vartan has two servants here, Sako and Yegho. They are brave and dependable men. Hurry and find them and let them know what the situation is. Just tell them that Mr. Tutukjian has been arrested and that our house has been searched. They will understand the rest."

Having imparted his instructions, Khacho left the women's section of the house confident that Sara, in her intelligence, would do whatever the situation called for.

Out in the yard, Khacho noted that the soldiers—those representatives of the government charged with maintaining law, order, and justice—were now displaying a Babylon of unruliness while enjoying the abundant blessings of a peasant's table, eating his food, and drinking his wine and *aragh*. He looked away and walked on, finding it unbearable to witness this flagrant insolence that he had no power to punish.

Turkish functionaries do not follow the principles of their religion strictly and, thus, drinking *aragh* had become a normal practice for them. Forbidden fruit is sweeter. When a Mohammedan drinks, he changes into a beast, the effects of intoxication leading to a raging madness. If there is anything that earns Mohammed a place beside the prophets, the greatest must be his prohibition on drinking alcohol among his adherents.

Meanwhile, the conversation taking place in the guest room was quite interesting. The sergeant had drunk a considerable amount and, whereas the earlier conversation between him and the Effendi had revolved around official business, now their conversation took on a friendlier, more intimate tone.

"How many wives do you have?" the sergeant asked the Effendi.

A special sort of smile appeared on the Effendi's bizarre face.

"They asked the donkey how many wives he had, and he pointed to the entire herd," he answered.

Whenever the Effendi began expressing himself in donkey metaphors, this was an indication he was really comfortable and felt in his own element.

"But I believe Christians are forbidden to have more than one wife," the sergeant observed.

"Well, by the same token, Mohammedans are forbidden to drink, and yet you have had more to drink than I," said the Effendi, quite proud of his own cleverness.

Just then, Khacho entered bearing a plate of dessert consisting of rahat-lokhum and Smyrna figs.

"It's a good idea to sweeten one's mouth after lunch," he said and placed the plate on the table, then left immediately

"That old fellow seems to be a very decent man," said the sergeant, after Khacho had disappeared. "It really surprises me that he would open up his house to that Russian spy and the troublemaker from Bolis."

"'A donkey is long in ears but short in intelligence.' If there are any stupid people in the world, they're the ones who are called 'good.' He's one of those," said the Effendi in his characteristic manner.

The Turkish sergeant, in possession of greater decency than the Armenian effendi, responded in a troubled tone:

"I fear the new commandant will really milk that poor old fellow."

"That's certain. He would be stupid not to take advantage of such a cow," responded the Effendi.

"Do you know anything about the new commandant, Effendi? This is the first time I've seen him," asked the sergeant.

"I know him well. I've known him since the time he was the kaimakam of Diyarbekir province. For ten years he stole; he got rich; then he went to Bolis and became a pasha," the Effendi responded in the manner of someone who was a specialist in such matters.

"What sort of a man is he?"

"The kind who searches for a dead donkey so he can pull off its shoes."

While the sergeant and the Effendi were thus engaged in conversation, while the soldiers were singing and bellowing and dancing in their drunken oblivion, the women of Khacho's house took their children by the hand and disappeared through the back door, on their way to the homes of their respective parents. The tears were flowing in torrents from their eyes for, as they saw things, they were bound for slavery and would never again see this home where they had been so blessed and so loved.

During this same time, Yegho and Sako took their weapons and exited by the same door as the women and children. They mounted their horses and rode off. With all his satanic cunning, it hadn't occurred to Tomas Effendi to have this pair of outlaws arrested, these two men who were capable of thwarting his evil plans.

CHAPTER 28

Tomas Effendi considered his plan only half-accomplished at this point; his main goal hadn't been achieved yet. He had known for a long time that Stepanig was a girl, for the priest who had baptized her, Father Marouk, had told him so. Having been invited to have lunch with him by Tomas Effendi one day, Father Marouk lost himself to drunkenness and gave away the secret that he had worked for so long to keep. From that day on, Tomas Effendi wanted Lala.

But what could love be in the heart of such a corrupt man? Only an instinctive craving and thirst; to eat, to drink, to become sated—that was all there was to it. Such a man is happy when his passions have been satisfied. The spiritual and ideal aspects of love were not accessible to Tomas Effendi. Having spent his entire life with the Turks, he had taken on their moral attributes. To Mohammedans, beautiful women and pretty girls are like toys to children; a child only enjoys a toy for a time, then, becoming bored with it, breaks the one in his hand, kicks it aside and looks for another.

To Tomas Effendi, a woman was just an object to be owned and enjoyed for a while in temporary satisfaction of his needs. Seeing another prettier one, he was ready to forsake the first and pursue the latter. This was the position Lala was in now. But why was it necessary for him to use such corrupt and satanic means to get what he wanted? Why was it he couldn't simply make his case to her father for her hand?

Tomas Effendi was systematic in the conduct of his affairs: to pursue the fulfillment of his various needs and imperatives in life, he picked his own particular time to act. He was an oppressor, and oppressors don't pursue their goals directly. An oppressor chooses circuitous paths. An oppressor is the type of hunter who lays out nets, and traps, and pitfalls for his prey. As a moral predator, this was Tomas Effendi's method. He employed diabolic cunning in pursuing the love of an innocent girl; his goal—to push Lala's father to such a state of desperation that he would be forced to yield and give his daughter's hand.

To Tomas Effendi, Lala was no more than her father's property, like some farm commodity. As tax-collector, he well knew how to tear whatever he wanted right out of the peasants' hands. He knew that unless you have completely tormented the peasant and reduced every fiber of his resistance, he won't yield what it has taken him so much work to produce. Thus, Tomas Effendi had tied old Khacho up into the sort of knots that only he, the Effendi, had the power to loosen.

There was yet another reason for betraying Khacho and his sons to the government. In portraying them as individuals who associate with troublemakers and welcome spies into their home in time of war, his loyalty and usefulness to the government would be clearly demonstrated. At that point he would be in a position to address Khacho, and say, "Now look. If you don't give me Lala, you and your sons will go to the gallows, your house will be burned down, and all you own will be confiscated. I'm the only person in the world who can save you from all that, and my price is beautiful Lala."

This evil man had every means to bring all that about. He was now poised to execute the very finest example of his treachery. Beneath the iron doors of Khacho's cellar, in a secret space, lay Mr. Salman's traveling bag with all his papers inside, and the key to those doors was in the Effendi's pocket.

But Tomas Effendi didn't want the harm done to go beyond certain bounds. He was convinced that Khacho's approval would be easy to get. Only one powerful contender remained in his path—Vartan.

Ever since that day in the guest room when Vartan had grabbed the chippoukh out of Stepanig's hand, thrown it out the window, and attacked Tomas Effendi because of her, the Effendi was convinced a secret bond linked the two of them and that they loved each other. On top of that, Vartan enjoyed a great deal of affection in Khacho's home, and everyone in the household would be only too happy to give Lala's hand to him. Even if, somehow, they were unwilling to do so, Vartan's love for the girl coupled with his being a smuggler could lead to his simply doing with her as he did with contraband and disappearing with her. The Effendi knew that Vartan was brave and daring enough to do such a thing. These were the Effendi's thoughts. What could he do to thwart the young man? He had to make sure that Vartan was securely conducted out of the province under the careful guard of Turkish soldiers. It was with this intention that he labeled him a Russian spy.

But of all Khacho's sons, why did the Effendi single out just Hairabed and Abo. Could he have suspected they were in league with Mr. Salman? He could have suspected no such thing as an Armenian peasant with the capacity to contemplate his own freedom. All the Effendi knew was that Khacho's other sons were simply docile donkeys and that only Hairabed and Abo would offer any resistance. He had long been aware that these two brothers were opposed to him, and it was for that reason he had them arrested and silenced.

And so it was in this uncertain position that Lala found herself: three men wanted her and each pursued her by different means. Being a fearless and notorious bandit, Fattah-Bek would swoop down upon his prey like an eagle that soars in the clouds then dives down to snatch a fawn grazing among the rocks. Thomas Effendi, on the other hand, oppressor that he was, intended to get hold of her like a boa and, squeezing and choking his victim, swallow her. But as we have said, Vartan was a self-confident, audacious smuggler, and he would look for an opportunity to flee with her if he didn't receive the family's permission for her hand. And as to which of these three men Lala truly loved, we already know.

At this point, the Kurdish *bek* gave little thought to Lala, involved as he was with all the preparations for war, and Vartan was preoccupied with Mr. Salman. Of them all, it was only Tomas Effendi who had so arranged his affairs that they promised success.

The sergeant fell asleep, completely drunk, right after the meal. His soldiers had taken their guard posts. Old Khacho's sons, Hairabed and Abo, were still not home. Tomas Effendi saw this as the best moment to speak to the old man about Lala. Leaving the sergeant asleep in the guest room, he thought to himself, "Now it's time to finish what I've started. Riding a donkey is disgraceful enough, but falling off it makes two disgraces."

He found Khacho sitting against a wall in the yard, sad and tired, trying to warm his frozen limbs in the warmth of the afternoon sun. Before him, the soldiers were brazenly wheeling about, laughing, and making crude jokes. As the Kurdish servant girls passed near them, they pulled at their skirts and tried to engage them in playful banter. They struck several of the servants to make them meet their various demands. The old patriarch was witnessing this vulgar behavior in a home where domestic order had always been maintained; where even an immodest smile on a stranger's face would have been punished. Yet now, before his own eyes, he saw a mob of debauched men issuing orders as if they were in their own homes. "What kind of situation is this? What are we living for? Why doesn't the earth just open up and swallow us? Why doesn't the sky just fall down and bury us? What kind of life can this be where we witness such disrespect and can't protest? And for whom were the flames of hell made by God? And for whom the lightning bolts of the heavens? Why is it that evil doers go unpunished?" These were Khacho's thoughts as he sat looking up at the heavens, his eyes brimming with tears. But he heard no answer.

He saw some soldiers come out of the house with various articles in their hands. Sara, after having seen her sisters-in-law off, remained at home, and she was now struggling to take a large bronze milk pan out of a soldier's hands, but he struck her in the chest with his fist, and she fell to the ground. "Without being asked, all my property is being divided up before my very eyes. And what is my guilt? Only that I took in a guest who protested that a peasant's labor and property should be defended. They are punishing me because I gave shelter to a man opposed to violence, oppression and bestial cruelty; a man who exhorted us to remain the masters of whatever land is still left to us out of our paternal inheritance; who told us that we should govern our own affairs, that we have to throw off the yoke of foreign domination… Where did we get such ideas, if not from nature itself? If they would just leave us alone; if they wouldn't dishonor our home; if they wouldn't take our livelihood away from us; if they treated us like human beings instead of tormenting us like animals—then we would be quite content. The young man used to say, 'Freedom's father is violence and its mother, injustice.' Now I understand what he meant when he said, 'The violent oppressor creates his own enemy.' If the Turk hadn't treated us this way, we would even love him, though he is not of our flesh and blood."

Such were old Khacho's thoughts, and his heart was turned upside down like a storm-lashed sea. But what could this old lion do against such wolves? He felt the bitterness of his situation and despaired of any hope. "One hand can't clap," he thought, repeating the well-known aphorism to himself. "If all our villagers only understood that, then there would be a way."

This was the state of mind in which Thomas Effendi found Khacho as he approached and shamelessly called out to him from a distance, as if to wound his heart yet more deeply, "The situation is bad, very bad, Mr. Khacho. The donkey isn't ready yet to be rescued from the mud."

Khacho didn't hear what he said, but seeing him approach, stood up.

"Sit down, and I'll sit beside you," the Effendi said, placing his hand on Khacho's shoulder in a friendly manner. "There's no better place for us to talk," he said and sat down with Khacho on the small rug that had been set out against the garden wall.

"When are those men going to leave?" Khacho asked, pointing to the soldiers who were not yet finished with their outrageous behavior.

"They took an oaf to a wedding, and he said, 'This house is nicer than ours.' Where would you expect them to go and why? Is there any shortage of food or drink here?" the Effendi said with a callous smile.

The old man didn't need this joke on top of everything else, and the Effendi, noticing that, changed his tone.

"Don't worry, Danouder Khacho. As long as Tomas Effendi is alive, he won't allow one hair on your head to be harmed."

"How should it not be harmed?" Khacho responded, quite distraught. "Can't you see they're destroying my house and dividing up my property right before my eyes, and I can't do anything to stop it?" he said, again pointing to the soldiers.

"That's the way they are," said the Effendi. "'When a dog gets into the meat vendor's stall, he's sure to snatch a bone.' You know very well a Turk will never leave an Armenian's home with empty hands. But that's not the most important thing; one should be thankful that only one's goods are taken, and not one's life..."

A shudder went through Khacho's entire body at these words; so sensitized was he at this point that the slightest word powerfully affected him.

"What else can I give them! What else! If there is something else, tell me. Otherwise, why torment me like this? If I have to die, let it be quickly!" he cried out, quite beside himself.

"I'll tell you. I'll explain it all to you, Danouder Khacho. Be patient," said the Effendi, now assuming a more accommodating and serious tone.

He then began explaining to Khacho (once again citing the life of donkeys for another example) that, "If a donkey doesn't want to hurt his foot, he shouldn't kick at the goad." From this saying he drew the moral that Armenians should take care not to oppose the Turks, especially in time of war. Then citing the burning of Van, he argued that this resulted from the great "folly" of not showing loyalty to the Turks. He explained why the Turks of Van had burned down thousands of Armenian shops and stolen the goods from them. He said that this was because the Armenians of Van were spying for the Russians. Having said that, he went on to state that in the coming war the Armenians could expect no help from the Russians. Then returning to the theme of loyalty, he made the point that the Turks were not as bad as many people believed; that the future of the Armenians was bound up with that of the Turks; and that, therefore, any rebellion against them must be considered "foolishness." For these reasons, the Effendi viewed Mr. Salman's activities as complete madness, and he found no reason at all to be troubled that the young man would receive the severest penalty of the law. His only qualm was that because of him a number of innocent men would also have to suffer.

"Who do you mean?" Khacho asked, turning completely pale.

"You and your two sons, Hairabed and Abo. And that other guest of yours, Vartan," the Effendi answered.

This came as a tremendous shock to poor old Khacho and might have paralyzed him in an instant but for the fact that a lifetime of torment, tribulation and ever-present danger had so conditioned his heart that he was able to withstand the Effendi's ominous words and maintain his composure.

"But what are we guilty of?" Khacho asked, interrupting the Effendi.

"Good Lord, not even a child would ask such a foolish question! How could you not know what you are guilty of?" the Effendi answered with bitter sarcasm. "What is the guilt of an entirely healthy person who is treated as if he is sick just because he has fled from a country infected by the plague and tries to enter another country? He is seized and stuck in some little hole and subjected to so much smoke and fumigation that his soul leaves his body…"

"So, are we to be stuck in some little hole, too?" Khacho asked, the wrinkles in his brow now quaking with extraordinary anger.

"Yes," was the Effendi's cold reply.

Yet his purpose in coming to see Khacho was to present his proposal for Lala's hand and declare his love for her. Why had he forgotten all that? Why was he tormenting poor old Khacho like this?

As we said above, it was Tomas Effendi's plan to place Khacho in such an unbearable position that he would be convinced, forcibly, that the only salvation for him and his sons lay in sacrificing Lala to him; for he knew that, in light of what Vartan had revealed about the many women the Effendi had married and abandoned in the past—and which he, the Effendi, had never challenged—Khacho would not readily consent to giving his daughter's hand to him.

But now seeing that he had gone too far and that he had made a mistake in bringing the old man to such a state of despair, he tried to comfort him.

"It's true you'll spend a few days in prison, but that will only be for appearances. Tomas Effendi has taken care that no great harm befalls you."

Khacho had nothing to say in response. He took note of the great difference between the way the Effendi had spoken in the morning and the way he was speaking now. A dark suspicion took root in his heart.

CHAPTER 29

After leaving the house in the morning, Vartan, Hairabed, and Abo had no idea what had transpired during their absence. They knew nothing about Tomas Effendi's satanic plot, nor the search, nor the disorderly behavior of the soldiers and police.

They went through several villages in search of Mr. Salman. Everywhere they went, they asked about him, and at last found the village and the house in which he had spent the previous night. The man of the house seemed a decent person, and told them he didn't know what had happened to the young man. He knew only that, up until midnight, he was talking with some of the village youngsters, discussing various subjects with them. When the youngsters left, Mr. Salman remained alone. He was served supper, given some bedding, and went to sleep in the guest room. In the morning they noticed he was gone, but no one knew where to.

Vartan and his friends went into the room where Mr. Salman had spent the night. They found a scrap of paper on the floor, and on it were the hastily written words, "I was arrested," and the initials, "L. S."

"I expected this," said Vartan, handing the piece of paper to Hairabed.

The three men stood motionless, deeply affected by this development. They now took stock of two great losses: on the one hand, a young man filled with the best of intentions, victimized by his own inexperience, and on the other, the certainty his arrest would be held up as an example and endanger the project they had all made such great sacrifices to realize.

The householder stood looking at them, puzzled as to how a scrap of paper could have occasioned such sadness in them. The young men left without revealing anything.

By now it was evening. Herds of livestock were bellowing as they returned from pasture and rumbled through a haze of dust. Happy peasants, laughing and joking with each other, returned from their toil in the fields. None of them had a thought or a care that on the previous night, in their village, two evil events had taken place—a young man arrested, and a girl violated—both perpetrated at the hands of the same man, a man with an Armenian name and benefiting from the respect of the Armenian community.

"Except for being full-grown, the peasant is like a child," said Vartan to his friends. "If you've noticed, a child will fall down and hit his head on a wall, and cry for as long as he feels the pain. But when the pain goes away, he forgets all about it as if nothing had happened, and he starts to play and laugh again.

"Working with over-grown babies like that is no easy matter," he continued. "They take the same blows for centuries; they hit their heads on the same wall; they fall down into the same mud; but they don't feel a thing. Tomorrow they will forget what happened today. They will be happy and go to work again, never stopping for a moment to reflect on why they are working or what they have to be happy about.

"Tomas Effendi knows these people very well in calling them 'asses,' and in calling those who sympathize with them 'fools,'" Vartan went on. "Try telling the villagers that this bright young man is going to the gallows—this man who, just last night, was speaking to them with such intelligence about individual rights, about the real nature of work and how it can be protected. They will all respond the same way and call that man a fool.

"But I'm convinced of one thing," said Vartan, changing his tone, "I believe that Tomas Effendi had a hand in Mr. Salman's betrayal."

"I agree," said Hairabed.

"But we have to prove it," replied Vartan.

It was now getting dark. The elderly men and women of the village were coming out of their houses for the evening. Vartan and his friends left hastily.

"Beautiful needles! Thread of all colors! Lovely beads!" the same peddler's voice rang out again.

He approached on the opposite side of the street, rocking from side to side with the same limp, with the same large box on his shoulder, and, in his hand, the same stout walking stick—like the club of Hercules. "Come and buy something now, gentlemen. It's getting dark, and my prices are right," he said on seeing Vartan and his friends.

"What do you have?" Vartan asked, walking up to him.

"I have everything," the peddler said, setting his box down.

As Vartan pretended to look at his goods, he slipped the peddler the note Mr. Salman had written when he was arrested. The peddler quickly read the note.

"Yes, I know," he said to Vartan in a low voice.

"What can we do?"

"We'll meet and talk about it."

"Where?…"

The conversation continued in total secrecy. Hairabed and Abo could hear none of it from where they stood.

The peddler shouldered his merchandise once more and headed toward a peasant's house, talking to himself as he went: "I've done a lot of selling today. Now it's time for me to take a rest."

Vartan and his comrades continued on their way. The peasant cottages were beginning to light up with the evening lamps.

As they were passing by tradesman Bedros's house, they noticed neighbor Oho standing at his own door. It was customary that whenever Armenian villagers noticed an outsider passing through the village unexpectedly in the evening, they would call to the traveler, saying, "Come, be our guest." They had heard this invitation from many villagers that evening, but had simply said thank you and proceeded on their way. However, when they stopped in front of Oho's house, it was not because he had similarly invited them in as guests, but because they heard a strange sound there, like the voice of someone calling for help, issuing from the darkness of a barn. Abo immediately took hold of the lamp burning in front of the cottage, and the three men went into the barn. Before them, they saw the following scene: A young girl with a rope around her neck was hanging from a rafter. At her feet was a woman trying to support the weight of her suspended body so that she wouldn't be strangled.

"Let go of me, let go of me!" the girl said weakly.

"Varvareh..." the woman called to her with anguish.

Vartan and his friends quickly cut the rope and lowered the girl from the gallows she had prepared for herself. If they had been a moment later, all would have been lost, for the woman's hands were growing tired, and she would have soon been too exhausted to do anything for the girl.

They carried Varvareh into the cottage; she was still unconscious. They quickly arranged her bed and laid her on it. Her rather bluish-colored face showed tremors from time to time, and from her pursed lips issued the same words, "Let go." Susann was weeping and cursing someone whose name she couldn't remember.

The poor woman went up to the girl several times, holding her pretty head in her hands, saying, "Why did you try to kill yourself? What wrong did you do? Let God punish the evil-doer."

It didn't take Vartan and his friends very long to see that some secret lay behind the girl's dire condition. It remained unclear just what it was, for Susann wouldn't talk about it, even though there was no one else present besides them and two little children. Hairabed knew the man of the house, for Susann's husband, Master Bedros, had been to Khacho's house many times to service his farming equipment. But even if Hairabed had met her several times and was acquainted with her, a villager's wife would never speak openly with a stranger. Susann just blessed and thanked them for their help and implored them to call her husband home.

"Where is master Bedros?" Hairabed asked.

"He's in the neighboring village doing his work," Susann answered.

They agreed to go out and find someone who could look for Master Bedros. Just then, Varvareh suddenly opened her eyes and asked for water. Susann promptly brought her the water, and she drank deeply of it. The blueness in her face now began to dissipate, but her eyes were reddened from the pressure of her blood. She lay her head back on the pillow and pulled the covers up over her face, and she could be heard sobbing. This sad, heart-rending sound cheered Vartan and his friends, for now they knew she would live.

They found a boy outside and confidentially gave him some money to go and find master Bedros. Neighbor Oho was still standing at his door and again extended an invitation to the young men to be his guests.

"Good Lord, where are you going on such a dark night? If you only knew what fun we had here last night! If you join me, we could do the same thing tonight!"

"What fun?" asked Hairabed.

Oho recounted with great animation how he had been asked to help entertain the Effendi when he was a guest at master Bedros's house: musicians were sent for, the girls danced, everybody had a great deal to eat and drink and, in general, a good time was had by all. In conclusion, he had one additional point to make.

"With God as my witness, that man, Tomas Effendi, is really a fine fellow. He provided enough *aragh* for us all to swim in!" he said.

"Yes, and enough to get you all good and drunk, isn't that so?" said Vartan.

"My good sir, how could you avoid getting drunk after drinking so much? The fun is in the drinking!" Oho said with a laugh.

"Was the head of the household home?" asked Vartan.

"I was taking his place."

"And after you got good and drunk, the Effendi took your place. Isn't that so?"

"I knew nothing. I was carried home completely unconscious."

Vartan and his friends left Oho and continued on their way.

As they went down the road, Vartan turned to Hairabed. "Now I know why that poor girl tried to kill herself," he said.

"And now it's clear to me who must have betrayed Mr. Salman," replied Hairabed.

"There's no doubt it was Tomas Effendi. With all his cunning, when he saw what Mr. Salman was up to, he decided to render the government a service by betraying him. And that makes a lot of sense, because Mr. Salman was still in the village by nightfall. Knowing the kind of man the Effendi is, there's no question that's just the way things happened."

The three young men fell silent as they walked slowly up the road. Each was absorbed in thought, trying to figure out some way to save Mr. Salman's life.

"Everything you say is true, Vartan, but what should we do?" said Hairabed.

"I'm very familiar with the shortcomings of Turkish officers and how sloppy they are in executing their duties," answered Vartan. "You know very well that I have two brave companions; our horses are ready. This very night, we'll mount a search for him. No matter how far they've taken him, we'll find him. If there's no other choice, we'll free him by force. I'm well acquainted with the cowardice of Turkish guards."

"We're prepared to go with you, Vartan. We can't let you go alone."

"Not only is that unnecessary, but downright dangerous," responded Vartan. Then remembering what the peddler had said to him, he decided to wait for him to show up.

"Let's sit down for a while. It's hard to think or talk properly when we're pushing ourselves so hard," Vartan said to his comrades.

He seemed tired; he seemed crushed beneath all the weight of grief and sadness, and an agitation began to stir in his heart that little by little became stronger.

The three of them left the road and found shelter in a shack next to a field of melons. There were no workers present to guard the field, since the melons were still unripe and there was no danger of theft. The field shack is a good place for tired travelers to take a rest, and it provides shelter not only against the scorching daytime heat, but as well against the torrential rains that occur in this region.

It was a clear and moonless night. In the distance could be seen the twinkling lamp-light of the village of O... and the remote barking of the village dogs could be heard from time to time.

Vartan continued the conversation they had been engaged in on the road. He repeated the importance of doing everything possible to free

Mr. Salman from a captivity that would surely result in the death penalty for him. But he considered the participation of Hairabed and Abo in this undertaking too dangerous for them, because whether it was successful or not, the two of them would not escape the vengeance of the Turks, for it was certain the action could not be carried out without the spilling of blood or even death. Being people who lived in the province, the two brothers could not evade punishment and, besides them, their entire household and all their relatives would be punished as well. But Vartan had no such fears to consider. As an outsider, he could do his work, then disappear and return to his own homeland where no one could trace him, especially in the topsy-turvy conditions of wartime.

Having listened at length to Vartan's argument and regarding him as someone with great experience in many dangerous undertakings, Hairabed and Abo gave their response:

"We'll disguise ourselves so that no one can recognize us," they said.

"It won't make any difference what you do, they'll still find out about you. There are plenty of people just like Tomas Effendi to betray you here. If they got the chance, the local Armenians wouldn't hesitate to betray a fellow Armenian to curry favor with the Turks. An Armenian is a greater danger to Armenians than any outsider."

Profoundly shaken by the events of the day, he uttered these last words with great disquiet. On the one hand, he was confronted with the arrest of his dear friend and, on the other, the cold indifference of the people. On the one hand, he was confronted with Varvareh's victimization and, on the other, all the evils perpetrated by Tomas Effendi. All this had driven his heart to a state of utter desperation, without even knowing yet about the latest evils the Effendi had inflicted on Khacho's home. Immersed in all this worry and desperation, he had almost forgotten about Lala, that lovely creature who had been foremost in his heart. Suddenly her melancholy image appeared before his mind's eye, seeming to say to him, "Where have you gone, and why have you forsaken me? Have you gone off to save your dear friend? Well I, too, am your beloved. You promised you would take me far away. It is so terrible here. I'm afraid, so afraid, of the Kurds."

And now began an emotional tug-of-war inside of him. Two beings were now posed before him: one, the beloved girl, the other, the beloved friend. He loved them both, and both their lives were in danger.

Vartan was not really aware of the danger posed for Lala by Fattah-Bek. But he did know about the trap that Tomas Effendi was laying for her, and knew that the Effendi would spare no effort in getting his way with her.

Inside the shack, a temporary silence prevailed. Hairabed was preoccupied with similar anxieties. He knew about the tie of love between Vartan and his sister, and had consented to it. But now Vartan was preparing to leave to rescue his friend. He would either be successful and rescue his friend or be killed by the Turks. In either case, Lala would be lost, for without doubt, by the time Vartan returned from his mission, she would already have been abducted by Fattah-Bek. Vartan knew nothing about this, of course, nor did he have any way of knowing, since no one had said a word to him about it. Why not tell Vartan about it? But how? Up to this point, Vartan hadn't told anyone in the household about his love for Lala and that he wished to make her his wife. Only Sara knew about this, and that, only by chance. The precipitous flux of events, one after the other, had given Vartan no opportunity to reveal what was in his heart. Now a new, dangerous mission would separate Vartan from Lala, and Hairabed had been robbed of any hope that Vartan would free his sister from Fattah-Bek's clutches.

Yet, Hairabed was also quite disturbed at Mr. Salman's fate. He liked this altruistic young man even more than Vartan. It would be cruel to abandon him to his fate with the Turks, leaving him to be thrown into the darkness of prison where he would be tortured and finally killed. For Hairabed, the cruelty involved in allowing that to happen would only be compounded by appealing to his sister's plight to prevent Vartan from setting out on his mission.

Thus, each man was thrown into perplexity and inner turmoil by the circumstances. Both Lala and Mr. Salman needed immediate help. But which one should be helped first?

And, meanwhile, what were Abo's thoughts, that stout-hearted and unspoiled son of this peasant household? In reality, he wasn't thinking at all. He was the type of man whose choices were simply determined by the wish to avoid the worst outcome. With good guidance, Abo was a fit and effective agent for saving a bad situation.

Vartan broke through this stalemate with a confession. Without holding anything back, he declared his love for Lala to Hairabed and Abo. He let them know that he had promised to take her away and that she had agreed. He made it clear that the only reason he had considered such an unusual measure was because he could see that old Khacho had made up his mind to give Lala's hand to Tomas Effendi.

"You don't need me to tell you about that man," Vartan continued. "You both know him very well, especially after today. Giving a girl to a man like that is like placing her in the jaws of a wolf or a dog.

"There's just one more thing: I have to find Mr. Salman, as I said, and nothing will keep me from doing that. My love for a comrade like this places me under the greatest obligation. On top of that, I hold myself responsible that he got into all this trouble, since I encouraged him and exhorted him, and stoked the fire that burns in his troubled heart. So doing, I hastened his fall. That's why I can't delay doing whatever I can to rescue him.

"On the other hand," continued Vartan, "there is one great obstruction in my path, and I really don't know what to do about it. Can I leave Lala here? If I do, sooner or later, for certain, she will end up in the hands of that monster, Tomas Effendi. Then what will become of her?"

Hairabed answered that Lala had told Sara all about her relationship with Vartan; that Sara had told him all about it, and that, therefore, he had long been aware of the spiritual bond between Vartan and Lala. He added that both he and his brothers would be very happy if Vartan disappeared with Lala as soon as possible.

"The Effendi isn't the only problem. There's another reason we have to get Lala away from here," said Hairabed, and with that he proceeded to tell Vartan everything about Fattah-Bek's plan to abduct his sister. He told Vartan how the *bek*'s life had been threatened by his wife, Khourshid, and how Khourshid had contacted Sara and urged her to send Lala far away. In short, Hairabed filled Vartan in on every detail that he would have had no way of knowing about until this moment.

Vartan listened to all of this with great bitterness, every phrase striking at his heart like poisoned arrows.

"You knew all of this, but told me nothing!" he said, greatly provoked. "You were just going to wait for Fattah-Bek to come—by day or night—and carry your sister off while you stood there with your eyes wide open and allowed yourselves to be dishonored!"

Now, at last, Vartan understood the sadness and despondency in Lala's words that night they had been in the garden together, a tone that until now had perplexed him. He finally understood why on that night, when their moments together should have been sweetened with kisses and filled with boundless joy and love, tears were pouring from her eyes, instead, and, in desperation, she spoke those words, "I don't want to join Sona. I'm afraid of the grave. I'm afraid of the Kurds. Save me. Take me far away, to another land." She knew of the terrible misfortune that awaited her. This was why she had told him the story of her friend Nargis, carried off by the Kurds, and now in such a tragic state.

There are moments in life when a man, confronted with trials, dangers, and bitter circumstances, takes heart and becomes stronger; his heart becomes impervious, and he finds himself at ease. From that moment on, seeing that misfortune has reached its limit, he meets the blows of fate with contempt.

That was Vartan's state of mind at this point. He was now at ease, and no longer struggled with thoughts and emotions and mental torture. Everything suddenly cleared up for him, and he knew what he had to do. His love for a comrade overcame his love for a woman; for the loss of his comrade involved the death of an ideal, the ideal of emancipation for the oppressed and victimized peasant, an ideal that involved not Lala alone, but the honoring and saving of countless thousands of women just like her. How could he abandon all of them for the sake of just one individual? This was what he was thinking.

"After all this, I have to repeat what I said before. I have to find Mr. Salman and do whatever I can to save his life. As for Lala, I'm clearly not going to forget about her, but first some arrangements have to be made. Listen, this is what I have in mind…"

"No arrangements are necessary," they heard someone say, and from the back of the shed appeared the gigantic figure of the lame peddler.

Vartan was extremely happy to see him. Hairabed and Abo, on the other hand, were quite disturbed that this vagabond had been eavesdropping on their conversation. They knew nothing about him so far, but on noticing how cordially Vartan took his hand and offered him a seat, they relaxed a bit, especially after Vartan reassured them, saying, "Don't be afraid, he's one of us."

But Melik-Mansour didn't look the same as he had a few hours earlier—a wandering peddler all dressed in tatters. Even Vartan had a moment's difficulty recognizing him. He was wearing the national outfit of the Laz people and was armed to the hilt.

"I can't spend much time with you," he said in a hurried tone. "You already know that our dudukji has fallen into a trap and has to be rescued."

"That's just what we were discussing," said Vartan.

"Don't worry about him; he'll be freed soon enough. Just continue what you've been doing. I bid you good night now," Melik-Mansour said as he stood up to leave.

"Are you going alone?"

"No, my comrades are waiting for me nearby," he said, pointing toward the mountains where a group of horsemen could be discerned through the darkness of twilight.

"Who are they?" asked Vartan.

"Some young mountaineers. Until we meet again…"

Vartan still had many questions to ask, but Melik-Mansour was already gone.

Hairabed and Abo were completely dumbstruck at all of this, knowing nothing about this mysterious fellow. Vartan told them what he knew about Melik-Mansour, and the two brothers were persuaded that a man of such calibre had a good chance of saving Mr. Salman's life. The three of them left the shed and continued on their way.

Vartan's two loyal companions, Sako and Yegho, had looked for Vartan all day to convey Khacho's warning to him, but, as yet, had been unable to find him.

"Yegho, the situation looks bad. We have to make sure we don't get caught; if we do, we won't be of any use to him if he gets into trouble," said Sako to his companion.

"That's just what I was thinking," Yegho answered.

The two comrades decided not to return to Khacho's house but to continue to watch out for Vartan from a safe distance.

CHAPTER 30

It was well into the night by the time Vartan, Hairabed, and Abo returned to the house. Having no knowledge of what had happened during their absence, they entered unsuspectingly. As soon as they were inside, the doors were locked behind them.

Two military guards were posted at the door. The sergeant was in the guest room with his disorderly soldiers. Some of the policemen went into the yard and wandered around from time to time, snooping here and there like hunting dogs for one more object to steal.

The daughters-in-law had already found shelter with various relatives and neighbors. Under such circumstances, with a house occupied by foreign troops, the women are sent away.

Vartan and his friends noticed this situation, but still didn't understand the reality behind this unruly mob, for in this locale one routinely found troops stationed in the home of a village leader or any other Armenian. With such guests on hand, in order to protect the women of the household from their passions, the head of the household would be obliged to send all the women to other homes, if indeed he was lucky enough to have a guest who would forego putting a sword to his throat and demanding that the women be kept at home to wait on him and his party.

Hairabed encountered one of his brothers inside. "Do you see what trouble that tramp has brought down on us!" he said to Hairabed with great anger. "I'd like to see how you're going to explain all this to the authorities. I would have thrown him out the first day he got here, but you opposed it like the devil and wouldn't let me. Well, what do you say now?"

Hairabed didn't say a word. He understood his brother's abusive remarks as referring to Mr. Salman, and he understood the unfortunate situation that had developed.

"We've fallen into a trap, my boy. That's all we needed!" said Vartan to Hairabed.

Several policemen immediately rushed up and seized them and took them to the sergeant in the guest room. Tomas Effendi was gone. After finishing his business for the day, he had left Khacho's house and gone to spend the night with the village priest, Father Marouk. Except for a few soldiers posted at the door, there was no one else in the room besides Khacho and the sergeant. Vartan walked into the room and sat down beside Khacho without waiting for permission. Hairabed and Abo remained standing.

Taking note of Vartan's severe demeanor, the sergeant spoke to him in a contemptuous manner.

"Where are you from, Armenian?" he asked, uttering the word "Armenian" with sarcasm.

"From Russia," Vartan answered, holding his anger in check.

"What has brought you here?"

"I'm a merchant."

"Do you have a passport."

"I did, but I lost it."

"That will be easy enough to check on. Just tell me what border crossing you took, and we can verify your name and number. It will be recorded there."

"I'm a smuggler. Smugglers don't get anywhere near border posts. I might as well admit I didn't have a passport to begin with."

"If that were the only problem, you might be forgiven, but you're accused of something else."

"What else?"

"Of being a spy."

"Is that so? It seems Tomas Effendi has told you everything; he's such an honest man," Vartan said sarcastically.

"It's neither here nor there who told me," said the sergeant, maintaining his cool, officious demeanor. "We don't allow suspicious people into our country, especially in times of war. You'll be detained here tonight, and then tomorrow you'll be taken to military headquarters. They'll deal with you there."

"If I'm going to be dealt with there, what was the point of all this interrogation? You could've simply put me in jail whenever you wanted to, and that's all. That's what you usually do. In these parts, even an ordinary policeman can dispose of the entire matter himself, and he has the power to do whatever any superior might do."

The sergeant took offense, but made no comment. He summoned four policemen and, without further ado, ordered them to take Vartan and hold him as a prisoner. Vartan offered no resistance at all and allowed himself to be taken into custody.

After he was escorted away, the sergeant turned his attention to Hairabed and Abo.

"We don't have to waste our time with these two. They're obviously guilty. Take them away and guard them carefully."

Like a man half asleep and half awake, old Khacho watched all of this as if it was happening in a dream. Why had the Effendi tricked him? Or was this all just for appearances, as the Effendi had assured him it would be?

Vartan, Hairabed, and Abo were placed in a small building that had served as a granary. The floor and walls were made of stone, tightly fitted together with lime to create a barrier impenetrable to mice. The windows were narrow and covered with an iron grille to keep birds out. This little building made a perfect prison. An oil lamp burning in one corner cast its light up into the obscurity of the arches.

Hairabed and Abo were silent, their faces etched with profound sadness and terror. They were well acquainted with the cruelty of Turkish officers who, for the slightest cause and often making up the charges themselves, would slander and extort and crush an innocent man, especially if he was an Armenian with any possessions at all. And now there was a considerable amount of evidence indicating their guilt. But what had brought the authorities here this time? Who had betrayed them? This they couldn't figure out.

Yet Vartan seemed at ease. He had the calmness of an ocean following a violent storm.

"I will explain everything to you with a parable," he said to his fellow prisoners:

"The trees of a forest sent word to their king, saying, 'A tool has appeared in our midst, and cuts us down without mercy.'

'What is this tool called,' asked the king of the trees.

'It is called axe,' answered the trees.

'How is it made?' asked the king.

'Its head is made of iron, and its handle of wood,' the trees replied.

'Then that is a most dangerous tool, since its handle comes from one of our own,' said the king."

"The handle comes from one of our own," Vartan repeated with emphasis. "The handle of the instrument that is used to oppress, torment, and subjugate us and destroy our home is furnished by our fellow Armenians—those Tomas Effendis who, from the village moultezims right up to the *amirahs* in the service of the Sublime Porte, provide just such a handle to be wielded in the hands of our enemy. Such dangerous handles have never been lacking in Armenian history. Wherever you see our nation and people betrayed to foreign powers, an Armenian hand will be involved. Wherever you see an Armenian king toppled from his throne and his scepter in the hands of a foreigner, you will find an Armenian hand involved. Wherever you see an Armenian king banished and the gates of his city thrown open to the enemy, there you will find the hand of an Armenian. Wherever you see our ancestral soil soaked with Armenian blood and the homes of our people burned down, our children carried off into slavery, there you will find the hand of an Armenian. Wherever you see plotting and intrigue in religion that affects the national life and the Holy Church, there you will find the involvement of an Armenian. In short, an Armenian axe is involved in every tribulation, in every persecution, in every atrocity and barbarity that is inflicted upon us by our enemy. It is the Armenian who has undermined the foundations of his national edifice, and it is the Armenian who, with his own hands, destroys its sacred establishment. Why should we place the blame on foreigners?"

Abo and Hairabed listened to Vartan with profound sadness.

"Then there is no hope, and what we are trying to build will be lost before we complete it," said Abo.

"I, like a prophet, could see that things were going to turn out like this, and I knew it would be stupid to expect anything else. Mr. Salman, himself, was caught in a dilemma and barely maintained faith in his own work. I remember his expressions of despair word for word, as when he once said to me, 'Before the idea of a people's movement has spread to a significant number of people, at the stage when it is just the musing of a few individuals, that is when it can be smashed in one mighty blow with the elimination of its leaders.' But with the masses it's a different matter. In them that consciousness can never be extinguished"

"He used to say, 'It is for us only to sew the seed, not to harvest it. The harvest will be gathered by the next generation.' That's why he worked right up to the last day to build solid, suitable institutions like schools. Rebellion wasn't Mr. Salman's goal, but rather revolution, and, in time, his activities took on a well planned form. He approached me once with a smile that I had never before seen on his usually somber face, and he said that those of us who have taken on the responsibility of educating the people, we, ourselves, remain uneducated and have a lot to learn— even from them; he said that the people are great teachers, and that just one of their smallest sayings abounds with philosophy. He said, 'Listen to how they express their relations with the Turks: be friendly with a dog, but don't let go of your stick. That proverb truly reflects everything about their relations with the Mohammedans. They are a snappy people, and to protect yourself from their teeth you always have to have your stick ready.' This is why Mr. Salman was trying to arm the people and prepare them for self-defense."

Hairabed and Abo listened with deep attention. They seemed to have forgotten their own ills and the trouble that was in store for them the next morning, and now their thoughts were on a larger scope of suffering. They, too, had heard Mr. Salman expounding these ideas before, but they had never, until this moment, grasped their meaning with such clarity.

Being a prisoner seemed to inspire Vartan, and he spoke without pause. He had been in and out of prison many times in his life, and that experience had always left him with a very sad feeling. Yet now he seemed at ease, like a condemned man on the gallows, looking down with contempt on an unjust world and with scorn on the stupidity of evil men, saying within his own mind, "With all the power you have, you can do nothing but destroy my body. There is nothing you can do to destroy all the ideas I have planted.

"Be friendly with a dog, but don't put down your stick," Vartan repeated. "That's the truth. Under such circumstances, life gives birth to monsters… monsters like me. You don't really know me, my friends, but this may be the last night we'll be able to talk, so listen. I'm a man who long ago learned to fight evil with evil. My hands have been bathed in blood, but never the blood of innocents. I was a monk, once, and all I learned from the Old Testament was "an eye for an eye." When I read how the prophet Moses killed the Egyptian man who was abusing his Hebrew brethren and hid his body in the sand of the Nile,[37] my heart was filled with boundless hatred for those who, in the same way, persecute the Armenians. When I read that Moses, Jehovah's prophet, exterminated entire peoples to clear the promised land of all foreigners and establish a homeland where the children of Israel could live instead, I saw that this was the best way to deal with the Turks, the Kurds, and the Circassians who have taken away the inheritance left to us by our forefathers. That's the same natural law Mr. Salman spoke of in relation to the plant world; one kind of plant oppresses and overwhelms another and takes its place. If we don't wish to be annihilated in this struggle, we have to have the power and the capacity to resist with that characteristic called self-defense. The cultivation of that characteristic in the people was Mr. Salman's principal goal. I made it my own long ago. The moralist will undoubtedly call me immoral, criminal, bestial, and priests will call me sinful, but that doesn't make any difference. I'm compelled to do whatever life demands. Whenever people put an end to their evil ways, when peace and brotherly love reign supreme in the world, I will be ready, then, to welcome the good and embrace my enemy."

And thus did the prisoners speak at length until at last the oil lamp sputtered and smoked and went out, and their prison was filled with the darkness of night.

CHAPTER 31

That same night, while Vartan, Hairabed, and Abo sat in prison discussing philosophy and pondering the tragic condition of their people, Tomas Effendi was spending his time as Father Marouk's guest. He was in a gay, talkative mood after dinner and was making jokes with the priest.

This was the very priest who had caused so much trouble for Mr. Salman, yet now hearing of the fate that had befallen the young man, he felt badly about it; not because a significant worker had been removed from the field of activity, but because the misfortune of any ordinary

Armenian was disturbing to him. The old priest wasn't an evil man, and if he resisted Mr. Salman's school project and wished to see it stopped, he meant well but opposed it only because he considered it harmful.

At one time in his life Father Marouk had been a common peasant. As a child, he had barely acquired the ability to read at the monastery of St. Hovhaness. He was an unsuccessful farmer and, after falling into poverty, went abroad to search for better fortune. He failed in that endeavor, likewise. For a time, he ran a café in Van but didn't make a go of it and returned to his native province. Finding no other work to do there, he became a priest.

Also present as a guest on this night was Father Marouk's son-in-law, the well-known choir master Simon, teacher of the village children.

This man had a very high opinion of his own knowledge (an opinion shared by the rest of the villagers) and was exceptionally proud of being the priest's son-in-law.

The topic of conversation was what had happened that day at Khacho's house. This event had made a tremendous impression on everyone in the village, especially the old priest.

"'The jackass judges, but the horse gets the hay,' Father," said the Effendi, continuing their interrupted conversation. "That's the way the world is, and that's the way it will always be. What God has ordained, man cannot change. He has made one man a gentleman and the other a laborer. He condemns one, and the other gets to eat. The Armenian has grown used to working, the Kurd and the Turk to eating. The one who is used to eating can't live without the worker, and the worker can't live without the one who eats. The Turks take care of us with the sword, and we take care of them with our work. God put a sword in the Turk's hand, and He gave the Armenian a hoe. The two can't trade places."

"So true," said the priest and crossed himself. "In the Holy Gospel, our Lord Jesus Christ says that not one leaf falls from a tree nor does one hair turn white on someone's head without God willing it. Everything is in His hands."

"That's certainly true," agreed choir master Simon, likewise crossing himself.

Next, they began discussing the increased pressures and demands the approaching war had placed on the peasants. The priest viewed their losses strictly in terms of his own interests, complaining that the government had raised the taxes so high that almost everything the peasants produced had been taken from them and that whatever they might have left was taken away by the Kurds. As a result, he made little money for his services, and often conducted weddings, baptisms, and funerals without being paid. The villagers would promise to pay him later, but they were either unable to pay or simply took advantage of him, so that by this time he was owed a great deal, and he decided to do no more baptisms, weddings, or funerals unless he was paid in advance, because after all he too was a man and had to make a living.

"Father, you don't know the peasant as well as I do," said the Effendi in the tone of a specialist. "God gave the peasant a soul, but can hardly get it back from him. Yet when the time comes, and the angel of death stands squarely before him sword in hand, then, at last, the peasant yields his soul. This should serve as our example. Without seeing this 'holy stick,' the peasant will give you no money. Write down what you are owed, and I'll give it to one of my officers to collect so that you get every cent of it."

"Great heavens! May God grant you long life! I've kept a record of everything," said the priest.

"Read it to me, and let me see how much it comes to."

Father Marouk pulled a yellowed piece of paper from his breast-pocket; it was soiled, stained, and tattered from years of being kept there. This was his record of what the villagers owed him. There were four pages covered with large letters in crooked lines; this constituted his account. He brought the paper close to his eyes but, try as he might, he found it too difficult to read.

"Take this and read it, Master Simon, my eyes are too weak," he said, handing the account to his son-in-law.

Master Simon took the account in his hands, coughed a few times, scratched the back of his neck and, bringing the paper up close to his eyes, began to read what was there as if declaiming an ecclesiastical pronouncement:

For baptizing Cholakh Muggo's daughter—five ghouroush. The girl died a week later, and I buried her—seven ghouroush. I married Khulo's son—ten ghouroush; I was given thirty bundles of hay; the amount came down to three ghouroush. Pano's wife got sick; I went to their house and read three healing chapters from the Gospels. Sako's son took the cross out of the water. Parso gave me thirty ghouroush to take it out. I accepted Sako's offer. It was short twenty ghouroush. The amount owed stood at twenty ghouroush. He said he would pay me in wheat at milling time. I went and asked him for it, but he didn't give it to me. The kizir is my witness.

And thus, one entry after another, an entire story was told. Strictly speaking, it was not so much an account as a chronology of his pastoral activities over the past few years. Despite its jumbled form, it offered many examples of the duties performed by a village priest.

"It's a proper account," said the Effendi, breaking in on the choirmaster's "reading," too impatient to wait until it was finished.

"Just let me have it, Father, and I'll have it all collected. The villagers of N...shen were late in paying the monastery the 'fruit' they owed. The Vartabed wrote me a letter about it, and I got it all collected in one day. As a result, I received an inscription of blessing from the monastery."

Finding this method of collecting his debts quite natural, Father Marouk not only assented, but once again began to voice his gratitude and his blessings upon the Effendi's precious life.

But why did the Effendi accept this responsibility? He was the kind of man who would never do a favor for anyone unless there was something in it for him. Why was he so decent as to promise he would even forego the tithe that was routine when debts were collected under official orders?

"May the blessing of Father Abraham be upon you!" said the priest on hearing these last words from the Effendi.

Master Simon himself had a similar account of debts that he kept in his breast pocket; these stemmed from the various services he had rendered to his pupils. He was on the verge of presenting this to the Effendi, also, when Father Marouk got his attention and whispered to him, "Let them collect mine, first. Then they can see about yours."

There were just a few people living in Father Marouk's house. His only son had died, leaving his widowed wife and two little sons behind. Following her husband's death, the widow had no contact with other men, but remained in Father Marouk's house and took care of her two sons. The priest himself had lost his wife long ago and had lived a completely single life ever since.

After she had served dinner to the guests, Father Marouk's daughter-in-law was totally involved in caring for one of her sons who was very ill. Sitting near his bed, she looked very sadly into his face, stroked his hot little hands, and listened to his labored breathing. In this child, she found the image of her husband and the only consolation she had since his death. She could barely hear, let alone pay any attention to, the conversation that was taking place in the house. Utterly consumed by love and worry, she was aware of nothing but her sick little son.

Father Marouk, on the other hand, was so cheered by the Effendi's promise that he wished to make everything perfectly delightful. The bottle of *aragh* was by now completely empty, and he told his daughter-in-law to fill it up again and also see to it that *mazah*[38] was served; for although dinner was over, local custom called for the drinking to continue as a special sign of hospitality toward the guest of honor.

His daughter-in-law was so distracted that Father Marouk had to repeat his order a couple of times before she grasped what it was he wanted her to do. Finding more *aragh* was a simple matter, since this commodity was never in short supply at the priest's house, and she refilled the pitcher. But how would she make the mazah? There was no kind of sweetener in the house, and it would be embarrassing to let that be known. In an Armenian home, everything for entertaining guests is supposed to be readily at hand. She decided to go next door and borrow some.

It was pitch dark outside, and the rain was pouring down from the sky. The poor woman traversed her yard, walking through the mud, then went up to roof level in order to descend to her neighbor's house. Meanwhile she heard her neighbor's door being pounded with great force, and threats and orders to open the door being shouted in Turkish.

From inside the house, she could hear voices swearing that whomever was being sought was not there. But whom could it be they were looking for? And what Turks were these, trying to force their way into an Armenian home at this ungodly hour?

Zoulo (for that was Father Marouk's daughter-in-law's name) was very frightened on hearing this commotion, and she could neither bring herself to go on to her neighbor's house, nor return to her own. She stood where she was on the roof, totally confused.

Just then some barely audible whispering caught her attention; it sounded like someone climbing the ladder, trying to escape from the neighbor's house, but unsure of which way to go.

"Slow down, Stepanig…"

"Which way should I go, Sara?"

Zoulo recognized who they were, and, realizing that these unfortunate people needed help, her fear vanished. She already knew about the disturbing events of the day at Khacho's house. She also knew that the women of his household had been sent out to hide in other homes in the village, and why. The Turks pounding on her neighbor's door must therefore have been connected with the arrest of Khacho's sons.

Sara and Stepanig now found themselves on the roof of Father Marouk's house and, like deer pursued by hunters, surrounded and threatened from every quarter, they didn't know which way to go. The rain was pouring down. All the village doors were locked, and the villagers were asleep. It was already past midnight.

Then there was a flash of lightning followed by a mighty clap of thunder. The lightning had cast its light on Zoulo's indistinct figure. Seeing it, Stepanig thought a Turk had climbed up to the roof, and she collapsed with fright against Sara. Zoulo approached them.

"It's me. Don't be afraid," she said.

"Oh, Zoulo, it's you!" Sara said, trembling. "For the love of God, hide us somewhere. They're going to catch us and take us away…"

Zoulo was unsure where to take them. There were untrustworthy guests in her house, and her father-in-law would scarcely welcome such asylum seekers. Yet, she had to help these poor people.

She knew what they would suffer if they fell into the hands of the Turks. And yet, she would accept whatever the consequences if it was discovered that she had given shelter to people sought by the authorities, people whose only crime was that they were women. This she understood. But compassion prevailed over her fear and hesitation, and the immediacy of danger inspired her with an idea for saving the situation.

"Let's go," she said, taking hold of Stepanig's hand. Zoulo and Sara supported Stepanig with their arms.

They began their descent from the roof. At that moment, they heard a tremendous crashing sound, which was then covered up by the roar of the storm. This was the sound of the neighbor's door being broken down.

The priest's barn was right next to his house, and a small door permitted access to it from the yard. Zoulo took the fugitives there and hid them in the hay.

"I'll be back," Zoulo said, then locked the door and left.

Due to the din of the rain, neither Father Marouk nor his guests were aware of what was going on outside. Zoulo entered the house but revealed nothing to them except for whispering to her father-in-law that everyone was asleep in the neighbor's house and that she was unable to borrow anything to make mazah with.

"I'll find something," said Father Marouk. He got up and started rustling around in a cupboard.

Taking advantage of the priest's absence, the Effendi turned to Zoulo and said quietly, "You yourself are mazah. What other mazah do we need?"

Choirmaster Simon was too drunk to hear this remark, but Zoulo was deeply offended at the Effendi's suggestiveness.

"Shameless man!" she said to him.

An Armenian woman is long-suffering and will silently bear every sort of provocation except being dishonored. Very upset, Zoulo went to be with her sick son. He was now awake and feeling better. "Give Toros a spanking, he took my knuckle-bones[39] away from me," he said on seeing his mother. The sick child must have dreamed that Toros, his big brother, had taken his knuckle-bones away.

"Look, my little darling, Toros gave your knuckle-bones back," said his mother, reassuring him. "See? Here they are," she said. She drew the knuckle-bones from underneath his pillow and put them in his hands. He started playing with them with his weak little hands, and his mother looked at him happily. On seeing that her child was feeling better, she forgot everything else, including the Effendi's crudity. But now the poor mother had to deal with yet another irritation. Father Marouk had been searching through his cupboard for quite a while, and now he asked Zoulo about some sugar that he had stored away but couldn't find. She answered that she herself had taken it a few days before, since her son had a high fever, and she needed to make a sherbet for him to cool him down.

"You should've given him poison to drink, or bile!" the priest roared angrily. "Didn't you know the sugar was saved for guests? Now what are we going to do?"

Zoulo said nothing, but sat silently, tears flowing from her eyes.

Father Marouk wasn't a truly evil man, and, in fact, had many good qualities; but sometimes in ignorant people, goodness becomes transformed into evil unconsciously. Besides that, he had become somewhat calloused because of his job as a priest. Priests, physicians, and hangmen, routinely in contact with the dead, have little sensitivity for life. Thus, Father Marouk didn't have as much regard for his sick little grandson as for pleasing a guest like Tomas Effendi, especially since the Effendi had promised to collect all his fees for him.

"Why are you crying Mommy? Don't cry. I'm well now," the little boy said to his mother, looking at her with compassion.

With this, his mother forgot all her worries and wiped away her tears. Nothing is so consoling as a few sweet words, an innocent stammering, from a beloved child. Zoulo was now thinking about Sara and Stepanig and what would become of them if the Turks suddenly burst in, conducted a search, and found them. But the unbearable guests continued with their bout of drinking. Zoulo waited for them to be done and fall asleep so that she could go and check on Sara and Stepanig.

But, meanwhile, she had at least to find out what had happened at her neighbor's house. Thinking about it was unbearable and kept her in a state of restless agitation. Finding some excuse to leave, she got up and went into a tiny room which was used for storage and was called the "secret room." In the middle of the wall of this room there was a narrow opening through which one could see directly into the neighbor's house. Openings like this existed in almost every village house and served as secret channels of communication in times of danger. If one house was confronted with danger, this could be communicated to the house next door, and, depending on relations between neighbors, some of these openings could be large enough to allow the transfer of small articles of property. Often when neighbors ran out of matches, lamps would be passed through them.

Zoulo looked through the opening and could see part of her neighbor's house and hear voices.

"We'll kill you all if you don't show us... Where did they go? We heard they were here... You hid them... Give them up... If not, we'll take your women away..." These were the kinds of threats the Turks were issuing.

Collapsed at their feet, neighbor Zako was pleading and imploring, "May God, the heavens, and the earth be my witness. They're not here... My whole house is before you. Take whatever you want..."

This was the same situation as in Sodom when the town bullies gathered in front of Lot's house and demanded that he yield his guests to them. The good-hearted patriarch implored them to leave his guests alone and offered them his daughters... But the Jehovah of Israel was hard-hearted and vengeful, and, in order to punish evil, destroyed that sinful city with fire and brimstone. Yet the God of Armenia, seeing evil much greater than that in Sodom, let the evil-doers go unpunished.

Zoulo was still looking and listening, her whole body trembling. She heard a crash and saw that neighbor Zako had collapsed and fallen to the floor... The lamp was extinguished and Zoulo could see nothing now. She could only hear a jumble of moans: "My God!... Oh!... Let go... Don't kill me!...I'm dying!... Where are you taking me?"

These were the cries of neighbor Zako's women and girls.

"Quiet down!" was the only answer they received to their pleas.

CHAPTER 32

Going back into the main part of the house, Zoulo found the guests as she had left them—still drinking. Joined by his son-in-law, the priest was reciting a verse, and the Effendi, for his part, was also murmuring slowly along beneath his breath. They were as happy as could be. How could they bother about what was happening next door?

Zoulo thought if she let them know what was happening, they might be able to do something about the situation. She went up to Father Marouk and, speaking into his ear, told him what she had witnessed in Zako's house, omitting the fact that Sara and Stepanig were hiding on the premises. Some inexplicable instinct kept her from revealing this fact to her father-in-law.

As is customary for Armenian women, Zoulo didn't speak to the guests at all, but conveyed her message to Father Marouk in such a brief and quiet manner that the guests heard nothing. But on noticing the change in their host's expression and his sudden uneasiness after Zoulo had spoken to him, they asked with great curiosity about what had happened.

"What beasts! What beasts!" the priest cried out, raising his arms heavenward. "May the curses of the twelve apostles and three hundred sixty-six patriarchs be upon you, oh, you roots of evil!"

"What happened?" the Effendi asked once more.

Father Marouk reported what Zoulo had said and begged Tomas Effendi to do something to help his poor neighbors.

Some people when confronted with the misfortunes of others, to assuage their own consciences, find fault with them rather than extending a helping hand and trying to find a way to protect them; and this is a judgement rendered in accord with each person's own level of understanding. The Effendi not only found nothing wrong with what was happening, but actually justified it as the outcome of unacceptable behavior.

"Tell me, Father, would even an oaf do what Khacho did: take in suspicious guests who go around driving the villagers out of their minds with all their foolish preaching?"

"It's stupid, very stupid," the priest replied. "But why should the villagers be blamed and thrown into the flames by the Turks because of a few fools? Our neighbor Zako is a very pitiful man; he's so timid, he's afraid of his own shadow. Why are they tormenting him and violating his home? Why this kind of cruelty?"

"'A green tree that grows tangled up with a dry one will also be burned,' That's the way the world is. Who will make a distinction between them?" the Effendi said, impressed by his own good sense. "When God sends misfortune to punish people, innocent children are sent to the grave as well as the old. Good and bad are mixed together… It's the same way with the vengeance of governments when the people have to be punished. I tell you, Father, the villagers will suffer, all of them."

The priest came up with no answer to this last statement. The Effendi had cited very telling examples, indeed. In times of cholera and pestilence when men were being punished for their sins, was there any distinction to be made between the just and the unjust? The green tree was burned along with the dry. These were Father Marouk's thoughts. He had, by now, even forgotten about his neighbor Zako, and the Effendi's latest comments had reminded him of one other matter, much closer to his heart:

"If they plunder and rob all the other houses in the village as they did Khacho's house today, I'll never get my fees collected."

"Don't you worry about that, Father, I'll have them all collected without any question. But tell me, Father, didn't Khacho deserve the punishment he got?"

The episode at Khacho's house had caught the attention of the entire village, and, though no one knew the details, everyone found fault with Khacho. "What good would it do for an Armenian to keep weapons? If you give fire to a child, he will burn his fingers," they all said. Father Marouk was of the same opinion.

"I know only one thing, my son, when the multitude approached with swords and staves to arrest our Lord Jesus Christ, the Apostle Peter drew his sword and struck at Malchus,[40] servant to the priest, and cut off his ear. At that moment, Jesus Christ chastened Peter, and told him to put his sword away, since those who live by the sword will die by the sword. We can't forget this warning without violating our Christian faith."

"Good for you, Father, well-said! And what about the pamphlets, have you read them?" asked the Effendi.

"Some of them fell into Simon's hands and I read them. We read through them over and over again, but none of it made any sense. I say, goodness, if you're going to write something it should be something that nourishes the soul or helps the body, something that you'll read then repent of your sins. But what's the use of blather like that? Isn't that so, Simon? You read them."

"I didn't go along with it," the school teacher responded, taking advantage of this opportunity to display his knowledge. "It was just a lot of devilish talk. If they had printed something from the lives of our saints or forefathers, then the people could have read it and been chastened. But I'm very pleased that Vartan is being punished. He was a very proud fellow. He came to my class once and said to me, 'What do you know about education? You should be out in the pasture tending donkeys.' Now is that any way to talk? You'd think he had more education than I."

"'The donkey's kick hurts more than the horse's.' That Vartan fellow has offended me, too, many times," said the Effendi.

And thus the priest, the school teacher, and the government official, each preoccupied with his own point of view, paid no attention at all to what was happening next door. And not one of them was in the least troubled by a thought as to what the situation would be like inside Khacho's house that night. That man thanks to whom all this barbarity had been visited upon the village now turned into an object of scorn to the villagers, because, from their point of view, his conduct had been inexcusable. Everyone was in the grip of terror and expected the worst; but Tomas Effendi, author of all these evils, was filled with satanic delight, deeply pleased that, at last, all the seed he had sewn now promised to bear fruit.

"I have to say again, the villagers will be greatly harmed by all of this," the Effendi said with the air of an expert. "These are bad times. Preparations for war are taking place everywhere, and under such conditions, incidents like this will be severely punished by the government."

On hearing this talk of war, Father Marouk was in shock, not because of all the troubles and destitution involved with war, but because of his uncollected fees.

"If a war starts, the taxes will be so high, I'll never be able to collect my fees," he said.

"Don't worry, Father. I'll make sure you get them all before the war begins," replied the Effendi.

At this juncture Simon once again approached Father Marouk to remind him of the fees he hoped to collect from his pupils. Once more, he was told to desist. People will talk about whatever it is that causes them the greatest discomfort; and so it was that the priest and the school master found their uncollected fees to be the issue of the moment.

"'Though, by itself, the donkey doesn't amount to much, you can make a good brush out of its hair,'"[41] said the Effendi. "You're familiar with this saying, Father. That's the way the peasant is, too. Though the peasant, himself, wears tattered clothes and goes around barefoot, it's from his sweat that the gentleman gets his clothing. Though the peasant stays hungry and without a crust of bread to eat, the gentleman's home is adorned with every fine thing. But you, Father, don't seem to know how to take advantage of the peasant; because if you did, you wouldn't have all these fees owed to you, and you wouldn't be having us drink tonight without any mazah."

These last words had a telling effect on the priest, and he responded with great affliction in his voice:

"What am I supposed to do, Effendi? We priests have our hands tied. We don't carry the same kind of stick you do, to beat and scare the peasant with. Our weapon is a very weak one. What can I do? To tell you the truth, sometimes I get fed up and start uttering curses. But these days the peasants have become such non-believers, they aren't even afraid of curses anymore. And what other weapon do we have? But it's really not their fault. The Kurds have left them nothing, and we can't expect to get anything from them. Ach, may those Kurds be cursed! If it weren't for them, I wouldn't have all these fees to collect, and now that war is starting, the Kurds will go wild..."

"'The donkey will be a donkey, but the mule is even worse,'" replied the Effendi in his characteristic manner. "The Kurds are as bad as mules because they are a mixed breed."

This idea that the Kurds were comparable to mules was not just the Effendi's idea, but was a view shared by Armenians in general, the bad behavior of Kurds being attributed to their being an impure, hybrid people. Our people always have a low opinion of the behavior of mixed people. But the truth is that, while losing their original type as a people by mixing with Armenians, the Kurds became a new and finer people. After centuries of picking the most beautiful of Armenian boys and girls and the tallest women (the Kurds have a fondness for tall women), they became a more beautiful people. And the Armenians, on the other hand, losing their finest members, became gradually uglier and odd looking. Anyone who has done any extensive study of Kurdish life and of Armenians in Turkish Armenia will see that the Kurds are no other than a new people that issued forth from the Armenians.

It was well into the night by now. Zoulo had sat with her sick child for a long time, overhearing the detestable conversation of the guests. She was anxiously waiting for them to be finished and go to bed so that she could at last go and check on Sara and Stepanig.

But the Effendi was far from going to bed; he still had a lot to talk about with Father Marouk and was prevented from doing so only by Master Simon's presence. For this reason, he let on that he was getting sleepy and was ready for bed, having to rise early the next morning to conduct some important business. Simon said good night, and when he was gone Father Marouk said to the Effendi, "The poor fellow has more knowledge than ten vartabeds but, alas, he drinks a bit too much. Did you notice how well he read out my fees?"

"You mean Master Simon? Oh, yes, he did a good job of reading them," the Effendi answered.

But the Effendi had no real interest in Master Simon or his high level of learning. He wanted to talk about the matter that had brought him to the priest's house in the first place.

The priest needed to take off his worn-out overcoat because he was feeling hot, partly from drinking and partly from the heat in the house. He accidentally tore one of the sleeves as he was taking it off.

"Father, your coat is so old. Why haven't you had a new one made?" the Effendi asked.

"Goodness, how could I have one made? You saw how much people owe me. This overcoat used to belong to fine old Garabed Effendi. When he died, it was given to me as a hand-me-down, and I've worn it for seven years now. On account of my sins, no rich men have died lately so that I could replace it."

"You're a good pastor, and I'll have a nice one made for you. Wear it and always bless my name," said the Effendi.

"May the blessings of the three hundred sixty-six patriarchs be upon you, my son," said the priest, and he began declaiming the prayer for protection.

"But there's just one other matter I have to ask you about, Effendi," the priest added. "People like you are the crowning honor to us Armenians. We're fortunate and every day thank God that there are men like you among us Armenians, men who can have frank audiences with moutirs and kaimakams and pashas, and say whatever they want to them. For the love of our people and our holy faith, I beg you, don't let old Khacho and his family fall into the hands of evil men. If you choose, you can save them. They stand in need. They are Armenian Christians. Help them. Whatever wrong they may have done, we have an obligation to cover it up, because they're our flesh and blood. I don't support what they've done, but who is without sin?"

Though the Effendi was not especially touched by Father Marouk's words, he was at last presented with an opportunity to mention the matter he had originally come to discuss.

The Effendi responded by saying that he was willing and able to save Khacho's entire household from the misfortune that had befallen it, and that he would not allow one hair of Khacho's head to be harmed if Khacho agreed with the proposal he would make. Then reminding Father Marouk of the fact that one year earlier he had revealed Lala's true identity to him, the Effendi went on to tell the priest of his love for her and his desire to make her his wife. If Khacho agreed, then he would be helped. If not, the Effendi would simply allow justice to take its course, in which case Khacho's entire household would undoubtedly be destroyed and his wealth confiscated. The Effendi asked Father Marouk to carry this message to Khacho in keeping with his priestly duties, since there was still time to forestall the impending disaster.

"On my honor as a priest, I will go first thing in the morning to carry out your wishes," said Father Marouk happily. "Khacho should give thanks to God and make offerings in the name of the saints that a man like you wants to be his son-in-law."

A cunning smile appeared on the Effendi's face, and he answered derisively, "When you've done all that, you'll get your new overcoat."

"But what about my fees?"

"Don't you worry about that."

CHAPTER 33

A bitter, frightful night passed by. The next morning Khacho's house resembled a home that mourned the death of several members, all taken away at the same time to be buried.

Vartan was led out first. He was relaxed. There was no trace of anxiety in his expression. It seemed that nothing had happened as far as he was concerned. All that could be read in his expression was a certain contemptuous sarcasm in the set of his lips, as if to say, "What do these stupid people think they are going to do with me?" Five soldiers were prepared to take him to the pasha's military headquarters. When they placed him on horseback and started to chain his feet around the horse's belly, he offered no resistance, though being transported in that manner, unable to move, would be an incredible hardship.

"That's unnecessary. If I want to escape, your chains won't prevent me," he commented. The soldiers paid no attention to what he said and continued chaining his feet. Not satisfied with that measure, they also tied his hands behind his back, and two soldiers mounted their horses, each holding one end of the rope, and they made ready to take him away. The other three soldiers fell in behind to act as guards.

Though ordinarily an event like this is fascinating to common folk, none of the villagers was present to see what was happening and how Vartan was being taken away—this man who had worked so hard for their welfare—and they all avoided Khacho's house like the plague.

None of the women were left in the house; they were all hiding in various places. Hairabed and Abo were prisoners. After Vartan, it would be their turn to be taken away. Khacho's other sons were still free, but nowhere to be seen. Only Khacho came out to see Vartan off. After all these troubles, the poor old man was totally overwhelmed. He had been entirely crushed by bitter persecution, violent oppression, and bestial cruelty. He went up to Vartan and embraced him. With all the pain in his heart, he couldn't find a word to utter. His tears were more expressive than any words could be.

"Keep a stout heart, old father. One who goes into water can't be afraid of getting wet. Farewell..."

The soldiers understood none of this, and they set forth with Vartan in front of them. Khacho stood looking for a long time until they were out of sight. Plunged in sadness, he turned back to his house. Why had they just taken Vartan? Why had they left Hairabed and Abo behind? Why hadn't he been arrested himself? Except for being under surveillance, why did he remain free? What was the secret hidden in all of this? These were the questions that nagged at his mind. Khacho had no idea of Tomas Effendi's real intentions at this point. The Effendi had so arranged his plan that in case Khacho refused his proposal for Lala, only then would the full force of his vengeance fall upon Khacho's home. He had Vartan banished, and betrayed Mr. Salman, because he considered them a threat to the Turkish government that he served. But he had nothing of the sort against Khacho and his sons. He only implicated them in wrongdoing to place them in a difficult position so that he could then come along and play the protector and savior obligating them to repay him with Lala's hand in marriage. Thus motivated by crass self-interest, the Effendi set in motion a series of evils the outcome of which, despite all his satanic cunning, he could in no way foresee.

But on this particular morning Tomas Effendi didn't appear at Khacho's door. Khacho wanted to see the Effendi and find out what he would say, at last, about how the situation was going to turn out. He continued to have faith in the Effendi, and recalled his saying, "Don't worry, Danouder Khacho, I won't allow one hair of your head to be harmed."

Instead of the Effendi, it was Father Marouk who appeared at Khacho's door, this go-between who had come to discuss Lala with him. Under the circumstances, Khacho found the priest's visit unwelcome, though normally the presence of a priest is regarded as a consolation in times of difficulty. Khacho had a strong prejudice against priests and regarded their appearance as a bad omen. But Father Marouk carefully drew the old man aside and said he had something important to discuss with him. This put Khacho somewhat at ease. The two of them sat down together in a distant corner of the garden beneath the shelter of some trees.

As a preamble to stating his main purpose in coming to see Khacho, the priest opened with a set of consoling sayings and counsel presented in his characteristic preaching style and supported with various examples drawn from the Bible. Referring to the trials of Job the Blessed, he said that God often throws difficulties in the path of his servants to test their faith; that they must to be patient and never yield to despair; and that, in the end, He would save them and make them worthy of eternal glory.

Concluding his sermon, the pastor moved to the main purpose of his visit. As is traditional for go-betweens, he started with a parable:

"The son of a certain king went hunting and was overtaken by nightfall," he said. "Being unable to return home, he took shelter in a shepherd's hut for the night. He was quite pleased with the shepherd's hospitality, but, in particular, he was struck by the shepherd's daughter. The next day on returning to the palace, the prince informed his father that he wished to marry the shepherd's daughter. The king thought his son had lost his mind and was very angry. For a long time he stood firmly opposed to the idea, but, still unable to dissuade his son, he finally sent one of his ministers to discuss marriage with the shepherd. On his return the minister reported that the shepherd had refused to give his daughter's hand. The king was shocked and sent another minister, this time a man of higher rank. This minister also returned with the same message. Next, the king sent his highest vizier. He also returned with the same answer from the shepherd. At this point the king had no choice but to go and see the shepherd himself. But he, too, returned home empty-handed. The king, confounded by this predicament, called all of his top advisors together to confer. There was one man among them who had more experience and intelligence than the rest, and it was he who proposed that the king send a fellow shepherd as a messenger so that he could talk to the girl's father in the language of shepherds. This man was warmly received at the shepherd's hut. After the two shepherds had eaten and drunk their fill and felt good together, the messenger conveyed the king's proposal to his host.

'Why did you refuse to give your daughter's hand to the king's son?'

The shepherd host replied, 'Good Lord, I'm just a man like any other, and I have self-respect. The king had never before sent such a decent fellow as you to persuade me to give her hand.'"

Concluding his parable, the priest added, "I, too, am a shepherd, Danouder Khacho. Both of us have responsibility over people instead of sheep, I the village priest, and you the village leader. I've come to present you a proposal like the one shepherd did to the other."

"What proposal?" Khacho asked with displeasure, finding the priest's absurd talk extremely burdensome to his heart at such a sad juncture.

Father Marouk responded that God wished to comfort Khacho in his time of need and open the door of salvation before him. Tomas Effendi wished to have Lala's hand in marriage and save Khacho's home from the misfortune that had been visited upon it. Khacho should thank God that a man such as the Effendi was extending the hand of friendship and help.

No matter how clever the priest was in making his case, his efforts were without success. In other times, and under different circumstances, he might well have been successful, for Khacho had intended all along to make the Effendi his son-in-law. But conditions had changed. Two of his sons were prisoners; he himself was under house-arrest; the women of his household were vulnerable and hiding in other peoples' homes; his two friends, Vartan and Mr. Salman, had been betrayed to the government; all his property had been plundered before his own eyes; and in the midst of all this, he was being presented with a proposal by the very malefactor who had perpetrated all these evils. Suddenly Khacho's eyes were opened. He saw before him the pit that the Effendi had cunningly dug for him. He remembered what Vartan had said about the Effendi's dishonesty in marrying and abandoning many different women in different places. And wasn't he about to do exactly the same thing with Lala? He recalled the Effendi's behavior which from start to finish had some clandestine purpose at its core, manifesting itself in a series of cunning acts with but one goal—to ensure success in his pursuit of Lala. It was the Effendi who had first informed Khacho of Mr. Salman's arrest. How did the Effendi know about it, since the arrest had occurred under the cover of night, when not even a single villager in the entire vicinity had seen a thing? It was the Effendi who had first announced to him that there was to be a search of his house, then took possession of Mr. Salman's papers, locked the doors where they were hidden and put the key in his own pocket, all under the guise of friendship and confidentiality. Why? He could simply have taken the papers and destroyed them. No, he left them where they were so that at the right moment he could throw open the doors to the secret room and turn the papers over to the police, saying to them that they held in their hands all the proof they needed of treasonous activity on the part of the arrested suspects. As this picture completed itself bit by bit in Khacho's mind, he was horrified at having been tricked, and addressed Father Marouk with considerable bitterness:

"Father, your parable is quite out of line with the role you're playing. Even if Tomas Effendi were a real king, I still wouldn't give my daughter's hand to that dog, come what may. I'd rather see my whole house and family destroyed than be saved by this malefactor who's prepared all this misfortune for us. Now I understand, I understand it all—he tricked me. But he won't be able to trick me again..."

The priest had no comprehension what lay behind Khacho's anger or his dark words. He didn't know any of the details of what had really happened, and Khacho felt no obligation to give him a full explanation, especially in view of the fact that Father Marouk was Stepanig's godfather and that, outside of him and Khacho's own family, no one knew that Stepanig was a girl. Therefore, who but Father Marouk himself could have divulged her true identity to the Effendi?

Father Marouk was very upset as he left Khacho's house, and he kept muttering to himself, "First God deprives a man of his senses, then he takes his wealth."

In the meantime, the Effendi was impatiently awaiting the priest's return. As soon as he got back, the Effendi asked him, "What word do you bring?"

"I don't know what to say. That man must be out of his mind," answered Father Marouk, quite befuddled.

"He refused?"

"Yes."

"That's what I thought."

Then it seemed the whole sky fell down on the Effendi's head, crushing him with its awesome weight. Everything went black before his eyes; he trembled and fell to the floor. There he stayed for a long time without stirring. Then he sometimes raised his hand to his head, struck his forehead and pulled his hair, saying, "What will I do now? Ach, now what will I do?"

There is nothing in the entire universe that can humble a man like love. The worst monsters among mankind—those who cause trouble everywhere they go, who are bathed in the blood of many peoples, who keep nations in fear and trembling—humble themselves and fall on their knees before the women they love. In this respect, they are simply men, with all the weaknesses of men.

Tomas Effendi loved Lala now, with a true and burning love. All his untamed impulses and bestial indifference now melted away into nothingness. A devil who has fallen in love turns into an angel, and, accordingly, the Effendi became remorseful.

He had never been in love before, and it was for this reason that nothing had ever been sacred to the darker side of his character. As shrewd as he was in his daily affairs, as quick as he was in his calculations, and as much satanic mastery as he applied in attaining his goals, he was to the same degree unconscious of his own psychological motivations.

Love for Lala kindled a fire in his cold heart and gave access to that fiery brilliance which brings light to a darkened soul. He took stock of what he had done and was overwhelmed. "What have I done?" he murmured and pulled at his hair again.

It was not until that moment that he understood the full horror of his crimes, operating until then under the assumption that anything was justified in attaining one's purposes. But he now saw what great evils he had perpetrated. In the beginning, he had only intended to play a little game with Khacho so that he could childishly snatch a little ember from the fire and use it to scare Khacho and get what he wanted from him. But from that tiny ember had come an enormous conflagration and not peace.

"Ach! What have I done?" he sighed again.

Father Marouk looked down with alarm at the tormented Effendi, thinking he was on the verge of dying; and, indeed, he was sprawled out on the floor in a weakened state, with occasional feverish tremors passing over his face. He lay for a rather long time in this tortured condition, then opened his eyes.

"Everything Khacho told you is true, Father. I am unworthy of his daughter. What kind of bond could there be between a criminal like me and an innocent angel. Curse me, Father, for I am worthy of nothing but curses."

He then fell again into unconsciousness, and the priest thought for sure that he had died.

"Ach, my fees, my fees!" the priest cried out."They're all lost!"

CHAPTER 34

Let us now return to the beginning of our story.

At this point, I believe the reader will recall who the young man was who, during the terrible siege of Bayazid, accepted the message from Commander Shedogvitch, and, passing himself off as a fool, proceeded unharmed through the enemy camp and a few days later successfully delivered the message to General Der-Ghugasov. The reader will also remember how the young man left the Russian camp, having declined the position of bodyguard to the general and other military honors, in order to save someone's life.

That young man was Vartan. Let us now see where he went. Riding the horse he had taken from the Kurd he had killed in the dale, he made his way toward the province of Alashgert. That is where he sought what was most precious to him. That is where Khacho's house was, a place in which he had spent so many happy times. Beautiful Lala was there, she to whom he had completely surrendered his heart. That is where his beloved friends had been, those with whom he had entered into a sacred task of self-sacrifice. All of this had been there in Alashgert, everything that was most precious and sacred to Vartan.

But what was the state in which Vartan had left all of these people when he had been taken away in chains to be delivered to military headquarters? Khacho and his sons had been made prisoners. The family had been dispersed, everyone going to a different hiding place. Lala's fate was bound up with the bestial competition between her two pursuers, Tomas Effendi and the Kurdish chieftain Fattah-Bek; Mr. Salman was under arrest; Melik-Mansour and his band had set out to rescue him, but Vartan had no idea whether they had succeeded or not.

And so, he had left all of them behind in the direst of circumstances. One and a half months had elapsed since that day, and Vartan had no knowledge at all about them. In that brief period of time so many changes had occurred: the Russians had declared war against the Turks.

General Der-Ghugasov's forces took complete control of the provinces of Bayazid and Alashgert and were approaching Erzeroum. The miserable and oppressed Armenian masses, passing under Russian control, were able to breathe freely once more. Then suddenly the fortunes of war were reversed. General Der-Ghugasov was forced to abandon the land he loved so much and retreat to the Russian border. Bayazid, which was under his control on April 18th, again fell to the Turks on June 27th.

Vartan had no knowledge of these events. He had no idea what had happened to General Der-Ghugasov's army during its retreat. So much had happened. He knew nothing about the massive exodus of Armenians from Alashgert nor the tragic circumstances that had led to it.

Enormous changes had occurred in the briefest span of time. One and a half months earlier,[42] he had been taken in chains from Khacho's house to be delivered to military headquarters, surrounded by Turkish soldiers. But on the way there, and before reaching the headquarters, his two companions, Sako and Yegho, attacked the soldiers who were escorting him. After a daring engagement, they managed to free their master. In the course of this fight Vartan was wounded, and, leaning on his companions almost the whole way, he was led to Russian territory in the vicinity of Sourmalou and an Armenian village there. When he was barely recovered from his wounds, he and his two companions volunteered for the Armenian militia. Sako and Yegho were killed during the siege of Bayazid, and the story of how Vartan managed to get out of the citadel is already known to us.

Now, sad and alone, he entered the valley where the village of O… was to be found. What a beautiful sight this valley had presented just a few weeks earlier! How beautiful and full of life its fields and dales and green carpeted mountains had been! The entire valley had been filled with an undulating expanse of ripened grain, tossing like a golden sea. Herds of grazing livestock were spread out like ants on the mountain slopes. The sweet and tender strains of the shepherd's flute could be heard. Nature in its abundance had joined together with the hard work of man to bring forth the blessings of the earth. But now—all was changed. Now the entire valley had the appearance of a terrible wasteland; the harvest had been scorched and devoured by fire; the vast surface of the valley was covered with ashes. Who had brought this evil to pass? Who had annihilated the fruit of the farmer's hand after he had put so much labor and sweat into it? It was difficult for Vartan to comprehend what he saw. He looked in the direction where beautiful, populous villages had once been, and there, too, all he saw were dots of ash, further evidence of the fires' destructiveness. Everywhere life had ceased. The joyous song of the farmer could no longer be heard. No longer did herds graze in their pastures. Everything had fallen silent. Everything was shrouded in death. It seemed that the "spoiling angel" had just passed through the land, nullifying everything produced by the hands of the hard-working peasants. What had happened?

The July sun was scorching hot. Vartan entered the village of O… in the late afternoon. It had the appearance of a town that had been laid waste by black magic, like towns in certain legends. Houses that had been so full of life only a short time earlier had been turned into tombs. Everything was buried in tragic, eerie ruin. Vartan found his way through the familiar streets like a man in a daze. Here and there he saw the remains of human bodies. Something truly horrific had happened here. He went toward the church. God's temple could hardly be distinguished from the surrounding rubble.

He went to old Khacho's fortress. Only the outside walls remained standing, with gaps in some places. As he went in a terrible sight presented itself. The garden had been totally stripped of its beautiful, shade-rich trees in whose shelter he had spent so many sweet moments with beautiful Lala. And now—where was she, she for whom he had returned, she whom he sought in the midst of this tragic ruin? Could it be that Fattah-Bek had come and carried her off? Or did she fall into the hands of a Turkish soldier? Vartan was gripped by a kind of terror, a kind of petrifying chill, when this scene opened up before him. All at once this man of iron seemed to give way beneath the enormous and painful burden of the reality he confronted. His blood was rushing with extraordinary force, pounding inside his head, and the light of the world dimmed before his eyes. After that, he neither saw nor felt anything. He sat down mechanically on a mound of earth and, holding his head in his hands for a long while, was lost in a state of deep, feverish stupefaction. Suddenly, there appeared before his mind's eye that lovely image as he had seen it that last night in the silence of the garden, the same despondent, tearful eyes, her imploring arms wrapped around his neck, saying to the man she loved, "Take me away from here… I'm afraid of the Kurds." Why hadn't he taken her away then? Why had he abandoned her? He couldn't even think about it any longer and, falling into a stupor, his thinking ceased.

Yet what painful memories those ruins stirred in his mind. Just a short time ago the walls were firm and fast, and within them a splendid family lived its rich and peaceable life. What had happened, and where was that family now? He glanced toward where the women's part of the house had been, and all he saw was the four walls covered with soot and ashes, the ceiling fallen down. It was here that Khacho's many daughters-in-law and grandchildren, had been engaged in lively activity all day long, working and chattering, always happily carrying out their tasks. Now, the hubbub of the children and their mothers' solicitous voices had fallen silent. Vartan looked toward where the guest room had been. It was now totally destroyed. He remembered those noisy evenings there, when he and Mr. Salman together with Khacho and his sons had engaged in spirited debates, proposing and assessing hundreds of ideas for saving the poor, oppressed people and building a happier future for them. And now what he saw was that all had been destroyed, both the thinkers and the thoughts.

Suddenly some people appeared on the scene. Until that moment, Vartan hadn't seen one living person in the whole valley. He felt quite cheered, seeing them in the midst of the ruins. These people were several pitiful looking Kurds, searching through the rubble with pick-axes—Khacho's shepherds accompanied by their wives and children. The men were breaking up the ground, and the women and children were searching for any articles that might be buried there. Many household items still remained beneath the surface of the ground, untouched by the flames.

"May God assist you," said Vartan with the customary greeting given to workers.

"Welcome to you," they answered.

"What are you looking for?"

"You can see for yourself, kind sir," the people answered and went back to work.

"Do you recognize me, Khulo?" Vartan asked, walking up to one of the Kurds.

"Of course I do, sir. You were one of our master Khacho's friends. You used to bring merchandise here to sell, and whenever you came, you never forgot to bring something for your servant Khulo's children. Look, you gave this to us," he said, pointing to his wife's dress, beautifully embroidered with red thread.

Vartan asked him what had happened to Khacho's house, why the village was left in ruins, and what had become of the inhabitants.

The shepherd stuck his pick-axe in the ground and wiped the sweat from his brow, since it would take a great deal to relax and tell the story.

"What happened at this house, may it not happen even to our enemies," he said with great feeling. "To tell the truth, we don't know the whole story. We weren't here when it happened. We were away in the mountains with our sheep. At nightfall, we drove the flock back toward the village. (My wife had had a bad dream the night before, and I was expecting the worst.) Before we reached the village, a band of Kurds suddenly attacked us and stole our sheep. I and my friends ran toward the village for help. We saw the whole village in flames. There were Kurds everywhere. We hurried to Khacho's house, but it was on fire, too, and there was no way to get inside."

"What happened to the family?"

"If anything bad happened to them, may our sons bear the guilt. Danouder Khacho, Hairabed, and Abo weren't there. They had been taken away several days before by the police. I heard they were in prison. All the women were gone, too. Only Khacho's other sons remained behind, and I don't know what became of them. We just came back and saw the house in flames.

"Old Khacho was a good man," the shepherd continued. "He was so God-fearing he wouldn't even step on an ant. All the people who lived in this house were so kind they'd never even hurt a fly. They took care of us like their own children. But may the Eshirat[43] be cursed! They turned everything upside down. They destroyed everything."

"What happened to the other villagers?"

"Some of them were massacred, some were taken as slaves, and many escaped."

"To a drowning man, a chip of wood is a great consolation." And thus, as painful as the shepherd's account was, it offered Vartan a glimmer of hope. "Then all is not lost," he thought. He knew that Khacho, Hairabed, and Abo were in prison. But even that fact might spare them from the cruelty of the Kurds—if they had not in fact already been killed in prison. Vartan also knew that all the women and girls, including Lala, had been sent to the homes of various friends and relatives during the search of their home to spare them from the terrible things that occurred there.

The shepherd had provided Vartan with one other consolation when he had said, "Some were massacred, some were taken as slaves, and many escaped." Perhaps some of Khacho's family were among those who got away. Perhaps Lala was among them, he thought. But in what direction would they have fled? Where would they have been headed? Vartan was tormented by these questions, and the shepherd had no answers.

Everything had occurred at night and so suddenly that all the details were hidden in darkness. But on entering the Alashgert region, Vartan had noticed that not one Armenian remained. It was inconceivable that the Armenians had all been killed or taken as slaves. There must have been some massive exodus. But where had they gone? What territory had they set out for?

CHAPTER 35

On leaving the ruins of Khacho's house, Vartan was uncertain what direction to take. Given the shepherd's vague and fragmentary account, he didn't know what his next step should be.

It was already evening, and the sun was setting. All Vartan saw before him was ruin: empty villages and fields unworked. That was all. Was it possible not even a single Armenian was left in the entire valley? His attention was suddenly caught by the figure of a human being in this wasteland, a man who slowly and unsteadily made his way up the mountain slope, struggling to reach the top. From time to time the man stopped and looked around, grasping at rocks to keep from falling down. Ascending in this manner, he finally arrived atop a steep, rocky cliff overlooking a great abyss. His small figure was profiled by the last rays of the setting sun, and for a moment he stood as motionless as a statue, looking down on the vast valley where so many atrocities and so much destruction had taken place only a few days before. He stood where he was for a long time as if trying to resolve something that weighed very heavily on his mind. Vartan couldn't help but be fascinated by this sight which foretold some terrible outcome. He pulled his horse's reins and moved forward, keeping his eyes trained on the scene.

He saw the figure of the man frozen in place at the top of the precipice, making despondent gestures. The man took one more look at the wide valley filled with destruction, then covered his eyes with his hands and threw himself off. His little body rolled down like a ball, hitting rocks and tumbling down without stopping. Vartan rode forward on his horse to help the man and reached the foot of the mountain in a short time. The man's body was still rolling down but then got caught in some shrubs growing around the edge of the rocks. Vartan was glad he would now have a chance at saving the life of the would-be suicide. Looking up, he saw that the body was more than fifty paces above him, held motionless by the shrubs. How could he get him down? That was the problem before him.

He dismounted and began examining the cliff to see if there was any way to reach the spot where the body lay, but he saw none.

The body remained where it was, totally motionless, without any sign of life. What had driven the man to suicide? The grim setting in which Vartan found himself was so eerie that every little object seemed to contain some secret.

Though the man might still be alive, Vartan saw no way to save his life without risking his own. But compassion overcame any thought he had of himself, and he undertook to carry out a very dangerous exercise. He observed that it might be possible to climb up by grabbing hold of shrubs and protruding rocks on the face of the cliff if they were secure enough to hold his weight. Vartan was endowed with the suppleness of a snake and the agility of a cat. He reached up, took hold of the first steep rock before him and started to climb, scratching at its surface with his finger-nails. He went up a good distance when, all of a sudden, the rock broke and he tumbled down. "This isn't the right spot," he thought, paying no attention to his hands which were wounded and bloody from scraping over sharp fragments of rock.

Vartan was the type of person whose will is only provoked into determination by adversity, as if failure to prevail would be a personal affront. He made haste; the sun was setting rapidly, and within a few moments everything would be wrapped in darkness, making success impossible. Just then he had an idea. He took a long length of rope from where he kept it on his saddle. This was one of his weapons. On the end of it was tied an egg-sized leaden ball.

He hurled the leaden ball up, and the end of the rope wound itself securely around the branches of a tree not far from the fallen man. Taking the other end of the rope in his hands, he climbed up with spider-like speed and quickly reached the spot where the breathless figure lay. He lifted up the body, and to his great astonishment saw that it was Tomas Effendi. All in a flash, his heart was assailed with a maddening succession of anger, disgust, hatred, and revenge. He came close to flinging this repulsive body into the abyss yet again so that the rest of its bones could be broken, so that it could be made a meal of by the wild animals and birds of prey. But such cruelty to a half-alive person was far out of keeping with Vartan's nobility. He carefully lowered the body down on the rope, then descended himself.

His first concern was to determine if the man were alive or not. His bones were broken in many places. His head and face were bloodied from striking and scraping against the rocks, but his breathing hadn't ceased entirely. He appeared to be unconscious.

This evil man who had caused Vartan such great suffering, who had brought about the destruction of thousands of homes and the devastation of an entire province, could now in his pitiful condition only arouse compassion in Vartan. If the Effendi had fallen into Vartan's hands in better circumstances, Vartan would very likely have killed him; but he now looked down on a body in need of help.

Vartan had considerable experience in the treatment of wounds, having sustained many himself, and he always carried dressings with him. He first had to bandage the wounds on the Effendi's face and stop the flow of blood. Night had already fallen; the sky was full of dark clouds. A fierce wind and thunderclaps gave signs of an approaching storm. His next concern was to find some kind of shelter. He lifted up the body and tied it on his horse, but he didn't know which way to go. Not a single Armenian was left in any of the nearby villages.

Vartan remembered there was a Kurdish village in the vicinity. With the Effendi's body tied on horse-back behind him, he drew rein and guided his horse in the direction of that village. It was at this point that Vartan began to sense what lay behind the Effendi's attempted suicide: an attempt to put an end to a stinging conscience. Was it possible he felt remorseful for being the cause of so much blood and tears and devastation?

Vartan's memory had not deceived him; he saw a glimmer of light in the darkness. That must be the village, yet it lay at a considerable distance. Now the rain began to pour down. He took off his overcoat and carefully covered the Effendi's body with it. It was well into the night by the time he reached the village. The houses, like Kurdish houses everywhere, were excavated earthen huts. Vartan approached the first house he came to, raised his hand to knock on the door, then saw that it was already open. What fortunate people, that they could just go to sleep with the door wide open without any fear of robbers.

There was no lamp burning inside, and the people of the house were in bed. Vartan rapped on the door. A few moments later he began to hear women's voices from inside.

"Who is it?"

"God's guest."

This identification was sufficient for him to be allowed in. A woman lit a lamp and received him. She was partially clad and sleepy, wearing only a red blouse that reached down to her bare legs. She helped Vartan carry the Effendi in, and they laid him down on a carpet.

"Is he sick?" the woman asked, immediately fetching a small box with various dressings and implements for treating wounds.

"I am the doctor of the house," she said, opening the box. "When my husband gets wounded in battle, I take care of him. My mother-in-law used to be a doctor, but now she's very old. I learned what I know from her."

As much confidence as Vartan had in Kurdish medicine, he thanked the woman and proposed that he assist her, since he also had extensive experience in treating wounds.

Though his response hurt her feelings, since she was so eager to show what she could do, she relented on seeing that the wounds had already been bound.

"You should take care of your horse now. You just left him outside."

"Never mind, just show me where I can tie him."

The young woman took the lamp, led her guest into the yard, and showed him where the horse could be tied. Vartan looked around and saw that the yard was surrounded only by a very low wall.

"Is it safe here?"

"Of course it is. A thief doesn't steal from another thief's house," she said with a laugh.

As he looked around the house Vartan saw no one but the young woman and two children asleep on the floor. But the footsteps awakened the old mother-in-law, previously hidden from sight. The old woman raised her head, then sat up and asked, "Saro, is that you? Are you home, son?"

"It's not Saro. It's a guest," the young woman said, going up to her mother-in-law.

On hearing that it wasn't her son, the old woman laid her head back down and went right back to sleep.

"Her eyesight is poor. She thought her son, my husband, came back."

"Where is he?" Vartan asked with curiosity.

"He is in Bayazid. He went there to fight. You won't find one man left in our village. All of them went there. I just got back from there two days ago. I went to bring back some booty."

"Did you get a lot?"

"It wasn't a small amount. Whether it's much or a little, you have to be content with what God provides."

"Ah, free daughter of a free people," thought Vartan. "How full of life and simplicity! Why should you feel guilty if you were raised thinking of booty as honest gain? If, in a better life, you had received an education, your talents would be a wonder to the world."

Now Vartan turned his attention to the Effendi. He touched his body and found him to be very hot. His breathing was more regular now, but from time to time deep sighs issued from him. The young woman started to insist on ministering to the patient. Vartan acceded, knowing how well developed the healing arts were among the Kurds, a people to whom wounds and blood were common occurrences and the knowledge of their treatment a matter of survival.

"There's nothing to fear," the young woman said, finishing up what she was doing. "The wounds are slight, but his bones are broken in several places. It seems he must have fallen a great distance."

Vartan said nothing.

"Now I have to make something for you to eat," his hostess said.

It was only now that Vartan realized how hungry he was, for he had not eaten all day. But there are times when a man is starving, yet has no appetite. That was Vartan's condition now. He was filled to the limit with affliction and heartache.

"Don't go to a lot of trouble. Just a piece of bread and some cheese will do," he answered.

Vartan's modest request offended the young woman's sense of hospitality, since she was about to make a hot meal for him.

"Don't you worry about us. We're not as poor as we used to be," she said with a smile.

"Yes, you got rich from Bayazid."

"Bayazid aside, we've made a good haul here... Last year sickness wiped out all our animals, and we were left without a morsel of bread to eat, but this year God made it up to us. The Armenians from this area all fled and left most of their possessions to us Kurds."

"Where did they go?"

"I don't know. But their exodus was sudden, and they didn't have time to take anything with them. They just tried to get away as quickly as possible so they wouldn't be massacred by the Turks."

"Did they succeed?"

"Out of those who stayed, a great many were killed."

Little by little, the awful reality of what had happened was being revealed to Vartan. There had definitely been a mass exodus of Armenians from this province. But where to, and why? The young Kurdish woman had no clear explanation to offer. Vartan was overwhelmed with agonizing thoughts. He became completely oblivious to his hunger and hadn't even looked at the pretty Kurdish woman who had promptly struck up a fire in the stove and was preparing an omelette for him.

In other times, with a lighter heart, what young man could have looked without wonder on this fresh young figure of a woman who looked so remarkable in her simple blouse. Having been roused from sleep in the middle of the night, she wore no veil; the only covering on her forehead being the thick, brown tresses of her hair, tied up on her head like a crown. Such abundant hair, such a face, such shining eyes could only be found in the half-naked maidens who catch the reflection of their own beauty in mountain springs.

CHAPTER 36

It was the middle of the night. The lamp was still burning in the little Kurdish cottage. The simple, traditional family slept within the same four walls. On one side, the mother-in-law was asleep and snoring. Near her were the little children, dreaming of the mixed excitement of their day, and in the sweetness of sleep constantly talking and smiling. The free-souled mountain girl considered it completely natural to get in bed in front of this stranger who was her guest. Because it was so hot indoors, she left her covers aside, and the contours of her bosom were half-visible beneath the thick locks of her hair. She slept as peacefully as a roe deer.

"Now I understand why the world's first couple lived completely naked," thought Vartan. "It was when they first felt a sense of sin that they covered themselves. These people still have no conception of sin; they are therefore unfamiliar with those things the world identifies as shame, or decency, or propriety. Behold, a beautiful people still existing in pristine simplicity, from whom something truly great could be made. When a wild plant is grafted to one more cultivated and advanced, its fruit will be remarkable. What would happen if this healthy, vibrant element were combined with the Armenians?..."

Everyone in the house was asleep except Vartan. He sat for a long time with a jumble of melancholy thoughts crowding his mind. In his tortured imagination, he sometimes caught images of the terrible exodus from Alashgert. "A transplanted tree won't send its roots into mother earth but will dry up." This people who had been oppressed and dried up and, for the greater part, reduced to nothingness in its mad wandering through history, still hadn't come to its senses. Behold, yet another exodus! And that was quite natural, for a tree that hasn't sent firm, deep roots into mother earth will not withstand the trials of the world. Wind and storm will wrench its roots from the earth and cast it into the abyss... Sometimes Vartan pictured Mr. Salman's passionate expression and seemed to hear his fine statements as he spoke interminably. Though some of his ideas betrayed a certain immaturity, he spoke with a heart full of devotion. Vartan pictured Melik-Mansour, that rough man of adventure who always found particular satisfaction in the thick of life's stormy tumult. And Vartan recalled old Khacho, that virtuous patriarch who, with love and care in his heart, had taken responsibility for governing the affairs of his people and would make any sacrifice to wipe away the tears of the sufferer. Vartan remembered Khacho's sons, some of whom had lost their sense of liberty and any concept of a better life, having lived under the harsh yoke of subservience; and there were the two who had protested against the governing tyranny, misrule, injustice, and violence. Lost in these preoccupations, awash in them, and passing through all that darkness, he at last arrived at that single point he had not yet faced—Lala.

Just then he was distracted by the Effendi. His breathing was more stable now; his hands were moving constantly, and from his lips there issued a mixture of sighs and vague mutterings, lost as he was in deep delirium. Vartan listened but couldn't understand anything he said. The Effendi seemed in some tormented state, in the throes of some intense spiritual battle. This continued for a long while until, at last, he became calmer. He raised his head, opened his eyes, and, after looking around with a wild expression, laid his head back down on the pillow and shut his eyes again.

"Oh, if there were just one Armenian around," he could be heard saying in his weak voice.

"There is," answered Vartan.

"Give me your hand."

Vartan drew back in disgust.

"Where am I now? Who brought me here? Why was I taken from hell so soon? It was good there, very good. I was rocking in a sea of fire; thousand-headed dragons were crushing and suffocating me. I can see them now, writhing in those distant flames, rising upon each other like mountains. How sweet it is for an evil man to be tormented in their monstrous clutches, to be devoured and, without daring to object, consider himself worthy only of yet more terrible punishments…"

His clouded eyes opened once more, but he didn't recognize Vartan and went on.

"It was into the most horrible judgement chamber of all that I fell, that's what I'm proud of! I didn't succeed to a very high position in this world, but there I did. There I had no rivals. There I saw Vasag, Mehrouzhan, Vest Sarkis, Cain, and many other evil men of their kind. All were jealous of my standing. Oh, what deep satisfaction to be awash in waves of fire; to burn, to roast, yet never turn to ash. It's wonderful never to come to an end. Everything is good when you can exist forever…"

As to what fevered visions the Effendi had seen, Vartan could well imagine, for in his utterances he had heard the voice of a humbled, repentant heart.

"Calm down, Effendi, you'll recover soon enough. Your wounds aren't so bad."

"I hear a familiar voice."

"Vartan's voice."

A shudder went through the Effendi's entire body. He pushed Vartan's hand away and cried, "Take your hand away from me or it will be contaminated…Vartan, I recognize you; you whose heart is both good and pitiless. Muster all the cruelty you have in you now, and kill me quickly. Cast my body into the wastes of Alashgert that I myself turned into a desert. Let the wild animals feed on it. Or else, if you would be so kind, throw my body into a ditch and cover it with dirt. I will find my way back to the abyss from there, back to the unquenchable fire and the everlasting punishment. But no, no! I'm not worthy to be buried in Armenia's soil. My disgusting body will defile its holiness."

"Get hold of yourself, Effendi. You're not going to die," Vartan counseled again. "I've done everything to make sure you live."

"I thought it would be so easy to die and close my eyes forever on the evil that I've done. But no—heaven's retribution is more powerful than one little man. I had to be left behind for a long time to see all the destruction I created; to see again and again the huts of those humble peasants whom I condemned; to see all that and be tormented by the sharp sting of conscience. That is true agony. It was I who became the instrument for all the killing in this province, yet I was powerless to kill myself."

He uttered these last words with profound bitterness, as an expression of a spiritual torment so deep it impelled him to seek the peace of the grave.

Just at that moment, the young Kurdish woman woke up.

"It seems your patient is very uncomfortable," she said. "Is there something you need?"

"Nothing at all. He has a fever. It probably won't last much longer…"

The young woman went up to the sick man and looked at him closely.

"I recognize him. This is Tomas Effendi, isn't it?

"Yes, it is."

"The poor man. A few days ago I saw him wandering around in this area, barefoot, bare-headed, and with tattered clothes. When people got close to him, he would scream and groan and run away. They said he had lost his mind."

Vartan recalled that he had also encountered the Effendi in just the same condition as the young woman described. In that moment before he threw himself off the cliff, he had shown all the signs of madness. But how did he lose his mind? Was it possible in a man so corrupt by nature as the Effendi for moral anguish to have reached this level of power?

"They say the Effendi was in love with a girl whom he lost when the people fled from Alashgert. They say some people secretly took her away," the young woman said.

"What people? What girl?" Vartan cried out with a look of terror on his face, his voice filled with agony.

"I don't know. That's what people said."

Vartan needn't have asked, for his questions were the involuntary outburst of a man in despair. He knew whose loss it was, whose being taken away that had thrown the Effendi into madness. With that, his last glimmer of hope had been destroyed. There was nothing left in his exhausted heart but the spent embers of melancholy memories.

The night had reached its end, unnoticed, and the morning light appeared. Outside, the joyous singing of the birds began, and a tempestuous, rainy night gave way to a rosy, summer morning.

All at once, a girl came running in joyfully, seeming to have come a great distance to reach this cottage, being wet from head to foot, and the hem of her dress covered with mud.

"Chavo!" cried Vartan's hostess, giving the girl a hug.

"Sister!" responded the girl, offering her red cheeks for a kiss.

Watching the warm greeting the two sisters gave each other, it seemed that Vartan momentarily forgot his own worries.

The new arrival was lean and tall, and had a pretty face. She had the same dark, glowing eyes as her sister, now more restless and active with all her joy. Her face and name seemed somehow familiar to Vartan, but he had difficulty remembering when or where he had met her.

"Do you know what?" the pretty girl said. "Chavo is going to stay with you for a long time, starting now. The lady dismissed me."

As welcome as this news was to the older sister, and as sweet as it would be to see Chavo for a long time, she was quite flustered on hearing she had been dismissed by her mistress. Why had she sent Chavo away now, when, in the past, she had always been so unwilling to let her go to pay a visit to her sister?

"What happened?"

"Don't worry, nothing bad."

Chavo began to explain how her mistress had dismissed her to go and live with her sister only temporarily, until she received the call to return. Her mistress had given Chavo money, clothing, and many other very nice things which she had brought with her.

"Look, I'll show you all the things I brought," she said, and started to open her bundle, but her sister was still unsatisfied with her explanations.

"What happened, Chavo? Why did she send you away?"

"Chavo will tell you later; it's a very long story, as long as the tale of Leyli and Majnoun."[44] She said she was very tired, had been on the road all night in the rain, and was famished. She asked her sister for some milk to drink.

Chavo's sister promptly fetched a milk pan and ran to the barn to milk the cow for her.

It was only at this point that Chavo noticed there was a guest in the house, and her fiery eyes met Vartan's fascinated gaze.

"Oh, lovely Chavo, you are Khourshid's maidservant, aren't you."

"That's right."

"Servant to Fattah-Bek's wife."

"Yes, exactly."

Seizing this unexpected opportunity, Vartan asked with calculation, "Doesn't the Bek have a second wife—an Armenian girl?"

"He wanted her, but, little devil that she is, Chavo stole her away."

"The Armenian girl?"

"Yes, the Armenian girl—Lala or Stepanig—she had two different names."

Vartan's heart began to pound with happiness.

"And where did Chavo take this girl she stole?"

"Chavo took her to her mistress, and her mistress had her taken secretly to the Russian border."

Vartan's face brightened with indescribable joy and, forgetting himself, he hugged Chavo, being at a loss as to how to express his boundless gratitude to her.

"Give Chavo a kiss. Chavo saved her life."

"Chavo is my sister," said Vartan and gave her a brotherly kiss.

Chavo's sister returned with a pan of frothy milk. Chavo took it from her hands and drank half of it in one draught. The warm milk relieved her hunger and fatigue.

"Now tell me what happened," her sister said.

In her own characteristic way Chavo related that Fattah-Bek, her mistress's husband, had long been enamored of an Armenian girl, the daughter of Khacho, the village leader of O... (Khacho was well-known to all the Kurds in the province.) Her mistress was opposed to the Armenian girl's being her husband's second wife, since she was beautiful and could win all his love in an instant.

Impelled by jealousy and spite, Khourshid did everything in her power to prevent this marriage, but the Bek forcefully resisted her efforts. When he returned from the battle at Bayazid, he was ready to go immediately and take the Armenian girl, but before he got a chance to do so, Khourshid sent Chavo and two loyal servants to steal Lala away (for that was the girl's name) and take her to another land. Chavo found Lala hiding in Father Marouk's house with her sister-in-law, Sara. Sara had long known about the Bek's intentions. On hearing of Khourshid's plan, she readily agreed to have Lala sent away from the village of O... Khourshid's two servants delivered Lala to Russian territory, and the Bek was reduced to a frustrated and helpless state. Khourshid privately gloated over this state of affairs, rejoicing that she had taken beautiful Lala out of her husband's hands. The two servants returned a few days later saying the girl had been safely delivered to Russia. Khourshid told Chavo to go away for a while and allow time for the Bek's anger to subside.

So fascinating was Chavo's story to her sister, but especially to Vartan, that no one noticed the Effendi had been listening with equal interest to it. When Chavo was finished with her account, the Effendi began to say something:

"Now I can die in peace. Lala is free…"

Vartan went up to him and supported his bobbing head, but it trembled, then fell back on the pillow again.

"'The starving donkey caught the smell of barley, but before he could find it, he gave up the ghost.'"

These would be the Effendi's last words. The two Kurdish women drew near also.

"He just died," said Vartan.

"The poor man," the two sisters said.

CHAPTER 37

The July sun was beating down. It seemed as if the entire atmosphere was charged with burning needles, glinting like a cloud of sparks, softly spreading out all over in waves. The heat was unbearable. The birds, weak and exhausted, had hidden themselves away in the densest foliage where not a single leaf stirred in the absence of a breeze. Only active were flies and bugs and microscopic gnats, buzzing about in their millions, entering people's mouths as they breathed, entering their noses and ears, stinging them with their poisonous bites which burned even more intensely than the scorching sun.

At this moment, ancient Vagharshapat presented an uncanny sight. Everywhere one looked, one saw an awesome mass of people: women and girls, old people and children; all half-naked, all destitute, and all deposited here together. The streets were full of beggars. All around the walls of the Echmiadzin monastery, and inside; all the way to the monastery of Gayaneh, to the outer fringes of the forest planted by the Catholicos, wherever there was a spot of shade that offered protection from the scorching rays of the sun; everywhere could be seen the same suffering, pitiful multitude—these, the refugees from Alashgert.

Having left their homes, their country, and all their possessions to flee the sword and fire of the Turks, three thousand Alashgertsi families had sought refuge here. There wasn't a house in Vagharshapat not thronged with ten or twenty such families. Barns, haylofts, animal pens were all filled with them. Feeding this vast number was not the only problem; they required medical care as well. Having left the coolness of their mountain homeland far behind, they were suddenly thrust into the hellish heat of Ararat province and fell victim to a host of diseases.

It was midday, the hour when peasants would take a break from their work in the fields and withdraw with their animals to some sheltered spot. Those more prosperous would take their rest in cozy rooms after an ample meal. One figure stood out from this multitude of Alashgertdsis who went begging from door to door, a young girl not more than sixteen years old. Her face had lost its natural color, like a rose that wilted on the verge of death. A deep sadness shone in her dark eyes; her pale lips revealed she was still in the grip of some terrible illness. This melancholy face, which at one time must have been quite beautiful, still retained an arresting charm despite its gauntness.

It seemed the demon of suffering had wished to play an evil trick on this beautiful person, wrapping her in tattered clothing and condemning her beauty and preciousness to obscurity. But this made her only more remarkable and worthy of compassion. Her old, worn-out clothing barely covered her half-naked body, and it seemed that each part of it had been given to her by a different person. Each piece was different in style and color from any other: one piece was wide, another narrow; one piece was too short, and another too long.

She walked with slow, tottering steps through one of the streets of the village. It was difficult to set her feet down on the ground, heated by the sun to the temperature of molten iron. Two little children accompanied her, and she led them through the street, one in each hand like little angels. She went a long way, her head down, stopping silently in front of houses, not bold enough to approach, mutely waiting for hours until someone inside would notice her and give her a crust of bread. She seemed unaccustomed to asking for anything, and gave the impression of someone who had been raised in privileged circumstances, yet now had fallen into an unusual state of affairs due to tragic events. More oppressive than the illness that was slowly depriving her of life was the loss of her former dignity and the moral torment she had endured, all of which combined to fill her heart with inconceivable suffering.

She continued on her way from house to house, but no one noticed her. Then, at last setting her pride aside, she approached a house and, finding the lady who lived there, spoke up timidly:

"A piece of bread…"

In her voice could be heard the full expression of a heart filled with pain and suffering.

"Get lost! Which one of you should I give it to first?" was the brusque reply she received from the woman.

The girl looked around and, indeed, saw that there were many others like her crowding about. She was on the verge of leaving, but stayed where she was for just one reason: Though she, herself, was starving, her only thought was for the two little children who had eaten nothing all day and for their mother who lay sick and hungry somewhere.

She wiped her tears away and was about to repeat her request when a little dog darted out from under the gate and began snapping at her clothing with its sharp teeth. Terrified, the girl went away, leaving part of her clothing in its teeth. The two children started screaming and their hearts almost burst.

The girl gathered her clothing up to her knees and set out toward the monastery. The crying and terror of the children came to an end when, with great happiness, they found a discarded melon rind in their path. One of them rushed forward, picked it up, and, after dusting it off, began nibbling at it. The other child tried to take it away, saying, "Give me some, I'm hungry too." A struggle between them ensued, and when the girl saw what was going on she took the rind and broke it in two, giving each of them an equal piece to calm them down.

At that moment, a young man was passing through the street in a great hurry, but on recognizing the girl and the two children, he approached them.

"You're not completely well yet," he said. "I gave you orders not to go out, but you're still out, walking around."

The girl was embarrassed and didn't know what to say. Indeed, she was not well—so emaciated that she could barely stand. The young man looked at the two little children nibbling on the melon rind. He snatched it from their hands and threw it away

"How can you eat that?" he asked.

Being bolder than the flustered girl, the children answered, "We are starving," the tears still in their eyes.

"Aren't they feeding you at the monastery?" the young man asked, turning to the girl.

Instead of answering, the girl looked down at the ground with her languid, beautiful eyes and said with great difficulty, "If only you could find somewhere else for us to stay so that we could leave the monastery."

"Well, it seems that no-good vartabed is treating you badly."

The girl made no reply but continued looking down as if trying to avert the young man's inquisitive gaze, careful to keep her face from betraying what she kept buried in her heart.

"I understand..." the young man said, greatly disturbed. "Go on now. You can't walk around in this heat. You're sick, and it will just make you weaker. I'll visit you in an hour and make sure you get the care you need. How is your sister-in-law doing?"

"She's not very well. She was quite uncomfortable last night," the girl answered sadly. Then turning her timid eyes to the young man, she asked, "You're not going to leave us in the monastery, are you, sir?"

"Very well then, I'll find someplace else for you," the young man answered and went off in haste, thinking to himself, "Poor creature. How soon you tired of being in the monastery..."

This young man was a doctor, the son of a wealthy landowner in Vagharshapat. Having just finished his studies at the University of St. Petersburg, he had thrown himself into the world like a knight who had newly joined his order and sought challenges to prove his heroism in the practice of his profession. The mass of refugees from Alashgert, with its multitude of sick people, opened a vast field of work before him. He was so full of pure intentions and undaunted fervor that he drew great satisfaction from his work in helping these suffering people. In him both professionalism and virtue were joined together. He not only charged nothing for his visits and medicines, but he took on responsibility for the lodging and feeding of the refugees. It was for this reason that the girl could appeal to him with such familiarity, beseeching him to arrange some other lodging for her.

After he had left her, the girl continued on her way back to the monastery. Weaving and tottering along, she could barely put one foot in front of the other. She stopped a few times and sat down to rest. Some men shouted to her from the taverns across from the monastery, offering her money. "Those men are worse than the Kurds," she thought to herself and stood up to continue on her way.

She passed through the gardens and by the main entrance to the monastery, then turned toward the western wall, coming to the gate which leads to the lake and the forest. She entered Ghazarabad through this entrance. On feast days, this part of the monastery was used to receive large numbers of pilgrims, but it was now filled with the refugees from Alashgert. She entered one of the cells in the interior. In this dank cavity lined with red brick and devoid of air or light, a woman lay on the floor without benefit of either mattress or bedstead, a thin layer of straw beneath her and a tattered sheet for a cover. The two little children ran up to hug their sick mother and kissed her bony hands. But she was asleep, or rather in an unconscious state, and she didn't respond to her children's caresses.

The girl told the children not to disturb their mother and to go outside and play. They went out as they were told and started playing just outside the door, fashioning things for themselves out of dirt and pebbles and bits of wood. The girl lay down on the bare floor, cushioned her lovely head with her hands, and gazed at the sick woman with tears in her eyes. She was so exhausted, so weak, so anguished that a little sleep would have been welcome to her; but she was so overcome by tears, she couldn't shut her pain-stricken eyes. She would have wished to close her eyes forever, never again to see the light of the world which, now, had become darkness to her. What kind of suffering had she not experienced? What torture had she not endured? She had lost everything that was dearest to her: her father, her brothers, her prosperous home—everything. Now, she wandered from door to door in a strange land, unprotected and condemned to a tragic fate. And now the person who had been her only support and protection in the world, the one person on whom all her hopes depended, was sick and might die tomorrow or the next day. What would become of her then? Who would take care of the poor children of an ill-fated mother? If only she were healthy, if only she could work, she would do anything, even the hardest work, to go on caring for these children. But she, too, was losing her strength, day by day wasting away, growing weaker and weaker, awaiting her own delayed end. As she lay where she was, assailed with all these thoughts, tears running down her pallid face, a disturbance suddenly erupted outside, and a cruel voice was heard and added to her anguish.

The children had fashioned little play huts for themselves on the ground near the door and had been enjoying themselves there. As they were playing, a fat-bellied monk wearing a black hood, black robe, and black look, came toward them—no light about him at all. He saw the two little children in his path, and roared at them, "Get inside you little rascals! Why are you making a mess on the ground?"

The children were a little slow getting out of his way, and had they not just managed to run inside with desperate cries, they would have been trampled beneath the monk's feet. The wailing of the children roused their mother to consciousness. She put her arms around them, comforting them without knowing what had made them cry. Just then, the monk appeared in the doorway with his severe look.

"Get out of here right now!" he shouted angrily. "Didn't I tell you several days ago that you had to find somewhere else to stay? But you're still here!"

Whomever he thought he was addressing with such words, the children's mother didn't hear him. She just clung to her children as if this were the first time she had seen them. She had been unconscious for two days, yet at the sound of her children's voices, she awoke. Whom was the monk addressing? No one in the room could hear or understand what he was saying. Gripped by terror at the sound of his voice, the girl lost her own, and the frightened little children hid themselves away, trembling, in their mother's arms.

The monk's tirade was interrupted by someone else's voice:

"What is all this bluster about, Holy Father?"

"Hello, Doctor. How are you? Are you doing well?" the monk said, smiling now and acting less bellicose.

"Never mind about how I am," the doctor replied, looking the holy father straight in the eyes, "Just state your demands, Holy Father. Why are you giving these poor people such a bad time?"

"You can see for yourself that I'm not making any demands; it's just that they should find other lodging and clear out of here. You know as well as I they weren't supposed to stay here for more than two days. New refugees are flowing in every day. Those who arrived earlier have to make room for them."

"And where shall they go? You can see they're dying."

"What can I do? Those are my orders."

The holy father was the monastery's official host, a buffoonish, talkative monk whom everyone felt free to mock, especially the young doctor who took particular pleasure in upbraiding the clergy.

"You're not going to fool me with that kind of talk," answered the doctor. "Tell me the truth, Holy Father, do you see a ray of light in that girl's eyes?"

"Oh, good heavens, what are you talking about?"

"Just get out of my way, out of my way!" the doctor said and went inside.

The doctor's visit was a great comfort to the miserable family. He gave them medicines and instructions for their use. He let them know he had arranged for them to move into their own place and would be able to rest and make a decent living there.

"But quickly, please, if possible," the sick mother beseeched the doctor, her voice full of gratitude.

"Don't worry, you'll be taken there in a few minutes," he answered, then left to attend to other patients in the monastery.

"So, Lala, don't you see, my child?" the sick woman said to the young woman, now sobbing, her hands over her eyes. "At the moment of greatest trial, God doesn't abandon the unfortunate, but sends a consoling angel. Don't weep, my child. A bright morning will follow the dark and stormy night. The day will come when you will find your happiness again…"

"After all we have been through, dear Sara? After all that, there is nothing left for me but to die…" said Lala, her anguished eyes welling with tears.

Their conversation came to an end when two men entered. These were the doctor's assistants, and they had brought some bread and a meal with them for the family. They had also brought a package that contained women's clothing for Lala and Sara, and clothing for the children. Sara and Lala had no appetite, but the two little children fell voraciously on the meal. The two men waited outside until they had finished eating.

Lala put on her new clothing, then helped Sara out of her rags and dressed the half-naked children. Now transformed in appearance, the family left the corrupt atmosphere of the monastery and set out for the new lodging the doctor had arranged for them.

CHAPTER 38

Now "The Illuminator's Gale" began to blow, and the oppressive heat of the day gave way to the cool of evening. That is the blessed wind that blows every summer day not only in Vagharshapat, but through the entire region of Ararat. It is for good reason that our ancient folk tradition holds that our patriarch, the Illuminator,[45] instituted this wind to protect his people from sickness.

After their midday rest, the monks of the monastery left their cells and came out in pairs to enjoy a walk around Nerses's lake, passing through its beautiful promenades sheltered beneath the dense forest canopy. It was to be noted that they didn't form into groups, but rather went about either in pairs or individually. In this, they showed themselves to be people who remain aloof from social contact out of their fear of each other. Suspicion, disunity, and disloyalty kept them apart from each other—and this took the name of monastic brotherhood.

The lake was situated on a man-made plateau made up of sculptured rock. Beneath it, and extending to the monastery of Gayaneh was an ancient cemetery. New graves were being dug in various places and, elsewhere, those that already contained bodies were being covered over. Shovels and picks were at work everywhere. A priest muttering and reciting prayers, or in fact reciting nothing at all, ran from one grave to the next to carry out the burial rite. All this transpired within a deep silence. There was no crying of friends, nor tears of family members to help the deceased on their way to the next world. They seemed very grateful that these sufferers had at last been released from a painful life and found rest in the grave.

"So many have died," said one monk to his companion as they walked along together.

"It doesn't make any difference," responded the other monk coldly. "The Kurds and Turks should have killed them where they were. Here they are dying their own death. But we have strayed from the subject," he said, referring to their conversation earlier. "I must repeat, you can't believe him. He got close to us and acted friendly and familiar, and gave us a thousand and one little distractions to think about, but that was all phony. He was just trying to get secrets out of us however he could. He's a spy—nothing but a spy—and that's why he gets such a warm welcome in Upper Jerusalem.[46] He has very high hopes of soon becoming a bishop and the prelate of some wealthy diocese."

"Everything you say is true, except that he won't get the last two. 'The Fourth' is very liberal with his promises, but very stingy in delivering on them. They only want to lead the fool on to suit themselves. After that, they'll cut off his tail and leave an opening for someone they like better… Look, they just arrived with more bodies…"

"For the love of God, stop talking about your dead people… But he's not the kind of fox that can be tricked that easily."

"'A smart fox can fall feet first into a trap, too.'"

"Quiet down until they're gone…"

Two other monks appeared on the opposite side of the promenade, and they, too, suspended their conversation as they approached. They were members of the same brotherhood. After they had gone by, the former pair of monks continued their conversation:

"We have to call for the auction now. This is the very best time to do it."

"Why?"

"Because, it's clear to us who took over those church properties through taxation: Mssrs. N... M... and KH... who were always the excisemen for them. Now each of them has set off in pursuit of his own affairs, one of them to Alexandropol, one to Iktir, and one, the devil only knows where the hell he ended up. We can take advantage of their absence. If we announce the auction now, it's very clear the whole tax will fall on Sadayelian, who will then take over under his own name, and, of course, secretly in league with us."

"But as far as I know, Mr. Sadayelian doesn't have enough money to take over the mortgage."

"I'm aware of that, too, but that won't prevent success. We'll provide him with the mortgage money, and he will pay it."

"Do you have enough?"

"I have bonds accruing interest."

"That won't do any good. Say we raise the question of the auction in the next meeting. I'm afraid the higher-ups will interfere."

"But they can't. Aren't those *hos-hos*[47] trying to do exactly the same thing we're trying to do? If "Little Devil" meddles in it, I'll whisper in his ear, and he'll quiet down immediately."

And thus, some among the monks were discussing the intrigues afoot in the monastery, offering their secret speculations to each other; yet no one paid any attention to what was happening right around them; no one was concerned with the Alashgertzis who had been uprooted from their native land, exiles without protection or care, being destroyed like flies. No one gave a thought to what had brought about this mass exodus, or what the fate of these unfortunate people would be in a strange and unfamiliar land.

A few monks had gathered together in the forest and were sitting on beautiful Persian rugs, enjoying their evening tea as was their custom. Not far off, young novices were murmuring among themselves, laughing and joking and teasing each other as they went about the large task of serving the tea. There was cream, butter, white bread, rum, and every other sort of delicacy. The cool of the evening and the pure forest air had opened the holy fathers' appetites. They ate and drank and enjoyed themselves without a thought for the hundreds of families who lay starving on the damp floor of the same forest.

"This is really good rum; it has such a wonderful aroma. Where did you get it, Holy Father?" one monk asked another, quaffing a cup of tea with rum.

"Where did I get it?" responded the holy father who had brought the fragrant beverage with him from his room. "Don't you know that my little cell is the kind of sacred spot where offerings arrive on their own?"[48]

"I know… It's a wonderful gift to have such magnetism," said the monk who had asked the question.

The sun had already set. The gloom in the forest was gradually deepening, though the clouds were still gilded with the last rays of the sun. "The Illuminator's Gale" had subsided, and the leaves in the forest stirred lightly with an enchanting rustle. The deep silence of the forest was broken only by the occasional sound of desolate sighs. Night was approaching. Painful memories are stirred in the darkness: out in the open, spread out on the ground, the naked and hungry Alashgertzis were only now beginning to feel the full horror of their situation, like a man who wakes up from a terrible dream, realizing that he once had wealth but must now live by begging; realizing that he once had his own house and home, but now must live under the open skies; realizing that he once had children, but that they are no longer there. And where had they gone? Who took them away? What had become of them? He has no way of knowing. They had all been lost in some terrible and tangled set of circumstances in which mother forgets child, in which brother forgets sister, in which a young man loses his wife—a situation in which all, withering beneath the sword and fire of the Turks, sought to save their own necks. All bore unhealable wounds in their hearts; all had lost something that was most precious and irreplaceable in the world to them. This was why, on this night, Vagarshapat reverberated with the sighs of the exiled, all in mourning together—in a mourning that could never be consoled.

At this hour, a tall young man was passing through the forest, looking closely at the refugees. He would approach and talk to them, then continue on his way. His grave, pensive expression, his virile face, his bold and self-confidant manner automatically drew the attention of the people in the forest. He emerged from the forest and set out toward the monastery of Gayaneh and its cemetery. Work was ongoing there… More burials were taking place…

The young man heard some singing:

> The Bulbul's put some shoes on his feet,
> And is seeking the Rose with a love so sweet…

"Go to hell," thought the young stranger as he continued on his way.

This song emanated from the middle of the forest where the monks, gladdened by rum, were bringing their evening excursion to an end.

The young man went to the lake. Here, too, looking like black phantoms, several monks were enjoying themselves. But one sat still and alone, like someone in mourning, finding solace in this position where no one asks questions nor meddles with the suffering in his heart. His somber, sun-burned face and his worn clothing indicated that he was one of the refugees—poverty-stricken. None of the comfortable, neatly-attired monks came near him—as if afraid of being soiled by his clothing, though it covered a man who had a great many fine and noble qualities. Seeing him in the darkness, the young man approached.

"Ach, Holy Father Hovhaness, that's you!"

"Ach, Vartan!" the monk cried out, hugging him.

This monk was both the abbot of the monastery of St. Hovhaness and the prelate of Alashgert. He had come to Russian territory with the exodus, because he didn't want to be separated from his people.

The vartabed and Vartan sat down on a rock which served as a lakeside seat.

"When did you arrive here?" the vartabed asked.

"Today, this very hour," Vartan answered, taking a look around to make sure no one overheard him.

"Didn't you see anyone?"

"Not so far. How could you find anyone in that jumbled mass of people? I was really hoping to find Melik-Mansour. I had heard he was among the exiles."

"I saw him two days ago," the vartabed responded. "He must have made it to Yerevan by now. I believe he was going to meet with some gentlemen there who were planning to call a meeting about the plight of the refugees."

"There has already been a special meeting in Tiflis about them," said Vartan.

"Well, the one in Yerevan must be connected with it," the vartabed replied.

"How is the work going here?" Vartan asked.

"Very poorly," the vartabed responded with sadness. "I've put up with this place for one whole week, and no one has paid any attention to me; no one has cared to ask what tragic circumstances brought us here. They promised I would be taken to the quarters of the Catholicosate and interviewed, but, unfortunately, the days have just gone by. I was compelled to present the entire story of the suffering people and their exodus in writing, and I had hopes that after doing so, I would be summoned to present an oral account. That effort led nowhere, either. Can they be so indifferent and uncaring? I have evidence that out of three thousand families, one thousand five-hundred have died from sickness or starvation up to this point. Those who are left will also die for sure if their condition continues as it is."

As terrible as this last news was, Vartan wasn't shocked; he considered this quite natural. He had long known what devastating consequences such exile entailed.

"Are all the exiles concentrated only here in Vagharshapat?" he asked.

"No, they came to Vagharshapat from Iktir, and from here they've dispersed in every direction. They're scattered all over—from Sourmalou, to New Bayazid, to Old Nakhichevan. You'll find them everywhere, in every town."

"How are the inhabitants here treating their exiled brethren?"

"They've been very generous. They've offered them lodging, food, and clothing, and they've spared nothing to help them. It must be said that the people who live here, themselves, are upon very hard times. The war has driven up the cost of everything. But the refugees need medical care more than food. They're suffering from a host of rampant diseases."

The darkness of night enveloped the monastery grounds. The monks had withdrawn into their cells, but the troubling song could still be heard, coming from the depths of the forest:

> The Bulbul's put some shoes on his feet,
> And is seeking the Rose with a love so sweet...

The vartabed stood up. "Where are you going now?" he asked Vartan.

"I really don't know."

"Then stay with me."

"I wouldn't want to be seen around here."

"No one will recognize you in the monastery now."

CHAPTER 39

Holy Father Hovhaness's room was on the top floor of Ghazarabad monastery. Vartan felt a shudder go through his body as he stepped into this monastery once again. It had been more than ten years since he had left it, and now very trying circumstances had brought him back. What was it about this place that had such a disturbing effect on him, this community cut off from the world and devoting all its time to prayer and monastic discipline? He remembered his youth—that foolish and idle youth he had spent here. He remembered that somber past, a mere glimpse of which now filled him with revulsion and horror.

Vartan couldn't hide his inner distress from Holy Father Hovhaness, and the vartabed asked him with concern, "What's the matter? Why are you so quiet?"

"Nothing. It's just that sometimes I'm overwhelmed with meaningless thoughts."

The two men sat on a bed in the vartabed's little room. Across the room was a simple table with a samovar set on it, heating up over a candle. The holy father poured two cups of tea, handed one to Vartan, then started to sip his own. The hot beverage was soothing to Vartan's frayed nerves.

They sat in dreary silence for a long time. It wasn't until they struck on a subject of equal interest to both of them that they fell into conversation.

"What is the attitude here toward 'the work?'" Vartan asked.

"I'll tell you a little story that says it all," responded his host. "A vartabed arrived here recently from Turkish Armenia to be ordained a bishop. (He is still here, and perhaps you will meet him.)[49] From his very first day here he spoke about the condition of the Armenians where he came from, depicting their situation in the darkest of colors, reporting the barbarities of the Kurds, the violent oppression of the Turks; and he cited a thousand and one examples of atrocities carried out in Armenia. It was out of the question to doubt his stories; everything he said was supported by irrefutable evidence. Yet, as soon as this man came under the sway of the hos-hos he changed his tune. He then took to praising the humane kindliness of the Turks, defending their sense of justice, and expressing admiration for their decency and generosity. What could he do? If he didn't betray his own conscience, something horrible and detestable for him to do, he would throw the possibility of getting the bishopric he wanted into jeopardy.

"I'll give you another example. There was another vartabed from Turkish Armenia. The Kurds raided and plundered his monastery, and he came here to seek help to protect it. This man depicted the suffering of his people in even starker terms, both in regard to government officials and the Kurdish Derebeys. When the hos-hos got word of what he had been saying, not only did they turn a deaf ear to the request for protection that he had come to make, but they ordered him to leave the premises. This poor fellow was also forced to change his tune. After that he was accepted with respect, and he forgot about his monastery, he forgot his flock, and he didn't give another thought to the atrocities committed by the Kurds. It doesn't stop there, either. On a certain holiday, he toasted the Sultan's health on the very day the Armenians were being massacred in Bayazid and Alashgert. After all this, you should have a very clear picture of how 'the work' is going here."

Vartan couldn't believe his ears. It was as if he had heard all of this in a dream. He couldn't conceive of a degree of callousness that reached the point of treason itself. In this awesome moment of crisis for the nation— with its life and future hanging by a thread that could be cut at any moment, suddenly casting it into an everlasting abyss—the eyes of the entire nation were turned toward Ararat for salvation, and they were met with the cold indifference of those who should have been the guardians of the nation, but, instead, were found standing on the side of the murderous enemy…

"They all have the same outlook?" Vartan asked with exasperation in his voice.

"No, just the hos-hos. They see the Turkish government as fair and honest in every way; and if Armenians protest or show any sign of disaffection with it, they consider that completely illegitimate and disloyal."

"Obviously," said Vartan. "They are just so many Tomas Effendis. Tomas Effendis always benefit from Turkish misrule. If only they had followed the example set by the patriarchs Nerses,[50] Khrimian, and Narbey,[51] whose names will always be honored in Armenian history…"

"That kind of talk is very foolish, my friend," responded the old vartabed. "I'll have you know that this very day, if they got the chance, they would wipe out everything Nerses has accomplished, and even now, perhaps… They're doing everything they can to portray Nerses and his followers as charlatans, saying that they're misleading the nation and don't have the interests of the Armenian people at heart, and—which is preposterous— that they're all simply willing tools in the hands of various European representatives who are trying to lay more sins at Turkey's door. They have nothing but scorn for the gullibility of those who expect anything to come of Nerses's efforts. They say that making more demands on Turkey amounts to insolence on the part of the Armenians, and that Turkey has given Armenians all it can, and that the Armenians deserve no more. They maintain that if there is still anything lacking to the Armenians, the Turks will graciously provide it for them, being a decent people, and that there's no point in embarrassing the government."

"Are you saying the whole order takes that position?" Vartan cried out angrily.

Instead of giving an immediate answer, the old vartabed went outside the room and peered around in the darkness, then came back in and sat down, saying in a very low voice, "We've been very careless in our conversation. In this place, the walls have ears. The room next door belongs to the host of the monastery. He has a nose like the devil, and if he heard anything, he'll tattle in the morning."

"I was asking about the viewpoint of the ordinary monks," Vartan said, repeating himself without paying attention to what the old vartabed had just said.

"Aside from the hos-hos, not everyone in the order takes the Turkish side. There are many who are good men and have the purest intentions and are clearly willing to make any sacrifice to relieve the suffering of the Armenians in Turkey, but only if…"

"If the hos-hos allow them to."

"Yes. What can the poor people do? They are so hemmed in, they can't even speak freely, let alone take any kind of action. There's a certain Mangouni here who is a complete monster, a person who keeps everyone down under his weight and stifles them."

"But I still don't understand what kind of politics this is, to see an entire people ground down by Turkish violence, and on the verge of extinction, and then to side with the destroyers."

"It's a complete riddle to me, too. I simply don't understand it," the vartabed responded with perplexity.

"But how do they account for the exodus from Alashgert or the massacre of Armenians in Bayazid? How do they explain the burning of Van?"

"They always have ready-made justifications for what the Turks do. They lay the blame on the Armenians, saying the Armenians are a restive, malcontent people. They have a saying, 'It's not the wolf's fault if the sheep gets mad at him.' As for the mass exodus from Alashgert, they see in that situation not the sword and the fire of the Turks and Kurds driving an entire people out of their native land. On the contrary, they make every effort to prove that some secret and powerful party is responsible for forcing those poor people out. As to how false that view is, you know better than anyone, Vartan, since you have been in the middle of 'the work' from the very beginning…"

"Given all that, Holy Father, I don't understand what hopes have kept you here. Please tell me, what protection or support can you expect under these circumstances?"

"None, I know that myself—none. But what can I do? To whom can I appeal? Where can I go? I'm totally at a loss."

"Take your case to the Armenian public."

The old vartabed didn't respond immediately, but after several moments of reflection, he said, as if talking to himself, "It's very difficult to make things clear right now… But there will come a day when time will lay bare the perverse reality of this situation…"

It seemed these words were pressed forth from the poor monk's heart with drops of blood on them. So despondent was he, caught in such extreme distress, that he couldn't suppress his true feelings. And what would have been the point of trying to be secretive with Vartan? Vartan was no stranger to him. He had worked with Vartan, and they had shared much counsel together.

They returned to the subject of the exiles. The old prelate of Alashgert recounted the sufferings of his imperiled people; he depicted the blows they had suffered, and detailed the measures that could be taken to save them from complete annihilation.

"I'm amazed at the enormous number of sick people among the refugees," Vartan said, breaking in on the vartabed's account. "Over half of them are sick. How did this happen?"

"If you heard every frightful detail of what happened in the course of their exodus, you'd be amazed that any of them survived at all. That is a miracle, a genuine miracle. But neither my memory nor my power to speak is sufficient to tell you everything that happened. I will just give you a few examples.

"After the siege of Bayazid—the details of which are well-known to you—General Der-Ghugasov was forced to withdraw his army. In that moment, he was able to accomplish two great feats: on one side he had to battle the enormous Turkish army, far outnumbering his small force; and on the other side, he had the job of saving all the Armenians of Alashgert and Bayazid from slaughter. Accomplishing these two purposes required the very highest level of strategic expertise—and he proved he had it. So effective was he in slowing the awesome advance of the Turkish army that, by the time they arrived, the Armenians had been able to flee. But they had the smallest amount of time to do so, and were unprepared for exile.

"They got sudden word that the Russian army had to retreat, and that they should flee; if they stayed, the Turks would exterminate them all. This word traveled through the provinces like lightning. The people were gripped with terror. The enemy was at their door, and there was no time for hesitation. They would have to leave their beloved fatherland. I can hardly describe that horrible night when the people were separated from home and hearth, overwhelmed with fright and alarm. They had just one night in which to make their escape. They left most of their animals in the fields. They couldn't be brought with them. Fathers didn't wait for their sons to come home. Brothers forgot about their brothers. All their household goods and heavy articles were either left where they were or set on fire. Mothers carried their small children, while fathers, loaded up with as much property as they could carry, took their sons by the hand and fled. Very few families had carts, because they had all been taken away to be used by the army. There wasn't a moment to lose; the enemy was hot on their heels. Whoever stayed behind was lost to barbarous atrocities. Those who fled considered themselves saved, but then they were confronted with new misfortune, even more merciless than the Kurds or the Turks—starvation and disease.

"This sickness came from the terrible suffering the people endured in their exodus. A trip that would normally take a few weeks had to be taken by them in just a few days, nonstop, without rest. Women and girls, young and old, all on foot. Many of them became weak and exhausted and were left behind on the road. Who could give any consideration to one's relatives, or friends, or even beloved children? Everyone was in the grip of profound anguish; everyone had lost their heart and feelings. Add to that the hunger and thirst and the unfamiliar climate of a foreign land, and you will see how easily they got sick. In order to avoid contact with the enemy, we were led over the most devilishly difficult mountain roads, something extremely hard for the women and children. So that is why one-fourth of the exiles were just left to die on the road. In short, the exile of the Armenian slaves to Isfahan under Shah Abbas, depicted with such terrible colors in our historical records, was just an ordinary event by comparison."

As the holy father was telling this story, Vartan was preoccupied with something else, and he had barely paid any attention at all. His thoughts were directed to Lala, his beloved. She certainly must have been among those exiles, subjected to the same terrors. Though Chavo had told him that her mistress, Khourshid, had made arrangements for Lala to be taken to Russian territory, her Kurdish escorts could not possibly have crossed the Russian border, being subjects of a foreign nation. Therefore Lala and her sister-in-law must have been caught up with the rest of the exiles. But how could they be found? And were they still alive? These were the questions that were tormenting Vartan now.

"Holy Father, don't you know something about old Khacho's family? They must be among the refugees. How could I find them?"

"It would be very difficult to find them, because the refugees have spread out to so many different locations. But their parish priests and village leaders are with them, and I've charged them with the task of making a record of all their names, where they're from, and how many there are from each town, so that it's possible to know how best to meet their needs. As soon as I get these records, it will be a simple matter for me to determine which group old Khacho's family is in."

"When will they be delivered to you?"

"I don't know for sure—tomorrow or the next day."

This "tomorrow or the next day," seemed an eternity to Vartan, and he spent the entire night in unbearable distress.

CHAPTER 40

The soft, harmonious pealing of the monastery bells heralded the morning rites. The more privileged of the monks still slept in their cosy beds, while those less privileged hurried off to God's temple to pray.

On this particular morning, Holy Father Hovhaness had arisen quite early and gone out, leaving Vartan asleep in his room. He didn't go to pray but to visit the refugees and see how they were, as was his practice. This morning, the suffering he encountered among them was so heart-rending that he couldn't even finish his rounds. Everywhere he looked, he saw horrible scenes: entire families sick, uncared for, collapsed in the filth of various barns. Not a single one of them had remained healthy enough to be of any use to the others.

Filled with despair, he made his way back to the monastery determined at any cost to go this very day to the Catholicosate and plea for help for his dying people. Just then a carriage was passing by, and the passenger ordered it to stop on seeing the Holy Father.

"I have good news!" the passenger said, approaching the old vartabed. "The prefect of Yerevan has established a committee to help the refugees, and some dependable people were elected to serve on it. There's also good news from Tiflis. There, likewise, a committee is hard at work. They've promised to send money and medicine."

"That's encouraging," the old monk replied. "Here, too, there are efforts to write to the representatives of the spiritual leadership to collect donations."

"Who will do the writing?"

In answer, the old monk motioned toward the monastery.

"That won't do much good," the man answered. "Very little of what they collect will get to the Alashgertzis..."

This new arrival was Melik-Mansour.

"You cheered me up with your good news. Now it's my turn to cheer you up," the Holy Father said.

"How so?"

"Vartan is here—in my room."

"Really? How did that devil get out? I didn't think people could come back from the other world. Let's go."

The two men made their way to the monastery. On their way, Melik-Mansour asked the vartabed a question.

"Do you know Vartan well?"

"I've known him for over five years. He has a reputation as a bold smuggler in our province. But for a long time, no one really understood that he sought no profit for himself in what he did. All he did was transport weapons and pass them out free to the villagers. If he brought merchandise with him, it was just to disguise his real business. He had good intentions, but difficult conditions prevented the success of his efforts..."

"I only got to meet with him on a few occasions," responded Melik-Mansour, "But up to this day, I've found no one who inspired my sympathy as much as that fervent young man. I saw that as brave and callous and bloody as he was in his deeds, all this was exceeded by his nobility, his decency, and his loyalty in friendship."

"Besides that, Vartan is also outstanding in the satanic sharpness of his mind. In his lifetime he's done a great deal, more than most men could have accomplished in a hundred years; yet he's extremely modest in everything he does, and he covers it all up in the guise of an ordinary person."

On waking up in the morning, Vartan found himself alone in the Holy Father's room. The sun's rays penetrated the windows of the little room and filled it with light, but the hot air was stifling. He went to one of the windows and opened it. The crisp, cool air from the outside flowed refreshingly across his inflamed face. But it seemed something weighed heavily on his heart; something was still oppressing him. He waited awhile for his host to return, but he was late. Vartan had become quite impatient by this time and went outside to breathe the open air. Not wishing to be seen or recognized by anyone in the monastery, he left by a back door that opened up facing the lake. Here he encountered an old bishop whom he immediately recognized, one of the elders of the monastery.

"Greetings, Grandad," Vartan said to him. (The old bishop was called "Grandad" by everyone in the monastery.) The old man sat facing the summer sun, warming his chilly bones. He resembled those Hindu fakirs who neither bathe, brush their hair, trim their fingernails, nor wear decent clothing, regarding those things as sinful. Hearing the young man's voice, he shaded his eyes from the sun and looked up.

"Your voice is familiar, son, but my eyes are too weak to see who you are," the old bishop responded.

"I am Vartan."

"Long may you live, son! Come, let me kiss you. How big you've grown!"

Vartan received the old bishop's kiss.

"Sit down here, son, near me. That's right. What a fine man you've turned into, son. Do you remember how you used to sneak into my room like a cat and steal my fruit candy? You were little then, very little."

"I do remember, Grandad. It was here that I learned to steal…"

"Well, son, who doesn't steal nowdays? They all do. Honesty has become as rare as the swallows' milk—you won't find it anywhere. Less than two days ago, some damned burglars stole several hundred rubles from my room. I was saving it for the benefit of my soul. How they found it, I'll never know. The devil himself couldn't have found it. I hid it behind some boards in the ceiling. But demons could take lessons from them. Oh, the scoundrels, the scoundrels!"

Money being stolen from Grandad's room was such an old story that Vartan had no interest in it. This old man, almost a hundred years of age, had never spent a cent in his life, but simply collected whatever came into his hands. When his treasure had reached into the hundreds or thousands, suddenly some unseen hand would gain entry and take it all away. But the latest series of burglaries had turned Grandad into quite the expert in such matters; he had little hiding holes all around his room, and would put a little of his money in each one. For this reason, there had never been an instance in which he had lost all his money at one time, though to hear him talk he had.

Grandad was an entirely typical miser, and Vartan had known him since childhood as someone whose miserliness had acquired legendary proportions in the monastery. He was considered one of the wealthier monks, but was distinguished in one respect from them, in that he had amassed his wealth by sheer frugality, whereas the others had amassed theirs by stealth.

"You really have a great love for money, Grandad. What are you going to do with it all?" Vartan asked.

"Well, son, there is a fox that can swallow a camel, but it is the wolf who has a bad name. Who doesn't love money nowadays? This is a time for money. Everyone is after it."

The old bishop took a snuff box out of his breast pocket, opened it with trembling fingers, and saw that it was empty. This might have been the hundredth time he had done so and every time had seen that it was empty, yet he still couldn't believe his eyes; he thought it might have been filled again by some miracle.

"That damned vartabed Simon—you must know him—I gave him twenty kopeks and my tobacco tin to go to town and bring me some snuff. He went, but he must have kept both the money and the tin. Don't you have any snuff, Vartan?"

"I don't use it, Grandad."

A cigarette butt had fallen on the floor not far from Grandad's bed. He noticed it, rose to his feet, went over and picked it up. He tore the paper away and threw it to one side; then, emptying the charred tobacco into the palm of his hand, he crushed it and rubbed it in his quaking fingers, then sucked the acrid dust into his nostrils.

"Are they taking such poor care of you here that they don't even give you enough money for snuff, Grandad?"

"Ah, my son, this world of mine has changed so much. What happened to the era of Nerses the Sublime? In those days there was love; there was the great and the small. But these days, everything has been turned upside down. Whoever can tell skillful lies and deceive people will go forward. Who cares about what people like us have to say? These days, 'there are chickens who lay iron eggs.'"

Grandad was one of Nerses's most devoted followers. On his lips, the name of this Catholicos meant sainthood, being a man worthy of eternal remembrance. Whenever Grandad was confronted with unpleasant, disturbing circumstances, it was his wont to recall the days of Nerses, which, to him, were the Golden Age of Echmiadzin.

And now, transported by deep feelings, he pointed to the beautiful lake and explained why Nerses had created it. He pointed out some ruins near the lake which had been a paper factory, built to eliminate the need for importing paper from elsewhere, but now a place used by the nearby villagers to keep their donkeys. He pointed out another set of ruins near the lake where a silk factory had been, standing in a large part of the forest that the majestic patriarch had ordered planted in mulberry trees to serve its needs. Remembering that forest, the old monk couldn't hold back his tears any longer, and went on to recount that Patriarch Nerses loved his trees as a father loves his children. Whenever Nerses went into the forest, he carried pruning shears to cut away unwanted branches; he knew each tree and how much it had grown that year, and, seeing that, he rejoiced like a father seeing how much his child has grown.

Seeing that this story was going to go on and on, Vartan sought some excuse to leave.

"Lend me your ear, Vartan," Grandad said.

Vartan bent his ear to the old man's mouth.

"Get away from here right away, son; you're not looked upon with favor here."

"But no one has even seen me yet, Grandad."

"It's enough that one person saw you. I heard some evil talk about you."

"But your hearing isn't good enough, Grandad. How could you have heard anything like that?"

"Grandad's hearing is only bad when it comes to things that don't concern him, but in the case of things that are important, he hears them instantly."

Laughing, Vartan walked away. Grandad called to him.

"Listen, Vartan, if you go to town, don't forget to get some snuff for me. You saw that I was out of it."

At this moment, Melik-Mansour appeared with Holy Father Hovhaness.

"What were you talking about with Grandad?" the latter asked Vartan.

"He's the only good man here," Vartan said, then turned to Melik-Mansour.

"I was hoping to talk with you in private. Do you know of a house where we could talk?"

"Yes, I do," answered Melik-Mansour.

Vartan didn't fall prey to any doubts about what Grandad had told him, since, in general, he was already doing everything he could to stay clear of the monastery. Furthermore, he was still worried about Lala. He had to find her. He had to get information about her. He asked Holy Father Hovhaness if he had received any word from his priests about the Alashgertzis.

"I got word that they'll be here by lunch time today and bring their records with them. I'll let you know right away."

"Do you know where we'll be?" asked Melik-Mansour.

"Yes," answered the holy father.

"Then let's go, Vartan."

Just at that moment a small group of people appeared in the square, moving slowly toward the cemetery—some Alashgertzis carrying a coffin. There was no priest, because the priest was already at the cemetery. He never left his post there, since new coffins were arriving one after the other. Three women were walking along with the coffin, one of them leaning on the other two. She wasn't crying, and there were no tears in her eyes. She was in some terrible stupor, such as happens to one's heart when one's feelings collapse under the weight of an unexpected blow. She appeared to be a close relative of the deceased. Two little children were trailing along, grasping her skirt, and crying.

No one from Vagharshapat accompanied the coffin, except for the young physician who is already familiar to us. This young man stood out from the group of destitute, half-naked mourners.

Vartan and Melik-Mansour noticed this pathetic funeral procession from a distance, but paid it no particular attention. One encountered such scenes here every day, every minute, and they had already become entirely routine events.

CHAPTER 41

On seeing Melik-Mansour it seemed that Vartan temporarily forgot the intense pain that had filled his heart. Moreover, he had been considerably heartened by the hope Holy Father Hovhaness held out that once the reports from the various Alashgertzi priests and peasants were presented, crucial information on the whereabouts of Khacho's family would be provided to him. With this information, Vartan counted on finding Lala and comforting her in her exile. But these feelings were only the outcome of a searing grief that bordered on numbness.

Melik-Mansour guided Vartan toward a house located in one of the oldest streets of Vagharshapat. Although the houses here were small and quite run-down, they had enormous yards which spread out in the shade of fruit trees.

"You won't be too pleased with where I'm taking you," said Melik-Mansour to Vartan.

"That doesn't matter," said Vartan in an off-hand manner. "I just wanted some information about Mr. Salman. I assume we won't be disturbed there."

"Not at all."

They arrived and knocked at the door. An old woman answered. They entered, and the door was closed behind them.

"Well, Grandma, I brought you a new guest," said Melik-Mansour.

"So I see…" the old woman said.

"Bring us some wine right away, Grandma. We're very thirsty,"

Then, Melik-Mansour went up very close to her and said, "If you let anyone else in, I'll have your soul."

The old woman nodded her head knowingly and disappeared.

The two young men entered a small but tidy room which was furnished in a half-asiatic, half-european style. They sat down at a small table. A few moments later a young woman entered with soft steps, and, without saying a word, placed a bottle of wine and two glasses on the table before them. She then left as quietly as she had entered. Her head being covered in the Armenian style, all that was visible of her face were her two dark eyes set beneath the arch of her eyebrows. But this was enough to give evidence of her beauty.

Melik-Mansour filled the glasses with wine.

"I'm glad that most of our monasteries have been built in remote mountains, valleys, and wild places, far from human habitation. There you won't run into the kind of scoundrels and immoral youth that you find here in Vagharshapat. You'll find no women anywhere with morals as loose as the women here. For instance, that pretty woman who just came and went so quietly and modestly is a monk's sweetheart. I had thought a monastery would at least preserve a certain level of religious commitment, but here no one believes in anything. The conduct of the monks scandalizes the people, and they lose their faith. Protestantism has already begun to make inroads here. You must have seen any number of beautiful houses as you came through the streets. If you look closer, you'll see that most of them are occupied by the near or distant relatives of monks, people who were poor when they arrived here, but now are rich, thanks to the monastery. To tell the truth, I can't bear to see such enormous sums wasted when every kopek is so precious to us. We have a thousand and one needs; money is needed for everyone. The nation's treasury in Bolis is empty. The patriarch there can't cover his expenses. Yet, he has so many projects piling up on him that delay in their implementation could well result in irreversible loss for the nation. Despite that, I don't see the possibility of reconciliation between the patriarchs of Bolis and Echmiadzin. Mangouni lost twenty-five thousand in investments, and, according to what I heard, he recently sent thirty-thousand for the devil only knows what. Yet, the Armenian patriarch, our only active agent, doesn't have a cent…"

"This wine is sour," said Vartan, interrupting.

"Weren't you listening to me?" asked Melik-Mansour irritably.

"I heard you. The patriarch is out of money…"

"It's impossible to have a conversation like this…"

"What is there to talk about? I only know one thing: any people that pins all its hopes on clerics is bound to lose everything in the end."

The young woman entered again, approached with soft steps, and set down two saucers of dessert. This time, the veil that had previously revealed only her eyes was pulled back, revealing her rosy lips.

"Bring us another carafe of wine, but not the same as before," said Melik-Mansour. The young woman left, once more without uttering a word.

"I'm surprised you picked a place like this to stay in," quipped Vartan.

"If you really want to learn something about a monk, you have to get acquainted with his sweetheart," said Melik-Mansour with a laugh. "Besides, I get very useful information from the people who gather here in the evening."

"Especially about the monastery, no doubt," added Vartan sarcastically. "But, for now, let's leave aside this talk of the monastery and talk about our work. I wanted to know what became of Mr. Salman and what happened in my absence. I'm still in the dark, and even though Holy Father Hovhaness told me a great deal, I didn't get the kind of information from him that I really need, because he didn't know anything himself."

With this it seemed that Melik-Mansour's cheerful expression became clouded; his bluish lips began to tremble with this sudden reminder of tragic events that, up to now, he had committed to non-remembrance. He took his glass of wine and quaffed it down, all in one draught.

"I'll tell you everything, because you have to know, But you won't be happy with what you're going to hear," he said anxiously.

"Mr. Salman was arrested at night. I found out the following morning. His betrayer was so careful that even his host didn't know where Mr. Salman had spent the night. He pointed out a friend of Mr. Salman's who, by chance, had seen what had happened. My first task was to get some of our horsemen together and carry out an attack on his guards. If we found him on the road, we could undoubtedly free him. But, unfortunately, they took him by another road that we didn't think of. We had twenty or thirty mounted men, ready to deal with anything. After asking a lot of questions, I was able to find the town and the military post the poor fellow was being taken to. I found out that, on the way there, he had been strangled to death. I couldn't even find the poor youth's body. It must have been subjected to the barbarities that only monsters like them can inflict. But that crime filled my heart with a raging vengefulness, and the blood of that innocent victim sealed my commitment to the cause that has bound us all together."

"As you know, Khacho and his two sons, Hairabed and Abo, were arrested after Mr. Salman. They weren't killed outright, but were kept in prison under strict security. Evidently their captors wanted to get their hands on all the old man's gold first, and then kill them. But the poor fellows weren't able to hold up under such terrible conditions, and they perished in prison."

"After all of that, I understood what was in store for the village of O... and I went alone to see Ismail Pasha who commanded the troops around Bayazid. He's a pretty level-headed man, and I was hopeful that something might be gained by talking to him. I even told him about the kinds of preparations I and my comrades were engaged in. I told him that, yes, a fair number of weapons had been distributed among the people, but that they weren't for use in any revolution, as he had been misinformed, but rather for self-defense. I told him the entire Christian element could be wiped out, given the intense fanaticism that had been unleashed among the muslim masses at that point. I told him it was crucially important for the government to make sure the tragic events in

Bulgaria weren't repeated here, something that had put Turkey in a very bad light. I told him the government should be grateful to us for arming the Christians to save them from the fury of the Mohammedans.

"The cunning pasha showed great sympathy; he promised that he himself would take every step necessary to prevent any harm from befalling the Armenians; he promised that every measure would be implemented to protect both their property and their life. This was at the moment the Russian forces were retreating, and there was word that the Armenians wanted to leave with them. The pasha asked me to convince the Armenians to stay put, something I gladly agreed to do. But right after he saw me off, he secretly ordered the Kurdish chieftain, Fattah-Bek, into action, and he descended on Bayazid with his bloody hordes, set fire to the town, and massacred its inhabitants. That event spread terror throughout the entire province and added to the exodus. All the efforts I and my comrades made to keep the terrified Armenians in their own ancestral land were in vain. The writing was already on the wall. After that, they wouldn't even have believed an angel from on high who told them they would be spared the fate suffered by the village of O…

"But the corrupt pasha's treachery convinced me more than ever that, directly or indirectly, the goal of Turkish officials was to aid and abet the destruction of the Christian population, and empty Armenia of the Armenians.

"After all our efforts, we were able to keep only a fraction of the Armenians on their soil—a very small number. Then, Ismail Pasha allowed the Turks to vent their hatred on the Armenians that remained. The Kurds set to work with unbridled cruelty, and there were terrible massacres in many places…"

"I'm convinced to this day that if the people had stayed put, they could have defended themselves. It was obvious that the regular Turkish army wouldn't attack an obedient and peaceful population. The local authorities wouldn't commit such blatant barbarities, especially since the provinces of Alashgert and Bayazid were full of English agents and European journalists. The local authorities would only go as far as they did; that is, secretly stir up the Kurds against the Armenians, then look the other way while the barbarities took place. But defending against the Kurds wouldn't have been so difficult. A small, but very telling, incident will demonstrate my point, and I'll summarize it for you. After the exodus, when the Russian army was totally withdrawn and the whole region passed under Turkish control, that was, as I said, the moment the Kurds began slaughtering the Armenians, torturing and exterminating them. Several households left their homes and fortified themselves in the mountains. Picture for yourself—a very brave people under attack by several thousand Kurds over the course of many weeks. The people not only fought them off with great self-sacrifice, but managed to attack them so effectively a couple of times that they were able to make off with considerable spoils and military materiel. Even now, it makes my heart throb to remember those unforgettable days. Not only did the youth fight, but the old, and the women, too. I'm convinced now that oppression can't destroy the courage that our forebears put into our people's veins. Oppression can only suppress and stifle the spirit of courage for a time, but kill it—never! When the hour comes, its age-old power will awaken with renewed force. That's what I witnessed with my own eyes. Out of all those horrible events, that was the one consolation."

At these words, Vartan's clouded expression brightened a little, and he lifted his sad eyes up in a prayerful manner, as if rendering praise to Heavenly Providence.

"How did things turn out?" Vartan asked.

"If we had only the Kurds to contend with, we could have held out for a long time; we were well prepared in inaccessible mountain reaches. But soon the regular army laid siege to us. We could have withstood them, as well, since we had one inexhaustible strength—the mountains of Armenia, which so lovingly protect those who seek their refuge. But the siege and the exhaustion of our food supplies finally caught up with us, like an enemy that can't be beaten. On occasion, some of our people would go down at night, make a foray into a nearby Kurdish village, and bring back provisions; but this was rarely successful, mainly because the villages were empty and the inhabitants had gone away to distant pastures with their herds. We certainly couldn't hold out for long when there wasn't one Armenian village where we could have looked for help or provisions. The enemy drew closer and closer. At that moment our side carried out an amazingly brave feat. Some of our people broke through the siege at night and got through the enemy's huge army. Imagine, these weren't just fighting men carrying out this bold maneuver, but entire households—women, girls, and children."

"Where did they go, then?" asked Vartan with animation.

"They crossed the border into Persia, but they had a lot to deal with along the way."

"So, you arrived here from Persia?"

"Yes, from Persia."

"What are you up to here?"

"I have just one purpose, and I think you will concur," answered Melik-Mansour, assuming an even graver tone. "The lives of the refugees here have to be saved, otherwise they'll perish immediately from hunger and disease. I'm convinced the Russians will gather their forces and be able to retake the land they lost. Peace will then prevail in those regions, and it will be necessary to get the people of Alashgert and Bayazid to return to their homelands. Otherwise, there will be a very unfortunate future for Armenia, with the uncivilized Kurds taking the place of the Armenians in the border provinces."

"Do you think the Russians will be able to hold on to those two provinces?"

"With a peace treaty, they could possibly pass into Turkish control again, but if so, the conditions will be different; the same disorders won't take place again. After such a severe beating, the Turkish people will come to their senses… There's also something else that gives me hope…"

Just then, the old woman came in and announced that a certain priest had shown up at the door and wished to be seen. Thinking this must be one of the priests that Holy Father Hovhaness had mentioned, Vartan ordered him to be admitted.

The man who entered was Father Marouk, parish priest of the village of O…

CHAPTER 42

Vartan and Melik-Mansour had just finished several glasses of wine when the old priest came in. It wasn't easy for Vartan to see him again, this man who had caused so much trouble for the village of O… as well as for himself and Mr. Salman. But circumstances change and bring about the reconciliation of old enemies. Seeing the sorry condition the old priest was in, his humbled manner, his worn, torn clothes—more like those of a beggar than of a servant of God—seeing all these signs of misfortune, Vartan was compelled to lay aside his hatred. Moreover, it would be from the lips of this old priest that he would receive information on the family he was so concerned with.

"Were you sent by Holy Father Hovhaness?" Vartan asked, offering him a seat.

"Yes, by Holy Father Hovhaness…" Father Marouk responded as he drew himself up to the table where a carafe of wine remained.

Vartan filled his glass, and the old priest, after blessing it, quaffed it all down. This alcoholic beverage seemed as refreshing to him as the dew that gathers on grass after it has been subjected to the wilting rays of the sun.

Father Marouk's expression, so stony a moment ago, now gave way to a brighter look. "Would you like some food?" asked Melik-Mansour, noticing the change of mood.

"I haven't eaten since yesterday," the priest replied in a tone so piteous that anyone would have been moved by it.

Melik-Mansour called for some food to be served to the priest.

It was hard for Vartan to begin asking Father Marouk questions. In a way, the position he was in was like that of an unfortunate person whose house has been robbed, and all his possessions taken, while he was gone. He returns home and finds it totally empty. But he still hopes to find his treasure where it was hidden. He approaches the secret spot, and, with a throbbing heart, stands before it, afraid to open it; he is seized by sudden apprehension, thinking, what will happen if he finds his treasure gone and himself deprived of his last hope and consolation.

This was the indecisiveness that held Vartan in its sway, pushing him, pulling him. He still had hope of finding Lala. His complete happiness or his everlasting doom hung on the words that issued from the mouth of this priest. Was he strong enough to withstand bad news? Though he wanted very much to ask a question, he was filled with such terrible forebodings, he couldn't.

Though Melik-Mansour knew nothing about Vartan's special relationsip with Lala nor anything about her family, he could tell that something was disturbing his friend. "You might want to be left alone to talk with the priest," he suggested. "I could just..."

"No, I have nothing to hide from you," said Vartan. Then addressing himself to Father Marouk, he said, "You presented Holy Father Hovhaness with a report on his diocese, didn't you? Well I, too, would like to know how many families from O… are among the refugees and where they are now."

"Good Lord, do you mean to say there are enough people left from my parish to give a report about?" the old priest said in the manner of someone talking about so many chickens. "I can count them and the places they've wandered to on my fingers!" he said.

Vartan's entire body began to tremble. "Could they all have been killed?" he asked, turning quite pale.

"I can't say that all have been, but on the other hand, no one was left. What happened to them, I don't know myself. May God forbid what happened in the village of O… to happen to any Christian. That was due to our sin. As in Sodom and Gomorrah, fire and brimstone rained down and destroyed everything. Those who survived the fire were either carried off into slavery or slaughtered by the Kurds, all in one night. The next morning, the whole village looked like a burnt-out fire. I lost all my fees, all of them… And there's no hope of getting them back… Tomas Effendi—may God give light to his soul—promised to collect them all for me, but he, too, was done in by all this evil… And so I ended up bankrupt and destitute. Don't you see what condition I'm in?" he said, calling attention to his tattered clothes.

At this point, tears started running from the poor priest's eyes, and he fell to sobbing bitterly. Was he remembering his daughter-in-law, Zoulo, and her tiny, angelic little children who, also, had not survived the exodus? Was he remembering his son-in-law, schoolmaster Simon, and Simon's wife, his own innocent daughter, who had likewise vanished in the general calamity? Was he tormented by the suffering of that flock whose shepherd he had been and whose destruction he had just recounted with such lack of emotion? There was no such thing behind his tears; his only thought was for those uncollected fees owed him by his people and now lost for good, alas!

But Vartan knew nothing about his uncollected fees, and paid the matter no attention. He was relieved the priest had guided the conversation away from the central question. He took another drink, trying to dissolve his anguish in the numbness of wine. But the wine only intensified the affliction in his heart, like oil being poured on a raging fire.

Melik-Mansour rescued Vartan from his difficulties. He had heard of Khacho's family, and he knew that both the head of that distinguished family and two of his sons had met a tragic fate, but about the other members of the family, he knew nothing.

"Who survived in that family?" he asked father Marouk.

"No one," the old priest replied without emotion. "Khacho and his two sons died in prison. You must know that. His other sons were massacred. His daughters-in-law and the girls were taken as slaves…"

"All of them!" cried Vartan in shock.

It was only after Father Marouk took stock of the expression on Vartan's face that he realized how careless he had been.

"Sara is here with her two children and Lala," he said.

Vartan was ecstatic. He found himself in the state of someone who, after a shipwreck, is beaten about by the waves, contending with death. His strength is fading; he closes his eyes with the conviction that when he next opens them, he will have been swallowed by the sea; then suddenly, the sea throws him back to land. Having been deposited where he is by a mighty whirlpool, he has no idea how he got where he is.

"Lala is here?... Sara is here?... Then I can see them. Praise be to God!" Vartan cried out, jumping up from his chair. "Let's go, Father. You know where they are. And you come with us, my friend," he said to Melik-Mansour, grabbing him by the hand.

The two young men and the priest left the house together. But Vartan's happiness would be short-lived, for the priest didn't have the very latest news about these refugees.

If Vartan had taken a closer look at the pitiful funeral procession he had seen when leaving the monastery in the morning, its tragic reality would have been clear to him. But it seemed that fate was working to add to his suffering, denying him the opportunity of seeing the girl he loved...

Sara and Lala were both very sick when they moved to the new lodging arranged for them by the virtuous doctor. The kind woman into whose care they were given was very touched by their condition, especially when she found out that they had come from a prosperous, privileged family, but fallen into their present unfortunate state due to a tragic turn of events.

Suffering in spirit and physically weak, the young girl showed signs of fever from the first night in her new home. The lady of the house immediately sent word to the doctor, and when he came, he found her in a bad state. "There is no hope for her," he told the lady. He stayed at the house most of the night, trying to turn back the tide of illness which threatened the girl's life. Toward the middle of the night, the girl was feeling a little better, and the physician left. The girl was even doing some talking, and told the lady of the house many things as she sat beside her.

But when the doctor came back to check on her in the morning, he found her dead. Sara was unaware of her death, though she slept in the same room. But when she heard the coffin-maker knock at the door and saw the coffin, she knew what had happened. The poor woman didn't even cry—she couldn't cry—for even crying takes a certain level of health. It seemed she was relieved; it seemed that was just what she wanted—for Lala to die, to be at rest, to be freed from a world in which not a single day of happiness would ever be hers again...

As the coffin was being carried out, she pleaded to be present at the burial; and despite the doctor's opposition on the grounds that she would be gravely weakened by doing so, she persisted. It seemed that this anomalous wish of hers infused her with new-found energy. She found herself happy and clear-headed. When the coffin reached the cemetery, she said, "I wanted to be buried with you, my beautiful Lala…" but then, noticing the children, she checked herself…

She was carried back unconscious to the house. Just as the young doctor was trying to revive her, there was a knock at the door. The servant opened the door and saw two young strangers and a priest.

"We heard there were two Alashgertzis here—a woman and a girl," said Vartan.

"Yes, they've been staying here, but the girl…"

"What happened?"

"She died…"

Like a tree struck by lightning, Vartan fell against Melik-Mansour.

CHAPTER 43

It was a dark and gloomy night.

The sweltering summer air bore down heavily and disagreeably on one's heart. There wasn't a sound or a breath. Everything seemed dead. It was only from a certain corner of Gayaneh's cemetery that any sounds could be heard, deep sighs. A young man was sprawled atop the freshly dug earth of one of the graves, murmuring. Tears poured from his sad eyes and wet the dry soil. At times, he clutched the little grave in his hands and kissed it; at times, he rubbed his face and eyes over its dampened surface, repeating the words, "Lala… poor Lala…" and it seemed that his very heart and soul flew out from his lips with those words.

That young man was Vartan. After all his long wanderings, all he had found was his beloved's grave. What was left for him? Confronted by the vicissitudes of life, constantly battling against adversity, there had been one brightly burning star to fix his eyes upon, to guide him to safe harbor. And now that star had been snuffed out. Bereft of that balm, just one drop of which could heal all his wounds, all that was left was a broken and aching heart.

This loss was irreversible. Vartan had never loved before; tender feelings had been unknown to this cool, severe-hearted young man. But in the face of Lala's love, the roughness of his character melted away like the burning of a taper. He was bewitched by her love. But where was his consoling angel now? There in that grave that he had embraced and dampened with his tears; there in that grave where his heart was also buried.

Thus gripped for a long while in a state of anguish, murmuring, contending with inconsolable grief, he was overtaken in time by a kind of numbness that was neither sleep nor wakefulness. His feverish head rested on the grave, and his eyes closed.

A confusion of dreams now crowded in upon his inflamed imagination: hellish visions that filled him with horror, yet also, comforted and enchanted him. The cycle of time had seemed to jump forward by many centuries, and he saw Armenia, once nothing but a wasteland full of ruins, now totally transformed and renewed. What kind of miraculous change was this? Could it be that paradise was restored after being lost? Could it be that the golden age which existed before God's earth was polluted with evil and injustice, now reigned again? No. This paradise that Vartan saw was not the paradise Jehovah had established between the banks of Armenia's four rivers, where the first human couple lived in perfect innocence and unknowing. This wasn't that paradise in which there was no need to produce anything by labor, where people could simply live off the fruit of the land—feasting at God's rich table, spread out before them by nature.

This was a paradise of a different kind, a paradise created by people out of their own labor; where instead of innocence, there was intelligence and consciousness; instead of a simple patriarchal form of life, an advanced culture.

Now it seemed that the meaning of those fateful words spoken by the Creator to the first-created had been fulfilled, "You shall earn your bread by the sweat of your brow." Now man didn't simply labor, but had lightened his work so much that sweat was no longer necessary. Now he worked for his own benefit; what he produced was no longer torn out of his hands by a violent oppressor.

And behold, Vartan saw a village. Could it be the village of O... in Alashgert? The surroundings looked familiar: the same mountains and hills, the same river, the same verdant valley—all looked the same.

The passage of centuries had taken nothing away but only transformed things. And how changed the village was! Those miserable cottages, excavated out of the earth and more fit as dens for animals than for human habitation, were no longer to be seen. These houses were made of stone, white as snow, and surrounded by beautiful gardens; broad, straight streets were sheltered by trees ever green, and bordered by crystal-clear brooks.

It was morning.

The village children were coming out of their houses, healthy, gay, well-dressed; boys and girls together, hurrying off to school with their books slung over their shoulders. Vartan looked at them and was amazed. How well taken care of they looked, and how happy they seemed. They must have had no fear of school or teachers. Could these be the same half-naked and sickly children that Vartan had known?

He stood alone in the street, looking around himself with wonder, unsure what direction to take. A beautiful sound struck his ear, the sound of the church bell. It appeared the morning service had not concluded yet. This was the first time since leaving the monastery and the monastic order that the sound of invitation to God's house had seemed so sweet to him. His hardened heart was filled with spiritual devotion, and he made his way toward the church, a place he hadn't set foot in for more than ten years.

He was amazed at what he saw. What a plain and humble church it was; no throne for dignitaries, no altar, no adorned sanctuary, no gilded images, no silver crosses or precious vestments. All the magnificence of the Armenian church was absent here, nor were there any choristers, or choirmasters, or deacons to be seen. There were only two pictures, one of Jesus Christ, and the other of Saint Krikor the Illuminator, both mounted in simple, black frames.

Men and women sat together, holding missals in their hands. The priest was delivering a sermon with the Holy Scriptures opened before him in the pulpit. His attire was no different from that of the congregation. His sermon was so simple and clear that Vartan understood everything he said. God's word flowed from his lips like the pure, living water of a spring. He took for the subject of his sermon those words from the Holy Scriptures, "You shall earn your bread by the sweat of your brow." Vartan was struck by the priest's explanation of this verse. Up until this day, Vartan had been given to understand that these words were a curse placed on the destiny of the first-created, a curse extending to all future generations. He now understood that this was an admonition intended to root out idleness and keep man in a state of indefatigable, industrious, self-motivated activity.

The sermon ended. From the midst of the congregation, an ordinary villager was reciting an extemporaneous prayer, asking God's help for the health, intelligence, and strength necessary to work the land He had created to bring forth its countless blessings. "What a prayer! What do they seek for themselves?" thought Vartan. "They don't ask for anything spiritual. Could it be they expect nothing beyond the grave, that they are asking only for that which meets their physical needs and what is required by real existence?"

The prayer concluded. The entire congregation, men, women, young, and old, started to sing a song with words taken from the Psalms, "Many said, who will show us the goodness of God? The light of your countenance fell upon us, and you granted joy to our hearts. You made us abound with the wealth of wheat, and wine, and oil."

"Again, the same material intentions..." thought Vartan. "Again, nothing spiritual... The farmer sings of the abundance of the earth, given to him by God to be worked with his own hands. How remarkable that these people have reconciled the abstraction of religion with the demands of real life conditions..."

How beautiful that song was, joined in harmony by the organ's lovely sound. What a sweet anthem flowing from the lips of hundreds of people. It seemed to Vartan that the voice of these people became one with the melody of the seraphim and lofted upward to the Eternal Throne. This was the first time in his life he had heard such holy music.

The service came to an end, and the people started to leave. Now, the school teacher stood in the pulpit where the priest had delivered his sermon; and the children of the village filled the pews where the congregation had just been singing and praying. Boys and girls mingled together listened to their teacher's lecture. "Has this place now turned into a school? Have they combined church and school?" thought Vartan. "Ah, such frugal people; they don't want to make a separate building for school. Materialism, all over again."

But the teacher looked familiar. Wasn't that Father Marouk? His features, his stature, and even his voice, were the same. It was truly he, the priest, but in ordinary clothing. Could this be the man who had so vigorously opposed the creation of a school; the man who had caused Mr. Salman so much grief—now the director of a regular school? Could this be the same priest who had sold church rites for money, and thought about nothing but his uncollected fees? So overwhelmed by this paradox, Vartan was compelled to step forward and ask a question.

"Father—what ever became of your fees?"

The priest just gave the newcomer a sharp look without saying anything, making the young man feel stupid. He indicated that the bell would soon be rung, marking the end of the class. Yet another fact that greatly surprised Vartan was that the priest had been teaching a class in the natural sciences. A priest as both theologian and scientist—that was truly impressive to Vartan.

Without waiting for the class to end, Vartan walked out of the church, or rather the school, and went out into the surrounding grounds. Instead of the graves usually placed around Armenian churches he found the churchyard filled with the beauty of rare trees and flowers.. He stood for a long while looking at the beautiful walkways. Noticing that he was a visitor, a villager invited him to his house for breakfast.

The villager's home, totally ensconced in the shelter of trees, was one of those tidy houses that contain everything necessary within modest confines. There were several rooms, each suited to the various requirements of life; each plain, clean, appropriately furnished. The villager's daughter approached her father joyously, a sweet song on her lips. It didn't seem that her young heart had ever been touched by sadness or grief or disappointment with life. She showed none of the timidity typical of Armenian women. She didn't shy away from the young guest, but spoke to him with laughter, as if they had been old friends. And how much she resembled Lala! So bewitched by the similarity, Vartan felt like embracing her and saying, "I found you at last!"

Breakfast was already on the table. The lady of the house poured coffee and thick cream into the large cups set before the guest and her husband. The daughter then brought the morning newspaper to the table and, putting it down in front of her father with a proud smile, she pointed out an article.

"Ah, your article has already been published, Lala," her father exclaimed, straightening up his glasses and picking up the newspaper.

"Lala!" Vartan cried out with irrepressible emotion.

"That name has been used in our family for generations," his host explained.

Though Vartan could understand his point, he still had difficulty accepting the idea that the girl wasn't Lala. If she weren't, then she must be her resurrected phantom. To be sure, people are transformed after resurrection and acquire a different character, yet keep their own likeness.

Vartan was as taken by the tranquil, prosperous atmosphere of the home as he was by the young woman's beauty. He had expected these people to be engaged in hard work, day-in and day-out; but, modest as it was, he now saw that their life was comfortable.

"The villager's happiness isn't based so much on heavy, constant labor as on his knowledge of what he's doing and how to make it easier," said Vartan's host. "There are so many helpful forces provided by God in nature, we just have to know how to recognize them and make use of them for our benefit."

"That's true," said Vartan. "If only the Kurds would leave the villager's earnings in his hands, he would be blessed."

"What Kurds?" his host asked with surprise.

"The Kurds who are always robbing you," Vartan replied.

"Oh, the Kurds..." said his host as if having difficulty remembering the name of a long-forgotten people. "In the history of our iron age, I came across quite a lot about the Kurds, and it's true that they robbed and even massacred our ancestors. But where are those barbarians now? They died out, and are no more. A people like that couldn't withstand the light of culture, so they faded away and were absorbed. By the beginning of the last century, they had accepted our religion and begun attending our schools. They gradually became absorbed by us and disappeared."

On hearing this Vartan couldn't believe his ears, and everything seemed as if in a dream to him; and, in fact, everything he heard and saw was part of a dream. His host continued:

"In our family history we find many passages about the Kurds, written in blood it would seem. The ancestor to whom our family traces its origin was named Khacho. He was the village host of this town. The Kurds destroyed his entire home. He and two of his sons died in prison. The only offspring left by his oldest son Hairabed was one male child..."

"Who was taken by his mother Sara to Vagharshapat during the time of the great exodus from Alashgert," Vartan interjected.

"Yes. It was from that male child that our entire family sprang."

"And his name was Hovakim," said Vartan. "He also had a sister named Nazlou who died later with her mother. The orphan Hovakim was taken in and raised by a doctor."

"Where did you read about that?" asked his host with astonishment at the level of detail his young guest had on his family history.

"I didn't read it but saw it with my own eyes. That all took place when the Kurds destroyed the town and the entire province of Alashgert," said Vartan.

"But that was almost two hundred years ago, and you appear much younger than I. You would have to be Methuselah's age to have witnessed those events," his host responded with a kind smile.

Vartan was at a loss to answer, for it seemed to him, too, that those events had transpired centuries ago.

From where Vartan sat surrounded by the happy family of his host, the windows revealed the verdant beauty of the valley, stretching to the foot of the distant mountains. The mountains were covered with thick forests, and an awesome sight was presented by the gigantic trees rising up to become one with the clear blue sky. The morning sun poured down its golden rays, and, bathed in its light, many rivers twisted and shimmered like silver snakes, winding their way through the open expanse of the valley. Vartan couldn't take his eyes off this wondrous vista. Cultivated by the hands of a hardworking people, untamed nature had taken on the appearance of a masterful painting.

"You were talking about the sad times of the Kurds and the Turks," Vartan's host continued with a special happiness in his voice, "But after those days, a great many changes took place. Do you see those breath-taking mountains. Well, a century and a half ago, they were totally bare, without so much as a shrub on them. In those days, the trees were destroyed by the barbarians with the same cruelty that the people had been destroyed. Everything was gone; the people used dried dung for fuel, for there wasn't any wood left, and they were forced to dig into the earth to live. But when peace returned, then hosts of people came back to the destroyed towns, and the mountains became covered with forests, all planted by our hard working, dedicated villagers. See that beautiful green valley? It had been turned into a totally dry wasteland, without any water. There was only a little river left, and it would dry up completely in the heat of summer. But from the moment the forests were planted, there was water in abundance. This is now one of the most fertile and fruitful places in the region. Yes, a great deal has changed… Before, there weren't even any roads, but now you can see level roads gleaming like mirrors and connecting all the towns of our province with each other. The vehicles speeding along on those roads are powered by steam, not animals. What we produce here is taken to market hundreds of miles away; and, in turn, we get whatever we need from the outside world."

Vartan listened with great surprise to all of this and, as his eyes fell again on Lala, it seemed quite natural for him to ask where she had received her education.

"She'll be completing her studies in just one week at the academy of New Vagharshapat. Right now she's preparing to enter the university to study medicine. She isn't in the best of health right now, and I wish she could stay with us a few more months, but she wouldn't have any of that."

"How many children do you have?" asked Vartan.

"Our family has always had many children; our forebear Khacho's family consisted of more than fifty people, but I have only five children. Lala is my only daughter. The other four are boys."

"What do they do?"

"One of them is a forester in those same forests that you see; one is a professor in Garin;[52] another is a colonel in the Van regiment; and the fourth has been studying rural economics at the school of New Bagrevant."

The name of this last town struck Vartan as unfamiliar.

"I don't remember a town by that name in this province," he commented.

"That's the name of old Bayazid. Many of the names of our towns, villages, and localities have been changed. Some still have their old, historic names, while some have been given new ones."

Vartan's host picked up the newspaper once more and, taking a look at one of the articles, seemed quite disturbed by it.

"What kind of news is it?" Vartan asked, quite curious.

"Nothing unusual… A general convocation of the assembly is going to take place in town tomorrow to discuss some controversial issues… The various parties seem to be quite worked up…"

"Will you be participating?" asked Vartan.

"I have no choice."

From the tenor of what his host said, it appeared he was an elected member of the assembly.

Breakfast was over. Vartan stood up, thanked his host, and was about to leave.

"If you like, I'd be glad to be your guide and show you some of the enterprises we have here in our village," his host said.

"Thank you, sir."

"And if you ever pass through our village again, our doors will be open to you," said the lady of the house.

"Thank you, madame" said Vartan, bowing his head.

"And may you never find our house boring," said the woman's beautiful daughter with a candid smile.

"Thank you, miss," said Vartan, giving her an even deeper bow.

It was only when he had left this country home that Vartan realized how ill at ease he had been inside. He had felt like a total wild man there, uncomfortable in the presence of people more cultured than himself, wondering why he just went on being rough, unpolished, unable to converse and express his opinions and carry himself like the others. What mystery was this? Khacho's descendants, having passed through the crucible of the centuries and subjected to its refinement and purification, had undergone a transformation in character and given rise to a new and noble generation.

Led by his host, Vartan walked through the village streets. They passed by peasant women dressed in simple, clean clothes, each busily engaged in some kind of handiwork. Their husbands were dressed in work clothes. No one was idle; there was something to do for everyone. Vartan was impressed to see how much their life had changed and how enjoyable it had become. The common coarseness of earlier times was no longer to be found, and everywhere there reigned the spirit of a warm and vital culture. One thing that had remained from former times was the Armenian language—but how cultivated and polished it had become; and how beautiful the turns of phrase that could now be heard on Armenian lips!

Vartan and his host were by now outside the village. Wherever Vartan looked, there were dense crops, beautiful farms, well-cultivated fields, and abundant pastures.

They passed by a sawmill where most of the labor was carried out with steam powered machinery. The mill produced lumber in many different sizes and styles, and supplied all the nearby villages and towns.

"Who owns the mill?" asked Vartan.

"The village owns it. Any enterprise you see here isn't the property of just one individual," replied his host. "All the facilities belong to the entire village community; each villager has a share in it. They are constructed of wood from the nearby forests. These, too, are owned by the entire village."

They left the sawmill behind.

"Look, do you see that large building there?" asked Vartan's host. "That's a cheese factory, and it makes the finest cheese in the area. It's also owned by the village community. Each villager gives the milk from his animals to the factory; then when the final product is ready for distribution, each one receives either a proportional share of it, or money."

They were now standing in the middle of a field. The ripened crop had been harvested, but not with the use of sickles or scythes; here, also, the task had been accomplished with machinery which did the work of hundreds of workers. Now, at last, did Vartan fully grasp the meaning of making work lighter.

They were walking near an enormous building which was the flour mill. Here also the work had been made easier with the use of steam power rather than water. Wheat from villages near and far was delivered here to be ground, and the final product, clean and snow-white flour, was sold abroad. This, also, was owned by the entire village community.

But one thing impressed Vartan beyond all else: all the workers in the village conveyed a striking boldness, self-confidence, and hardiness of spirit wherever they were encountered and under whatever circumstances. Judging from their manner, it would seem they had grown up in freedom; that they had never suffered a slap at the hands of a Turk, nor ever had any fear of a Kurdish spear. He saw that these people had done their duty when called upon to do so; they had laid down their shovels and ploughs to take up arms, instead, and they had wielded them with equal skill and effectiveness.

"Those people were soldiers during wartime," said Vartan's host. "Most work came to an end in those times. War has always had the worst consequences for us here, though it's also had certain positive effects."

Leaving the fields behind them, they went back toward the village. There they stopped in front of a different sort of building, one more similar to the buildings found on ordinary farms.

"That is our village school of rural economics," said Vartan's host. "The school you saw this morning was an elementary school."

And what a school this was! Vartan had never seen a school like this before, though he had once been a vartabed. Inside of it could be found everything connected with the village economy. Next to this enormous building was a vast farm divided into sections, cultivated by students, both male and female. Plants from almost everywhere in the world could be found here: herbs, flowers, shrubs, etc.

The students here did not engage in book learning or dead literature. Everything they learned, they took from nature's wondrous book. At set times, they engaged in both callisthenics and military exercises. Vartan thought to himself, "This is the kind of education that produces both good cultivators and good soldiers."

Vartan thanked his host and went on alone. As to where he should go next, he had no idea. He saw something resembling a street car with people sitting on either side of it. On learning that it was going to the railway station he took a seat onboard. The railway station was filled with a crowd of people waiting for the next train. Suddenly from the surrounding crowd a familiar voice rang out . . .

"Vartan!"

Vartan turned around to see Mr. Salman standing before him, and the two old friends threw their arms around each other.

"And so, my friend, we find each other again after exactly two-hundred years..." Mr. Salman said, still holding on to Vartan's hand. "That's been a very long time. You look the same; you haven't changed a bit... But in those two-hundred years, there have been great changes in our country. Didn't I used to tell you, Vartan, that Armenia in its infancy was the cradle of humanity, a paradise in the age of innocence, but that the day would come, in humanity's maturity, when it would become a paradise of advancement? Now, that has all been fulfilled. Now, the existence of the Armenians on their own ancestral land is entirely secure, joyous, and peaceful; if you only knew how hard we had to work to get there... So much work... In these last two hundred years, we passed through so many trials... We won our well-being at the cost of much blood and sweat."

"Where are you going now?" Vartan asked his friend.

"I'm on my way to town. The representative assembly is going to meet. I represent my district there. Come on, Vartan, let's go together. I'm going to give a speech and you'll find our debate interesting."

The final whistle for departure sounded, and they mounted the car. It was nighttime. They reached the railway station just before day-break. The beautiful, lively town was now in slumber. Only a few workers could be seen in the streets, hurrying off to their factories.

"Take us to 'Noah's Dove,'" said Mr. Salman to a coachman.

The coach sped along straight and smooth, through streets lined with splendid, colorful buildings which looked like palaces to Vartan. Mr. Salman pointed out some of the more noteworthy buildings:

"There—that is the university. That is the academy of science. That used to be the ancient royal palace, but it's now used as a museum. That is one of the town's outstanding theaters. That is a hospital. Those are the statues of the heroes who distinguished themselves in our last revolutionary war. That is the newspaper building which produces one hundred fifty thousand copies per day. That..."

"Is there no military installation?" asked Vartan.

"No, there isn't, for here every citizen is a soldier."

"What a beautiful town! What a remarkable town!" Vartan exclaimed with great admiration.

The coach came to a halt in front of "Noah's Dove Inn."

Vartan and Mr. Salman went into a small room to the side of the main hall. Here, a lively discussion was going on between Tomas Effendi and Melik-Mansour.

"That would be a purely asinine kind of martyrdom," Tomas Effendi was saying.

"Well, as far as I'm concerned, that would be the most direct way to achieve the desired goal," responded Melik-Mansour in a state of considerable agitation.

"That path will take us far out of our way, and get us to the goal on a donkey's Easter," answered Tomas Effendi with a laugh.

"Oh, here's Salman; let's see what he thinks," they said, suspending their debate for the moment.

Great was their surprise when they saw Vartan who had seemed to appear out of nowhere.

"Where did you come from?" asked Tomas Effendi with his usual sarcastic smile.

"Well, I feel just the same way about seeing you," said Vartan, shaking his hand. "I found your broken body at the foot of the Alashgert mountains; then I buried you in a Kurdish cemetery... and now..."

"I have been resurrected," Tomas Effendi responded with a laugh. "You may not believe in the doctrine of reincarnation. My suffering soul passed through the bodies of the most impure of animals. For many decades, I prowled around in the body of a wolf, attacking animals, surviving as a hunter... For decades I barked in the body of a dog... I cringed and attached myself to whomever would offer me food... For some decades I slithered around in the body of a snake and struck with my fangs... For several decades, I brayed in the body of a donkey, and my ears were pulled so many times, I went out of my mind. Then, at last, my suffering soul entered the body of a lion, and there it became cleaner and purer. That cycle took two hundred years. The mummies of Egypt have remained in the pyramids for thousands of years awaiting the return of their souls, but my soul completed its cycle even more quickly."

"And I got the chance to see the transformation of Tomas Effendi." said Vartan, interrupting.

"Yes! The Tomas Effendi that you knew before was a true child of his age, but he was changed by time. Now, he is one of the best representatives of his generation. And this new generation has made tremendous progress, my dear Vartan. Do you remember the days when Melik-Mansour used to go around through all the villages of Alashgert, crying 'beautiful needles!' Well, now he is the general of a great army."

Vartan turned to Melik-Mansour and respectfully shook his hand.

"We're late, gentlemen. The assembly is about to begin," said Mr. Salman.

"He's the leader of our freedom-loving party," Tomas Effendi whispered in Vartan's ear, pointing at Mr. Salman. "He has an outstanding speech to make today. Ah, how well he talks…"

"Let me go with you, gentlemen. I want to listen, too…" said Vartan eagerly.

"Let's go…" he heard an unfamiliar voice say.

Vartan opened his eyes and grasped that everything he had seen had been a dream. He was still surrounded by the darkness of night at poor Lala's grave; but whose voice was it that had awakened him with the words, "Let's go?"

Suddenly, four powerful hands seized him, and everything was buried in the dark of night.

THE END

ENDNOTES

1. Translator's Note: Nestorian Assyrians native to the mountains of Jolamerik.
2. Translator's Note: A renowned Russian general of Armenian origin
3. Translator's Note: The foremost leader of the Muslims of Chechnya and Daghestan in their resistance to the expansion of the Russian Empire into their territories during the early 1800's.
4. Raffi's Note: The young man's actual name was Samson, but the hero of my novel is one of a different type. May I be forgiven for digressing from strict historical fact in the exercise of poetic license. Translator's Note: The reference is to Samson Der Boghosian, the hero of Bayazid, whom Raffi encountered and interviewed with great interest in Vagharshapat.
5. Translator's Note: *Allah* is Arabic for God, and is not a name restricted in its use to Muslims.
6. Translator's Note: Kurdish chief of Haidar tribe. He led his army of *bashibozuks* in their plunder and slaughter of the Christian communities of Haghbag, Bayazid, and Alashgert during the war of 1877-78. Upon completing these tasks, he was poisoned to death by Ottoman authorities. One of Raffi's other historical novels bears his name.
7. Translator's Note: Using pillage and plunder to extend his power, Ibadullah became a formidable threat to both the Christian population, as well as Turkish rule in general, in the regions of Van and Bayazid. On returning from a pilgrimage to Mecca, he was warmly received in Constantinople by Sultan Abdul Hamid II. The Sultan presented him with gifts and imparted his instructioins to him. This was later referred to by Raffi as "that hellish meeting." Taking the Russo-Turkish war as an opportunity to unleash a holy-war, he led his *bashibozouks* on a campaign of plunder and killing to Bayazid.
8. Translator's Note: A legendary hero of the Azeri and neighboring Turkic peoples, similar to Robin Hood.
9. Translator's Note: Antar was an Arab poet of the 6th century who, in the following two centuries, became the central figure in chivalric tales.
10. Raffi's Note: A *Majitia* can mean both a military decoration and a coin.
11. Translator's Note: Flat bread.
12. Raffi's Note: The Armenian girls of Alashgert, just as Armenian girls throughout Turkish Armenia, wear a multi-colored silk cap decorated with coins, gold coins for wealthy girls and silver coins for poorer ones.
13. Raffi's Note: I have had occasion to witness this sort of fanaticism in many different places, and it is astonishing that the masses entirely go along with the clergy in this kind of thinking.
14. Translator's Note: The shortened Armenian form for Constantinople.
15. Translator's Note: According to folk tradition, Bahloul was a king who renounced his throne upon the counsel of an angel and wandered from land

to land teaching his wisdom. He was then miraculously transported to "The Everlasting Kingdom" by God.

16.   Translator's Note: A mullah of the twelfth century, celebrated in many stories for his unpredictable and unconventional ways of stating the truth.

17.   Translator's Note: The most beloved Armenian patriarch of modern times, known affectionately as "Khrimian Hayrig." He was Patriarch of Constantinople from 1869-1874 and was forced to leave that office due to government pressure. He and Raffi knew each other and worked together for the emancipation of Armenians. Khrimian was Catholicos of All Armenians from 1892 until his death in 1907.

18.   Translator's Note: Egyptian statesman of Armenian origin. He and Khrimian Hairik were sent as delegates of the Catholicos to advocate for Armenian interests at the Congress of Berlin.

19.   Translator's Note: Krikor Odian was a lawyer and writer who took part in drafting the Armenian National Constitution of 1863 and the Ottoman Constitution of 1876. He later became secretary to the Armenian National Assembly in Constantinople. He was persecuted for his activism and forced to live his final years in exile. He was a batchelor and had no children.

20.   Translator's Note: Grand Vizier Midhat Pasha was the chief architect of the Ottoman constitution of 1876. He was dismissed in 1878, after the constitution was suspended by Sultan Abdul Hamid II.

21.   Translator's Note: The word used here by Raffi is *shvi*, a wooden pennywhistle used in Armenian folk music.

22   Translator's Note: Mesrop Taghyatiantz, 1803-59, prolific writer, teacher, world traveler. He wrote in numerous genres and translated into Armenian from the works of numerous English writers, including Shakespeare, Locke, Milton and others.[81]

23.   Raffi's Note: Doing *kagh-han* means uprooting all unwanted and harmful plants. This is the struggle of life, in which every being not only strives to preserve its own existence, but tries to wipe out its enemy, in order to secure its own unimpaired existence.

24.   Translator's Note: The problem presented to European nations by the gradual weakening of Ottoman control over its European territories, and the source of political and military rivalry among them from the 18th to the 20th century.

25.   Translator's Note: Van was burned several times. The instance cited here took place on December 1, 1876, when a suspicious fire broke out in Armenian shops. By the time the shop keepers found out and arrived on the scene, they were prevented by the police from entering their shops to save them. They were then killed in the street in front of their shops. Thereafter, troops and police looted the shops and set fire to those which hadn't caught fire yet. They then withdrew and turned the streets over to violent mobs who finished the business. [91]

26.   Raffi's Note: The Turks use the term "Chelebi" as a name for Armenian and Greek merchants.

27.   Translator's Note: Ankara.

28.   Translator's Note: The ancient chanted prayers of the Armenian church.

29.   Translator's Note: Raffi's question-mark.

30.   Translator's Note: Also called "Bulgarian Horrors" by the British statesman William Gladstone, the Bulgarian atrocities were a series of massacres in 1876, when Ottoman irregular forces (*bashibozuks*) killed the populations of several Bulgarian villages in suppressing a revolt by Bulgarian revolutionaries. About 20,000 people were killed..

31.   Translator's Note: A chewing confection, common to the region, made up of resins mixed with flavored spirits, mastak in Turkish.

32.   Raffi's Note: "Shapash" is the money bestowed on the dancers by the crowd, then handed over to the musicians when the festivities are over.

33.   Raffi's Note: No such custom is practiced in any part of Armenia. It is practiced only by asiatic gypsy boys or girls who employ this captivating gesture to win money from the celebrants.

34.   Translator's Note: A water-pipe.

35.   Raffi's Note: The rug on which Mohammedans pray is called a sachata. For praying in the home, they choose the most beautiful of rugs.

36.   Translator's Note: An infidel, or non-Muslim subject.

37.   Translator's Note: Exodus 2:11-12.

38.   Translator's Note: Mazah is a confection, such as candied fruit, etc., that customarily follows the drinking of spirits in this region.

39.   Translator's Note: Knuckle-bones are toys similar to jacks.

40.   Translator's Note: The Gospel of John 18:10.

41.   Raffi's Note: This is a Turkish saying, since among the Mohammedans of the East, the hair of a pig is considered unclean, and they use the hair of a donkey to clean their clothes or other articles.

42.   Translator's Note: The original text at this point mistakenly states "two and a half months earlier," but has been corrected by the translator in the interests of clarity. [162]

43.   Raffi's Note: The Eshirat are a wild, nomadic Kurdish people who are not well-regarded by their sedentary brethren because they subject them to the same barbarity as they do any other people.

44.   Translator's Note: A classic love story by Nezimi, a famed 12th century Trans-Caucasian writer. [174]

45.   Translator's Note: Gregory the Illuminator who converted the Armenian king and state to Christianity in 301.

46.   Translator's Note: The inner circle of the Catholicosate.

47.   Translator's Note: *Hosos* is a derisive term used in certain circles among Eastern Armenians to designate Bolsetsi Armenians. The term refers to the dominant clique within the Catholicosate which favors accommodation with Turkey in hopes of gaining high ecclesiastical positions in Turkish Armenia, especially Constantinople. The specific reference is to Catholicos Kevork IV and his closest adviser, Bishop Vahram Mangouni. Mangouni

was loathed and dreaded within the monastic order for his many machinations.

48. Raffi's Note: There are traditions regarding half-ruined chapels and monasteries located in out-of-the way places, such as deserts and other places far from people, that animals approach them on their own during feast days and are taken by shepherds and turned into offerings.

49. Translator's Note: Raffi's punctuation.

50. Translator's Note: Nerses of Ashtarak, Catholicos 1843-58.

51. Translator's Note: Distinguished bishop of the Armenian church and a poet. He served as translator in the Armenian delegation to The Congress of Berlin in 1878. [188]

52. Translator's Note: Erzeroum.

GLOSSARY

Aragh	An anise flavored brandy common to the region.
Bashibozouk	Irregular units of Ottoman army.
Bek	Lord, chief.
Bolis	Armenian shortened name for Constantinople.
Bolsetsi	A person from Bolis.
Bulbul	A famed song bird of the region, similar to the nightingale, a prominent figure in medieval poetry.
Catholicos	The head of the Armenian church.
Chalgis	Folk musicians.
Chipoukh	A very long-stemmed Turkish smoking pipe with a clay bowl, or, a long stick used by herdsmen or farmers to prod and control animals.
Danouder	The elective headman of a village, the official host and innkeeper for travelers, and most often the wealthiest peasant of a village.
Derebey	An independent feudal lord.
Duduk	A double-reed wind instrument similar to the oboe, made of apricot wood; emblematic of Armenia.
Effendi	Gentleman
Fakir	An Indian ascetic who engages in feats of self-mortification.
Gavour	Derogatory term for non-Muslims.
Ghouroush	Ottoman coinage equivalent to about 6 *kopeks*.
Hamals	Load bearers or porters in shipping enterprises in Constantinople
Julos	Nestorian Assyrian Christians native to the mountains of Jolamerik, noted for their martial values and independence, who were led in peace and war by their Catholicos called Mar-Shimon.
Kadi	An Islamic judge who applies Islamic law.
Kagh-han	The systematic weeding that preceded the planting of crops.
Khan	A title meaning 'lord' among the Tatars.
Khodja	See *Mullah* below.
Kizir	Official appointed by the central government to assist the danouder of a village.
Kopek	One hundredth of a *rouble*.
Krikor Odian	Odian was a batchelor and had no children.
Machitia	Ottoman currency equivalent to about 20 *kopeks*.
Madzoon	Yoghurt.

Mazah	Customary dessert, usually with a base of preserved fruit, served with wine and spirits following a meal.
Mufti	A professional interpreter of Islamic law who has a specific following and can issue *fatwas*.
Moultezim	A tax official.
Mullah	A teacher and interpreter of Islamic doctrine.
Pasha	A high Ottoman official or dignitary.
Pilaf	A specially prepared rice dish.
Rouble	A basic unit of Russian currency.
Saraf	A financier or banker.
Sheikh	An Islamic secular leader. Among Kurds, the spiritual leader.
Shvi	An Armenian pennywhistle made of wood.
Tonir	The principal stove-oven-heater in a house, consisting of a circular fire pit in the center of the main room lined with ceramic and covered with a circular metal membrane.
Tahn	A refreshment made of diluted *madzoon*.
Vartabed	A learned monk who engages in scholarship and teaching.
Vizier	An Ottoman minister of state.

www.ingramcontent.com/pod-product-compliance
Lightning Source LLC
Chambersburg PA
CBHW031122030726
47496CB00002BA/646